TROUBLE MAKER

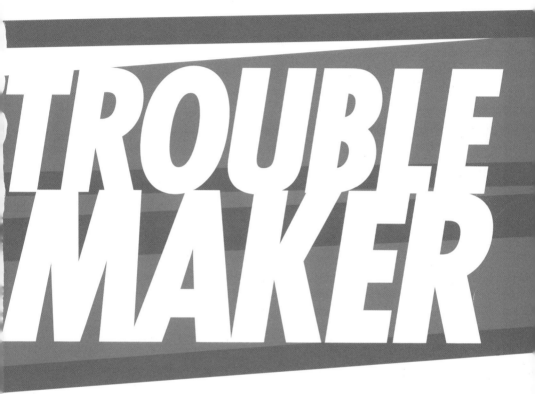

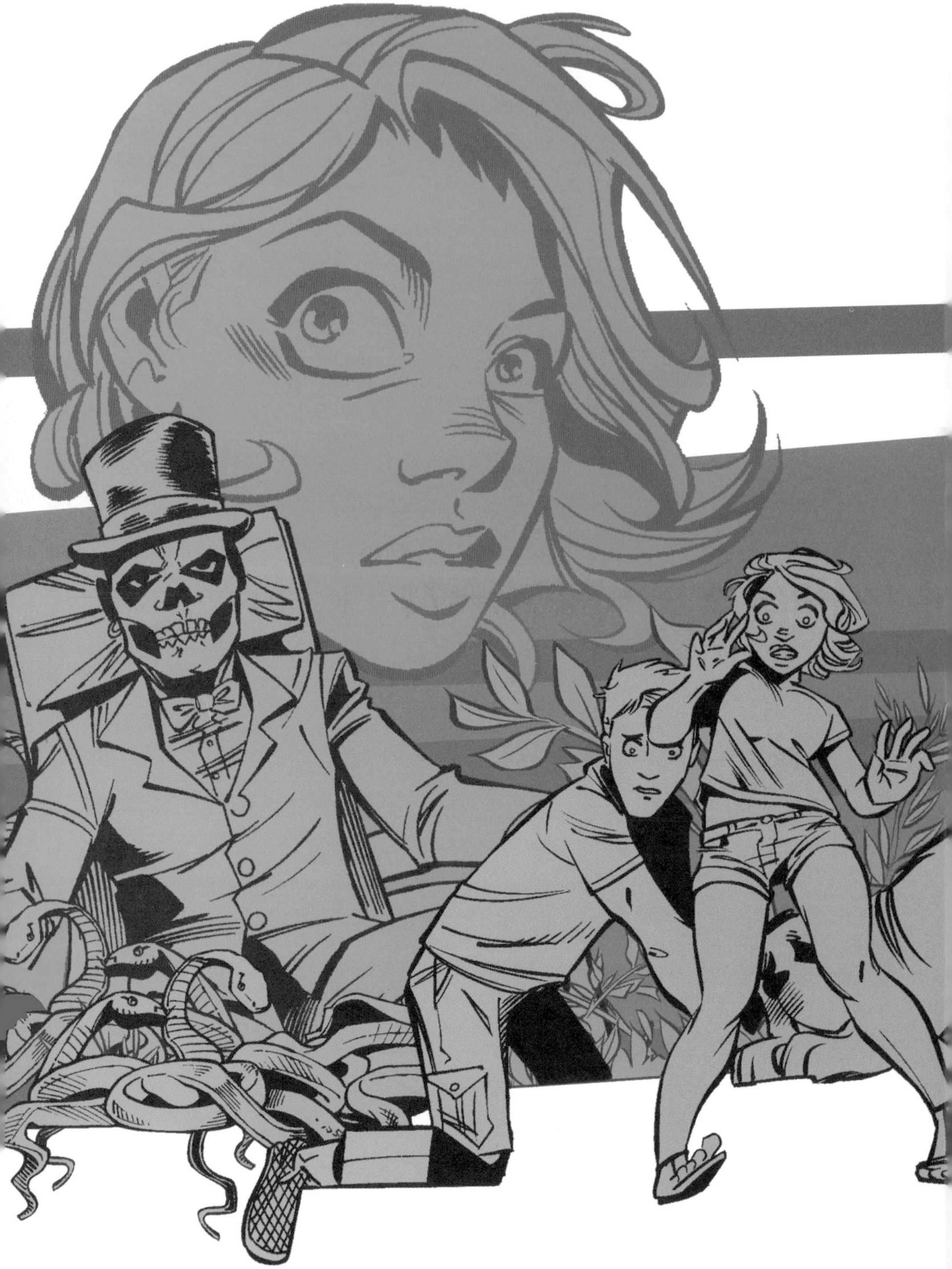

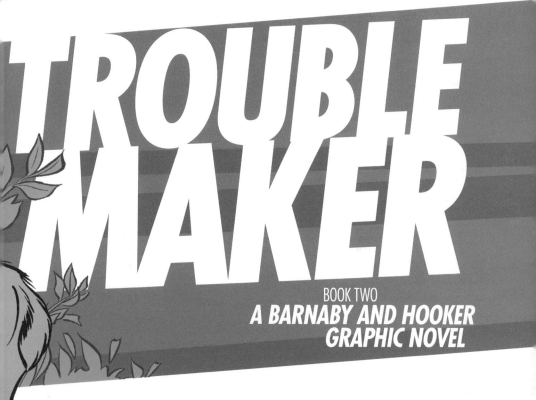

TROUBLE MAKER

BOOK TWO
A BARNABY AND HOOKER GRAPHIC NOVEL

WRITTEN BY
JANET AND **ALEX EVANOVICH**
DRAWN BY **JOËLLE JONES**

BACKGROUND PENCILS — BEN DEWEY | INKS — ANDY OWENS
COLORS — DAN JACKSON | LETTERS — NATE PIEKOS of BLAMBOT®

DARK HORSE BOOKS®

President & Publisher
MIKE RICHARDSON

Editor
SIERRA HAHN

Assistant Editor
FREDDYE LINS

Collection Designer
DAVE NESTELLE

Special thanks to Matt Dryer and Lia Ribacchi.

executive vice president Neil Hankerson • chief financial officer Tom Weddle • vice president of publishing Randy Stradley • vice president of business development Michael Martens • vice president of business affairs Anita Nelson • vice president of marketing Micha Hershman • vice president of product development David Scroggy • vice president of information technology Dale LaFountain • director of purchasing Darlene Vogel • general counsel Ken Lizzi • editorial director Davey Estrada • senior managing editor Scott Allie • senior books editor Chris Warner • executive editor Diana Schutz • director of design and production Cary Grazzini • art director Lia Ribacchi • director of scheduling Cara Niece

Published by Dark Horse Books
A division of Dark Horse Comics, Inc.
10956 SE Main Street
Milwaukie, OR 97222

www.darkhorse.com
www.evanovich.com
www.joellejones.com

To find a comics shop in your area, call the Comic Shop Locator Service toll-free at (888) 266-4226.

First edition: November 2010
ISBN 978-1-59582-573-5

10 9 8 7 6 5 4 3 2 1
Printed at Solisco Printers, Ltd., Scott, QC, Canada

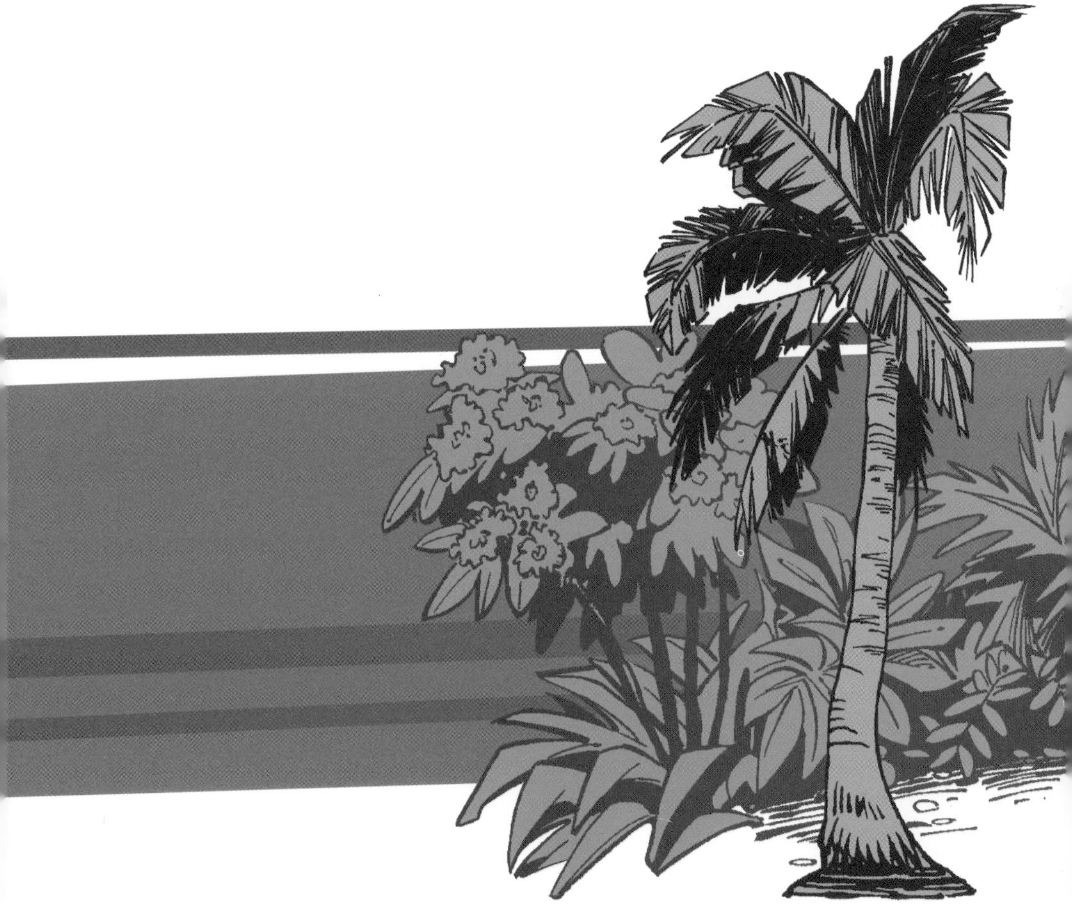

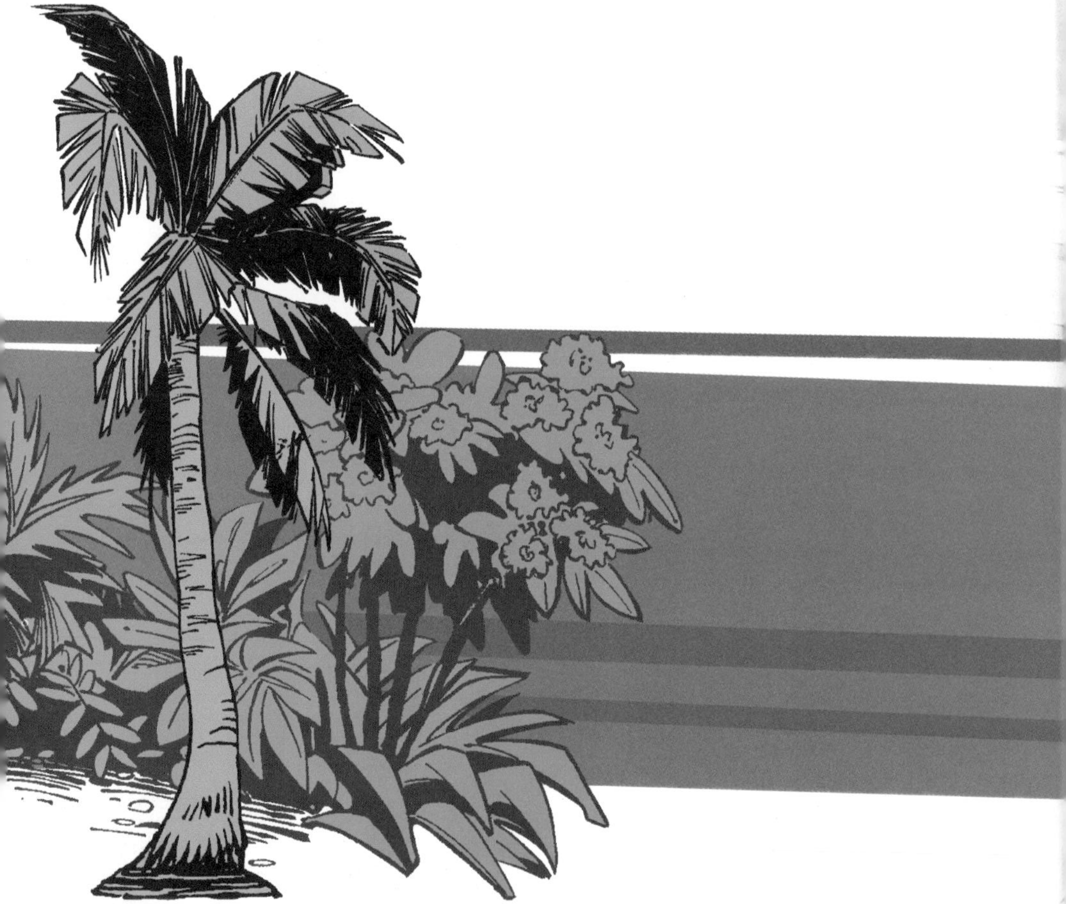

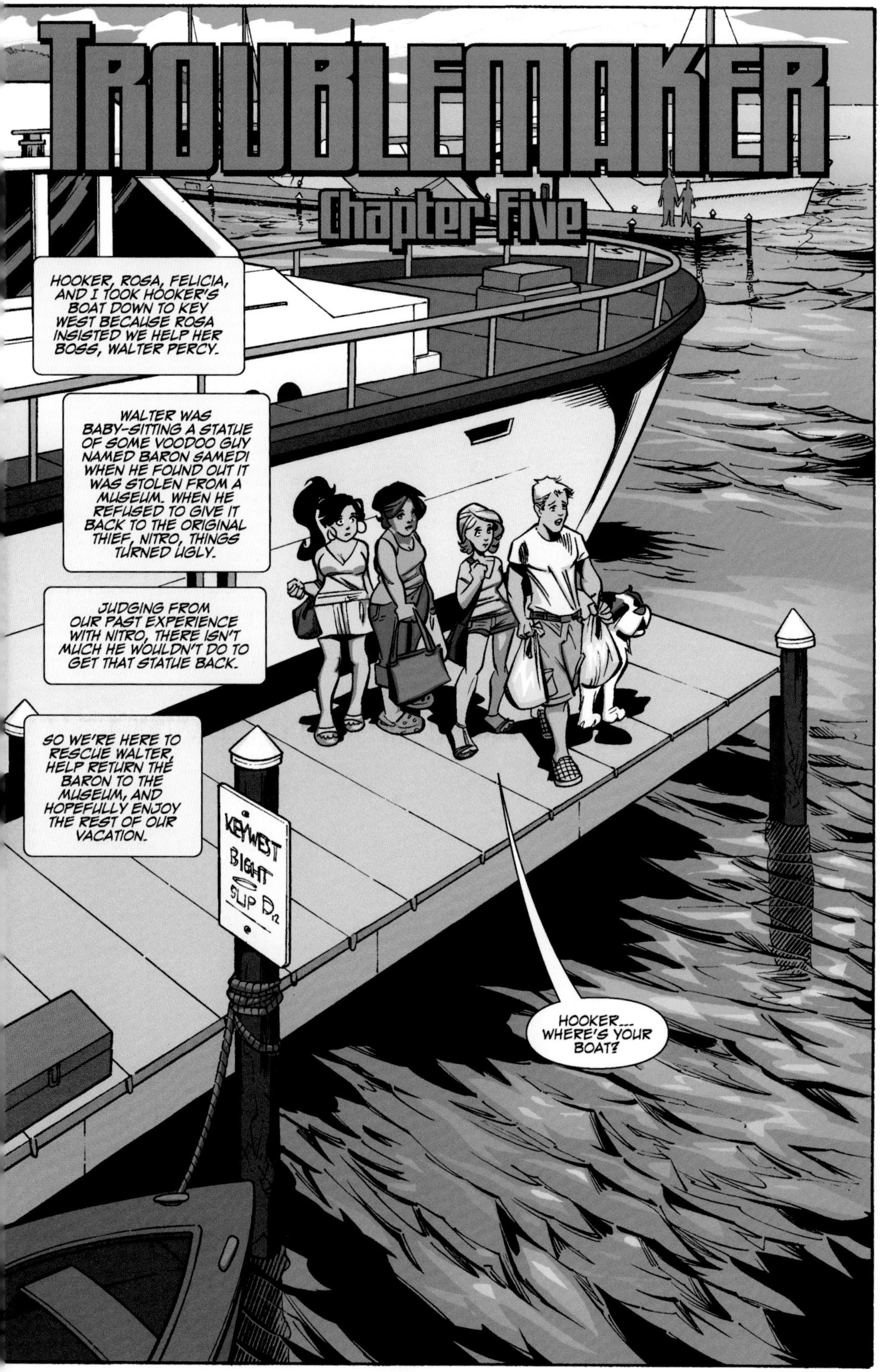
TROUBLEMAKER
Chapter Five
HOOKER, ROSA, FELICIA, AND I TOOK HOOKER'S BOAT DOWN TO KEY WEST BECAUSE ROSA INSISTED WE HELP HER BOSS, WALTER PERCY.
WALTER WAS BABY-SITTING A STATUE OF SOME VOODOO GUY NAMED BARON SAMEDI WHEN HE FOUND OUT IT WAS STOLEN FROM A MUSEUM. WHEN HE REFUSED TO GIVE IT BACK TO THE ORIGINAL THIEF, NITRO, THINGS TURNED UGLY.
JUDGING FROM OUR PAST EXPERIENCE WITH NITRO, THERE ISN'T MUCH HE WOULDN'T DO TO GET THAT STATUE BACK.
SO WE'RE HERE TO RESCUE WALTER, HELP RETURN THE BARON TO THE MUSEUM, AND HOPEFULLY ENJOY THE REST OF OUR VACATION.
KEY WEST BIGHT SLIP D12
HOOKER... WHERE'S YOUR BOAT?

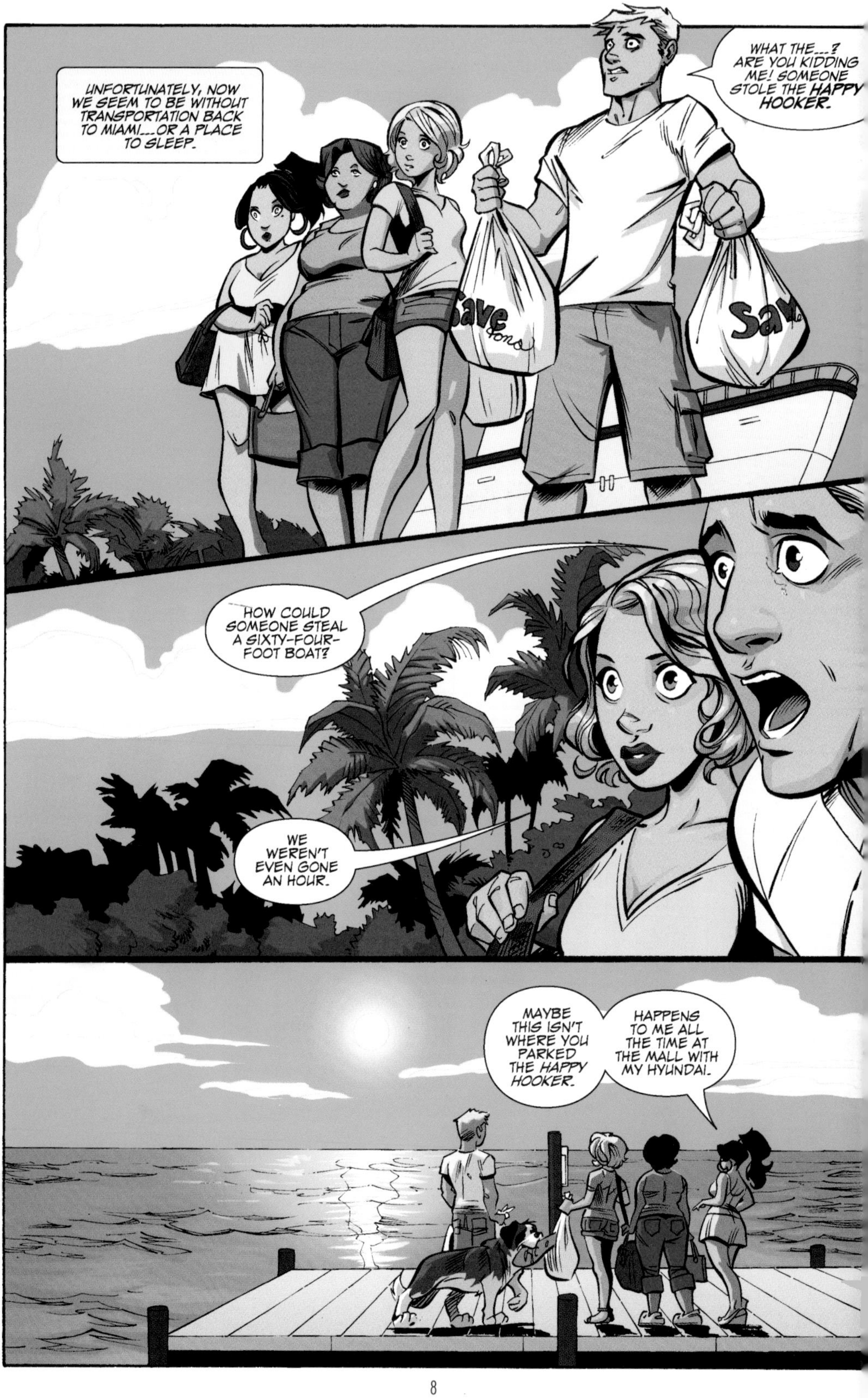
UNFORTUNATELY, NOW WE SEEM TO BE WITHOUT TRANSPORTATION BACK TO MIAMI...OR A PLACE TO SLEEP.
WHAT THE...? ARE YOU KIDDING ME! SOMEONE STOLE THE *HAPPY HOOKER*.
HOW COULD SOMEONE STEAL A SIXTY-FOUR-FOOT BOAT?
WE WEREN'T EVEN GONE AN HOUR.
MAYBE THIS ISN'T WHERE YOU PARKED THE *HAPPY HOOKER*.
HAPPENS TO ME ALL THE TIME AT THE MALL WITH MY HYUNDAI.

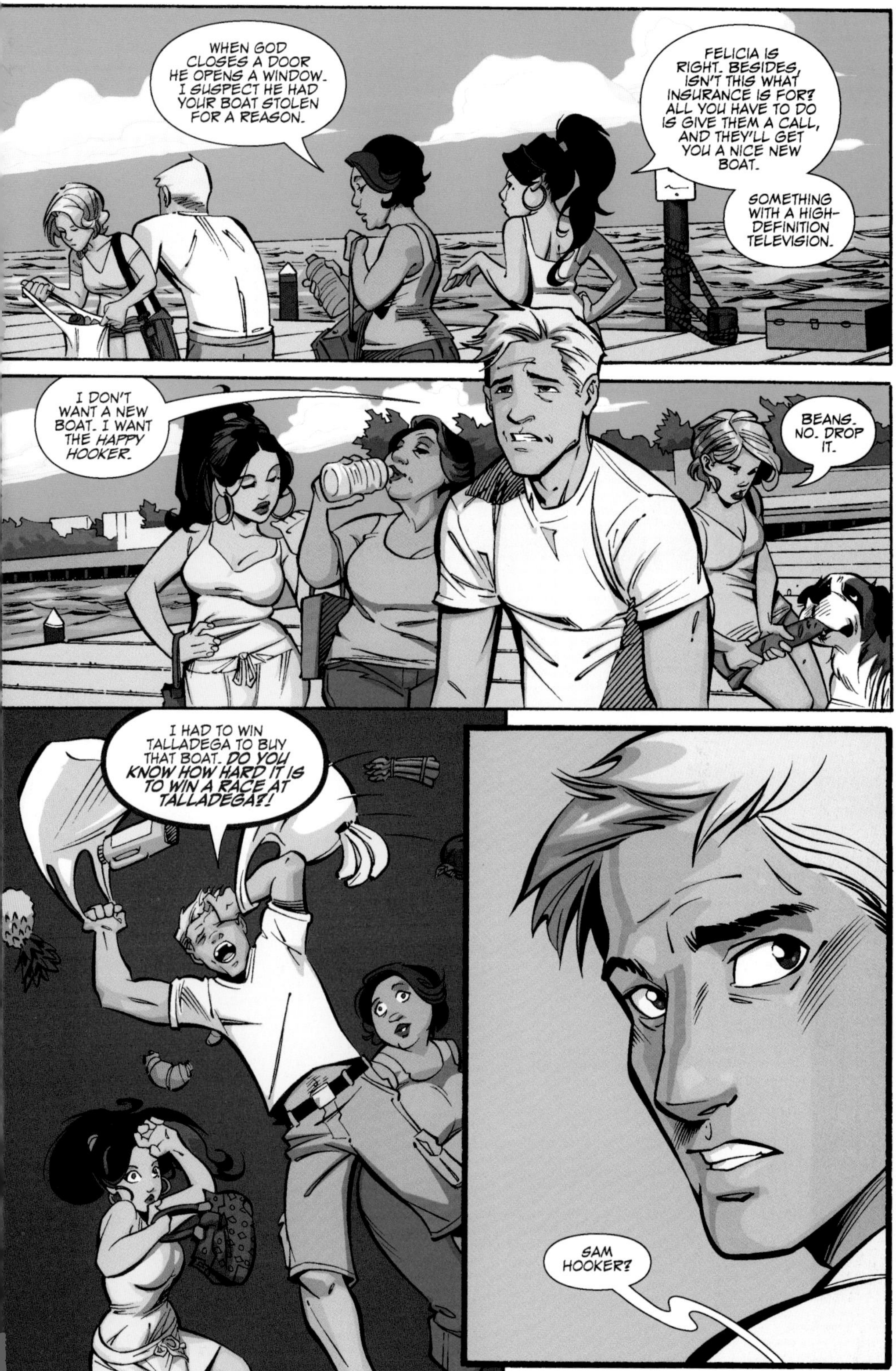
WHEN GOD CLOSES A DOOR HE OPENS A WINDOW. I SUSPECT HE HAD YOUR BOAT STOLEN FOR A REASON.
FELICIA IS RIGHT. BESIDES, ISN'T THIS WHAT INSURANCE IS FOR? ALL YOU HAVE TO DO IS GIVE THEM A CALL, AND THEY'LL GET YOU A NICE NEW BOAT.
SOMETHING WITH A HIGH-DEFINITION TELEVISION.
I DON'T WANT A NEW BOAT. I WANT THE *HAPPY HOOKER*.
BEANS. NO. DROP IT.
I HAD TO WIN TALLADEGA TO BUY THAT BOAT. ***DO YOU KNOW HOW HARD IT IS TO WIN A RACE AT TALLADEGA?!***
SAM HOOKER?

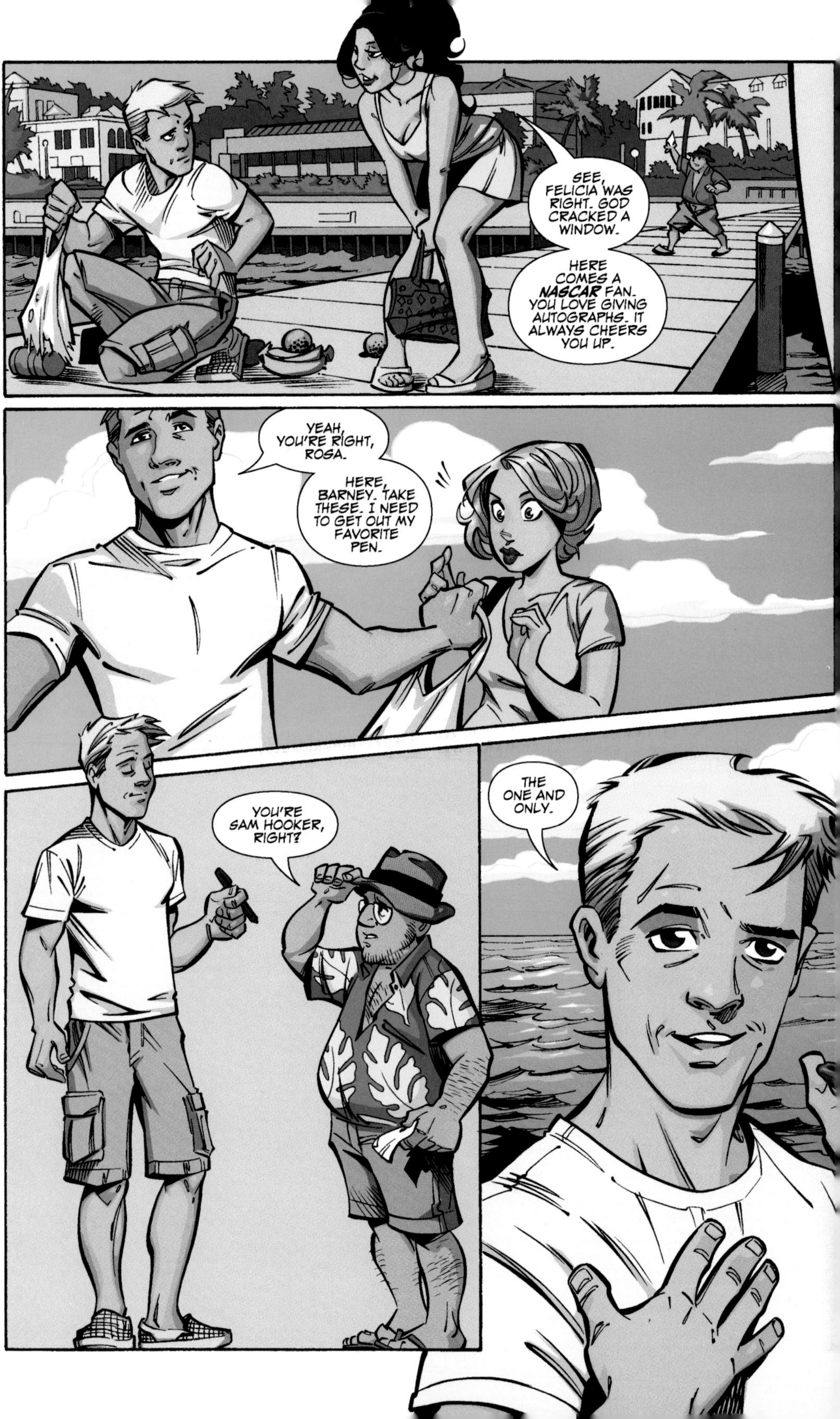
SEE, FELICIA WAS RIGHT. GOD CRACKED A WINDOW.
HERE COMES A NASCAR FAN. YOU LOVE GIVING AUTOGRAPHS. IT ALWAYS CHEERS YOU UP.
YEAH, YOU'RE RIGHT, ROSA.
HERE, BARNEY. TAKE THESE. I NEED TO GET OUT MY FAVORITE PEN.
YOU'RE SAM HOOKER, RIGHT?
THE ONE AND ONLY.

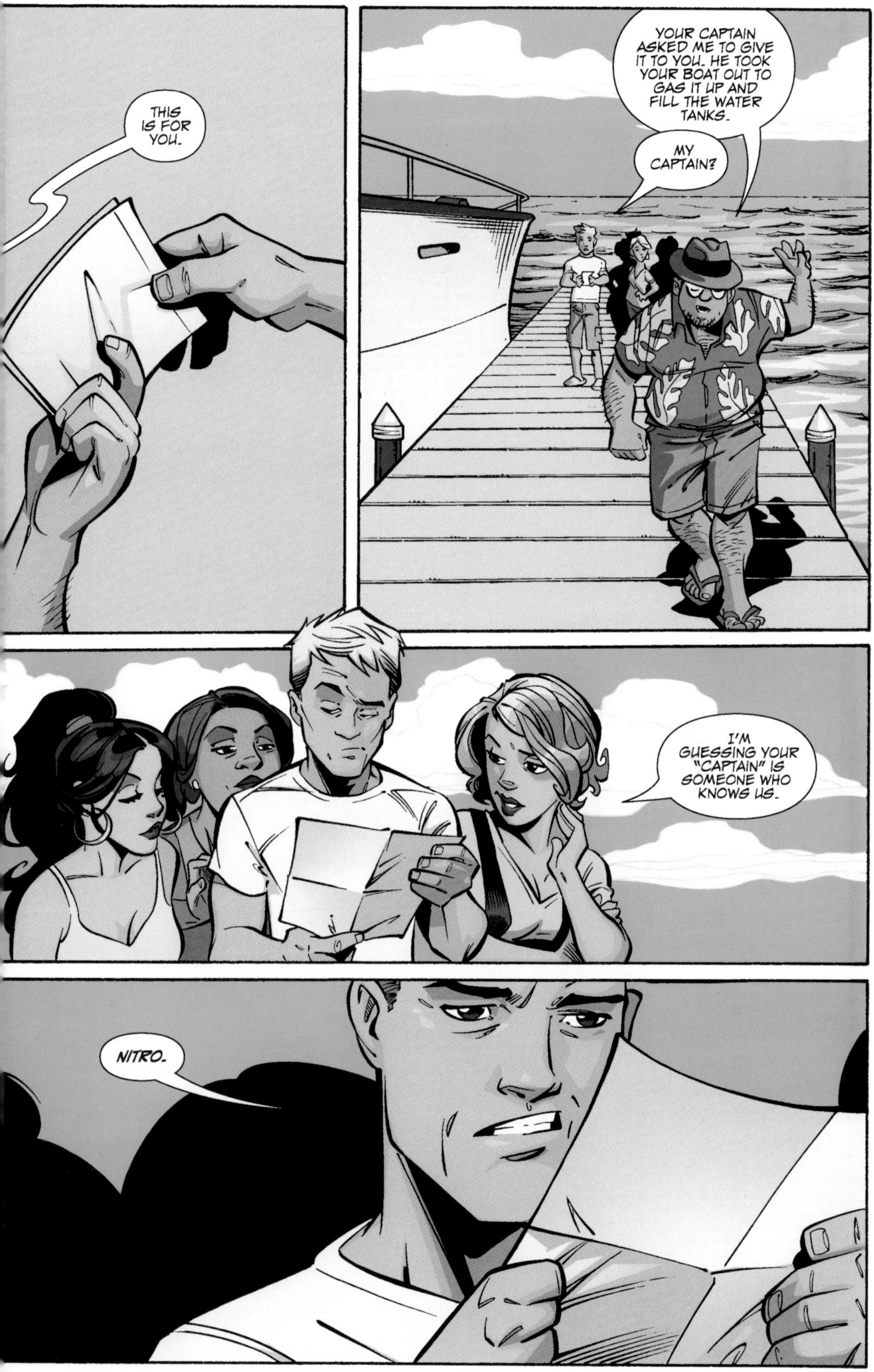
THIS IS FOR YOU.
YOUR CAPTAIN ASKED ME TO GIVE IT TO YOU. HE TOOK YOUR BOAT OUT TO GAS IT UP AND FILL THE WATER TANKS.
MY CAPTAIN?
I'M GUESSING YOUR "CAPTAIN" IS SOMEONE WHO KNOWS US.
NITRO.

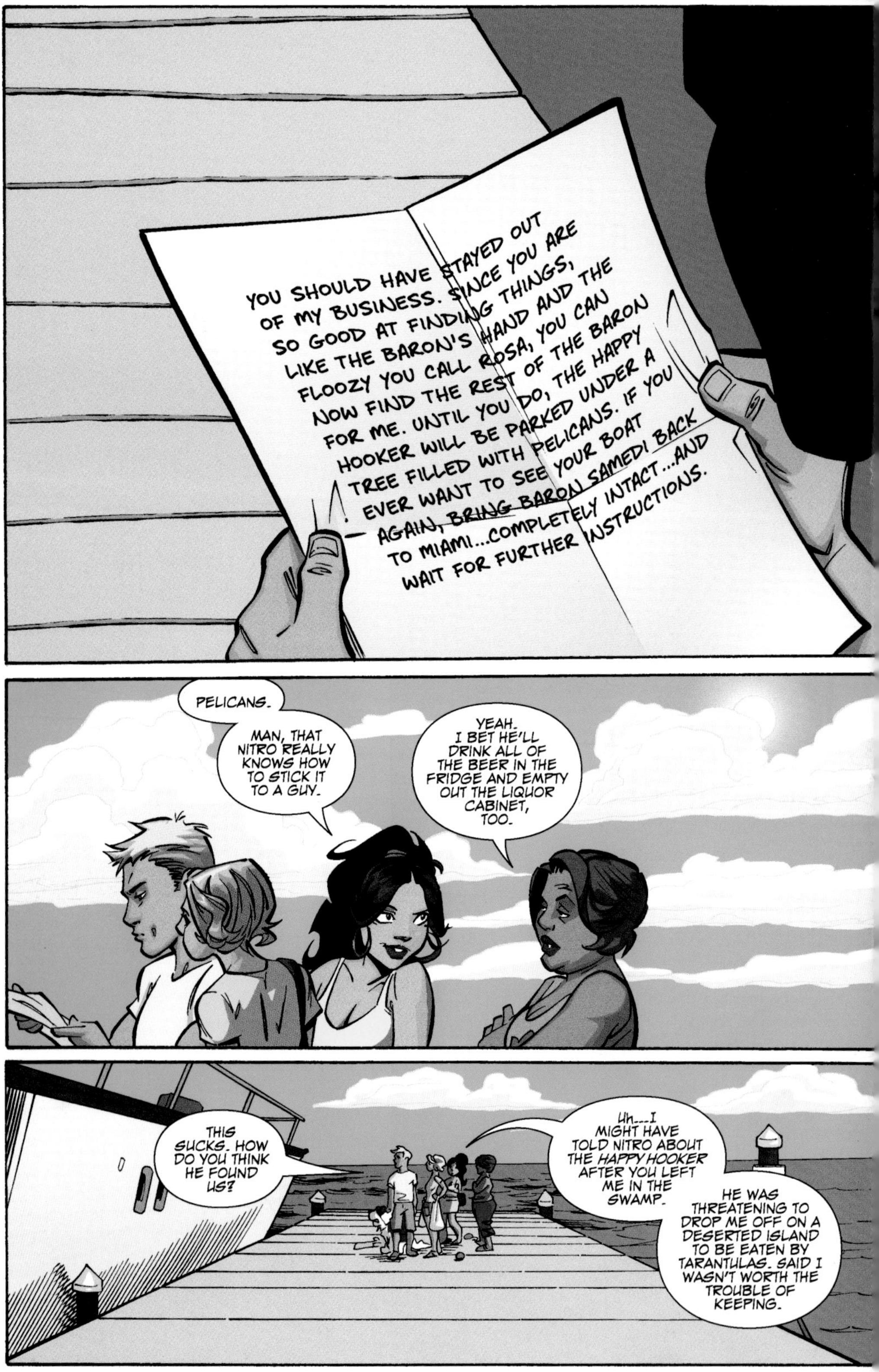
YOU SHOULD HAVE STAYED OUT OF MY BUSINESS. SINCE YOU ARE SO GOOD AT FINDING THINGS, LIKE THE BARON'S HAND AND THE FLOOZY YOU CALL ROSA, YOU CAN NOW FIND THE REST OF THE BARON FOR ME. UNTIL YOU DO, THE HAPPY HOOKER WILL BE PARKED UNDER A TREE FILLED WITH PELICANS. IF YOU EVER WANT TO SEE YOUR BOAT AGAIN, BRING BARON SAMEDI BACK TO MIAMI...COMPLETELY INTACT...AND WAIT FOR FURTHER INSTRUCTIONS.
PELICANS.
MAN, THAT NITRO REALLY KNOWS HOW TO STICK IT TO A GUY.
YEAH. I BET HE'LL DRINK ALL OF THE BEER IN THE FRIDGE AND EMPTY OUT THE LIQUOR CABINET, TOO.
THIS SUCKS. HOW DO YOU THINK HE FOUND US?
Uh...I MIGHT HAVE TOLD NITRO ABOUT THE HAPPY HOOKER AFTER YOU LEFT ME IN THE SWAMP.
HE WAS THREATENING TO DROP ME OFF ON A DESERTED ISLAND TO BE EATEN BY TARANTULAS. SAID I WASN'T WORTH THE TROUBLE OF KEEPING.

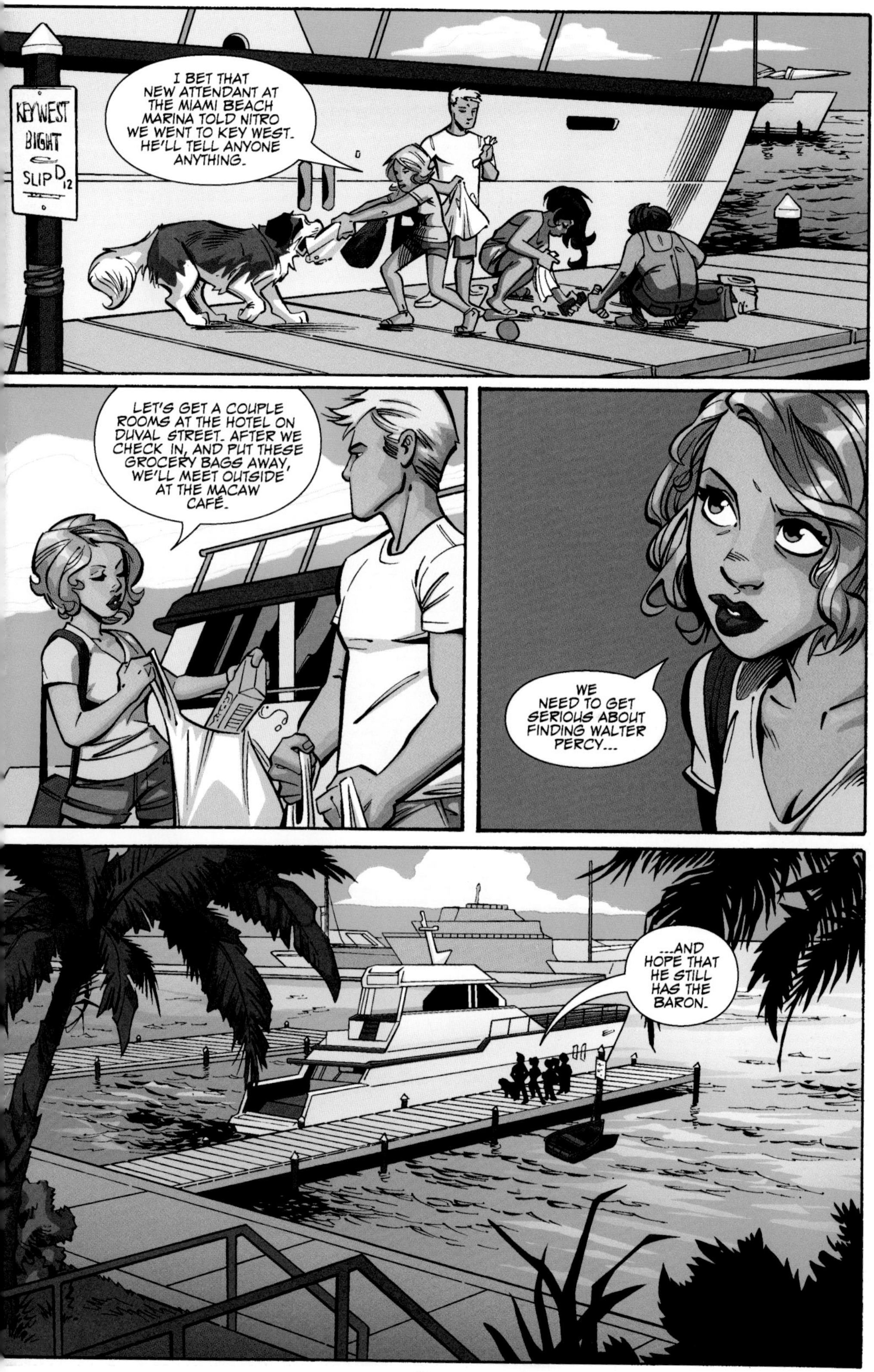
KEY WEST
BIGHT
SLIP D12
I BET THAT NEW ATTENDANT AT THE MIAMI BEACH MARINA TOLD NITRO WE WENT TO KEY WEST. HE'LL TELL ANYONE ANYTHING.
LET'S GET A COUPLE ROOMS AT THE HOTEL ON DUVAL STREET. AFTER WE CHECK IN, AND PUT THESE GROCERY BAGS AWAY, WE'LL MEET OUTSIDE AT THE MACAW CAFÉ.
WE NEED TO GET SERIOUS ABOUT FINDING WALTER PERCY...
...AND HOPE THAT HE STILL HAS THE BARON.

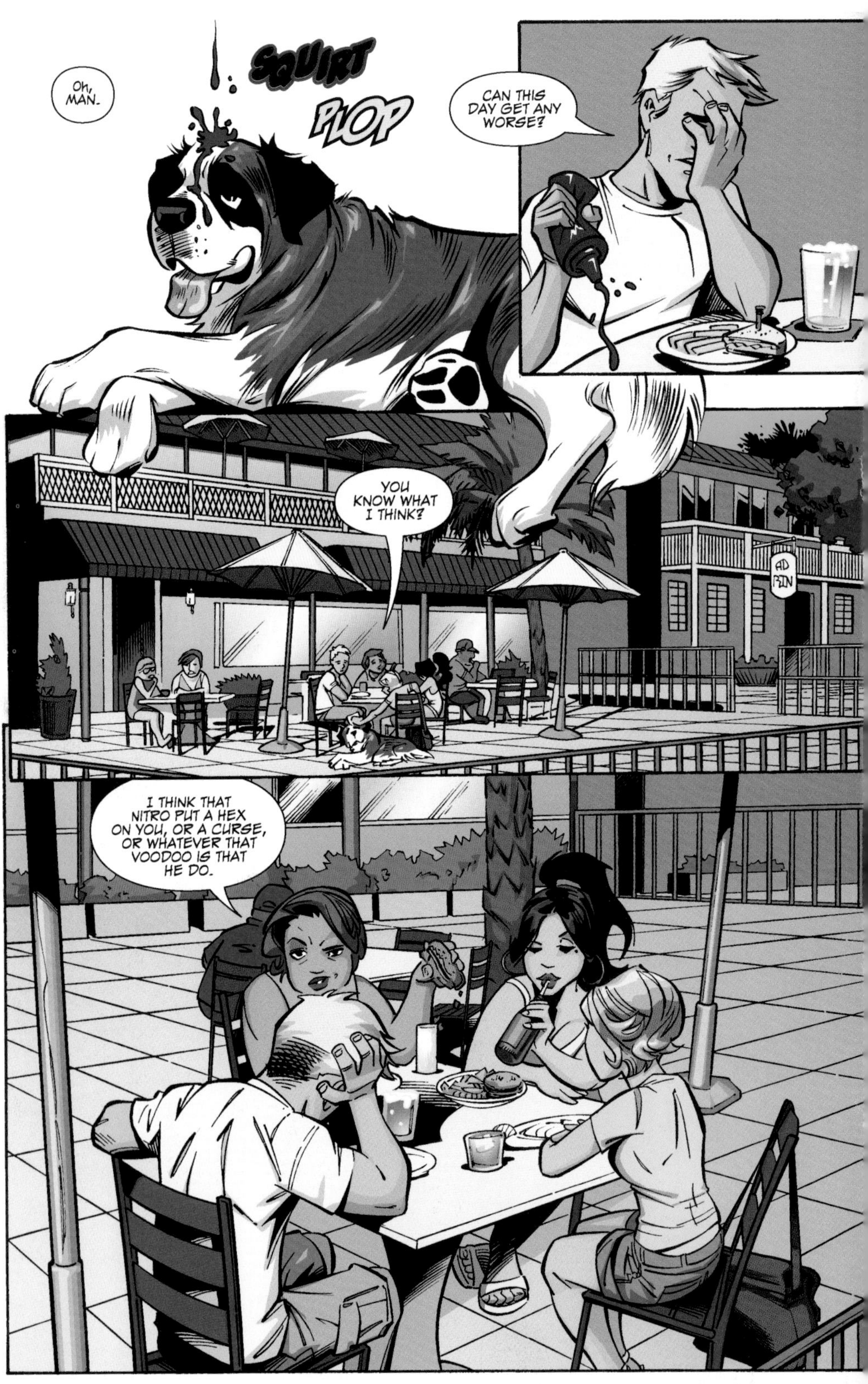

OH, MAN.
SQUIRT
PLOP
CAN THIS DAY GET ANY WORSE?
YOU KNOW WHAT I THINK?
I THINK THAT NITRO PUT A HEX ON YOU, OR A CURSE, OR WHATEVER THAT VOODOO IS THAT HE DO.

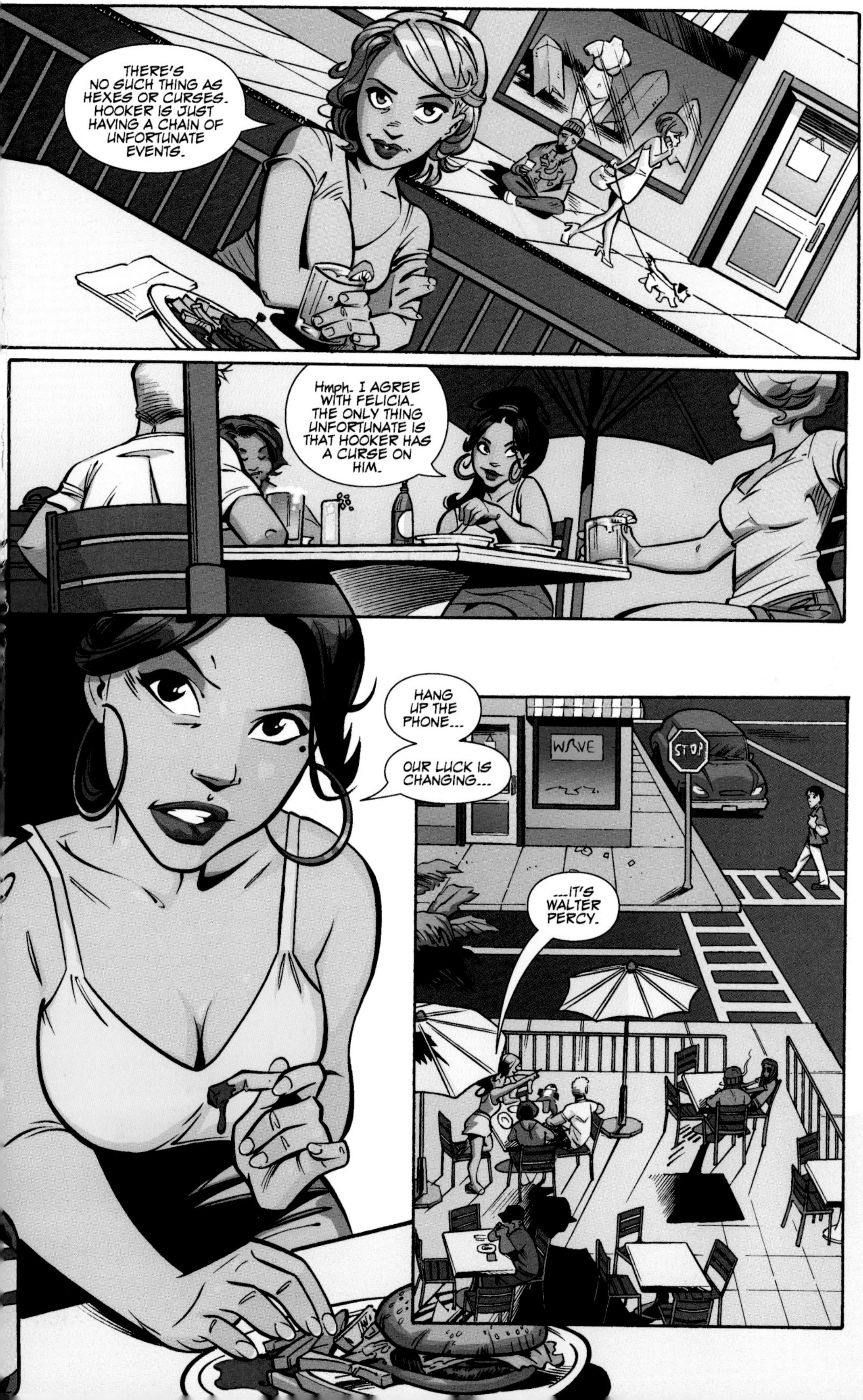
THERE'S NO SUCH THING AS HEXES OR CURSES. HOOKER IS JUST HAVING A CHAIN OF UNFORTUNATE EVENTS.
Hmph. I AGREE WITH FELICIA. THE ONLY THING UNFORTUNATE IS THAT HOOKER HAS A CURSE ON HIM.
HANG UP THE PHONE...
OUR LUCK IS CHANGING...
STOP
...IT'S WALTER PERCY.

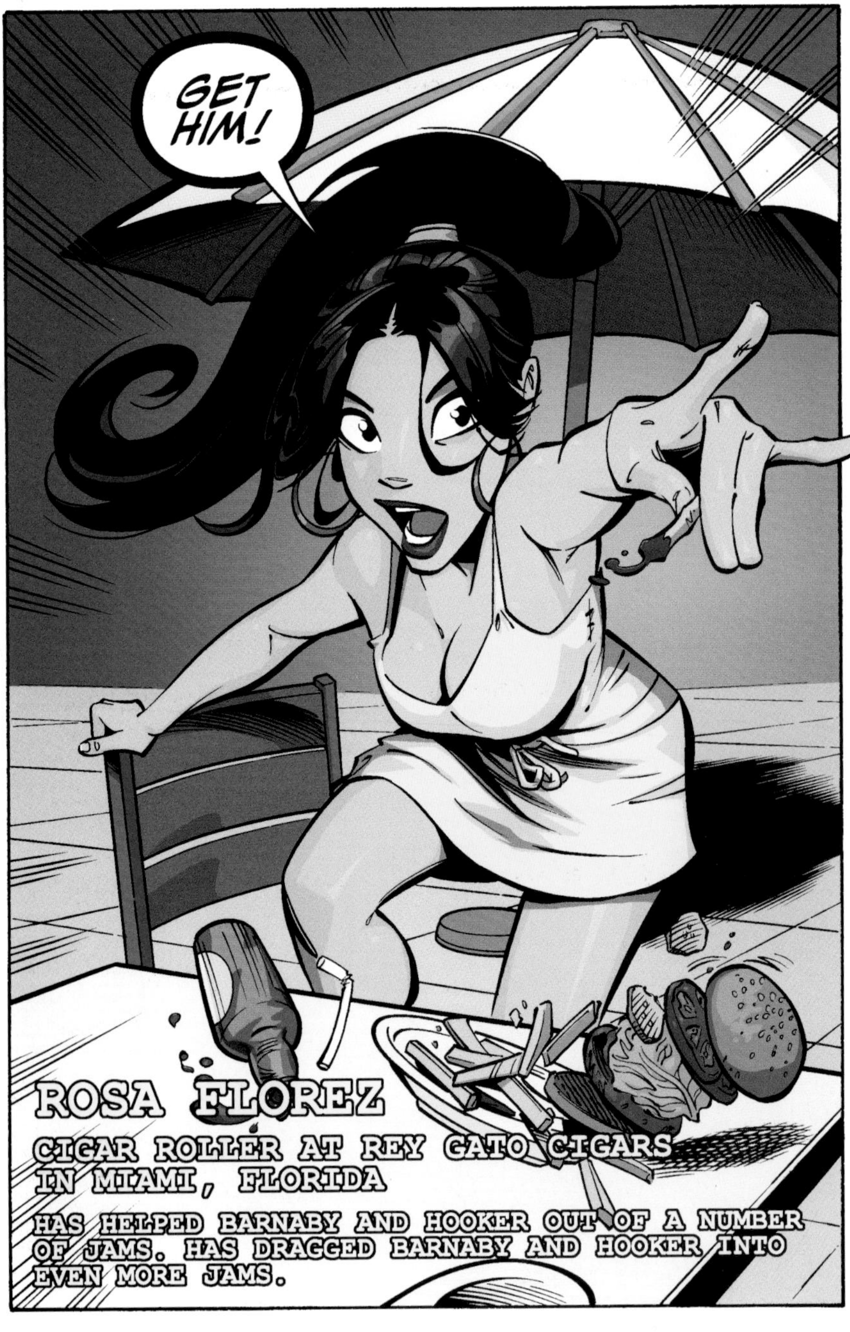
GET HIM!
ROSA FLOREZ
CIGAR ROLLER AT REY GATO CIGARS IN MIAMI, FLORIDA
HAS HELPED BARNABY AND HOOKER OUT OF A NUMBER OF JAMS. HAS DRAGGED BARNABY AND HOOKER INTO EVEN MORE JAMS.

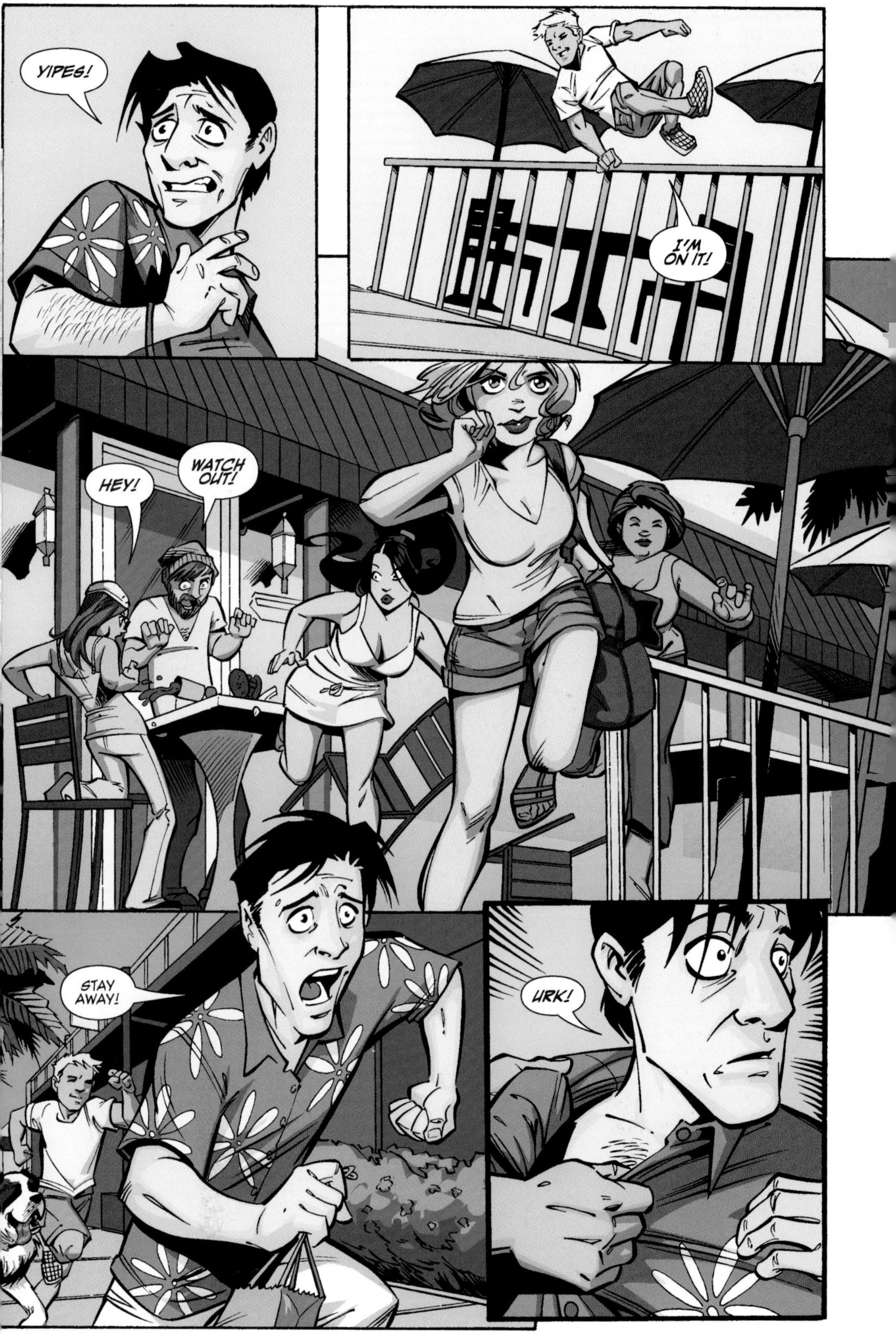
YIPES!
I'M ON IT!
HEY!
WATCH OUT!
STAY AWAY!
URK!

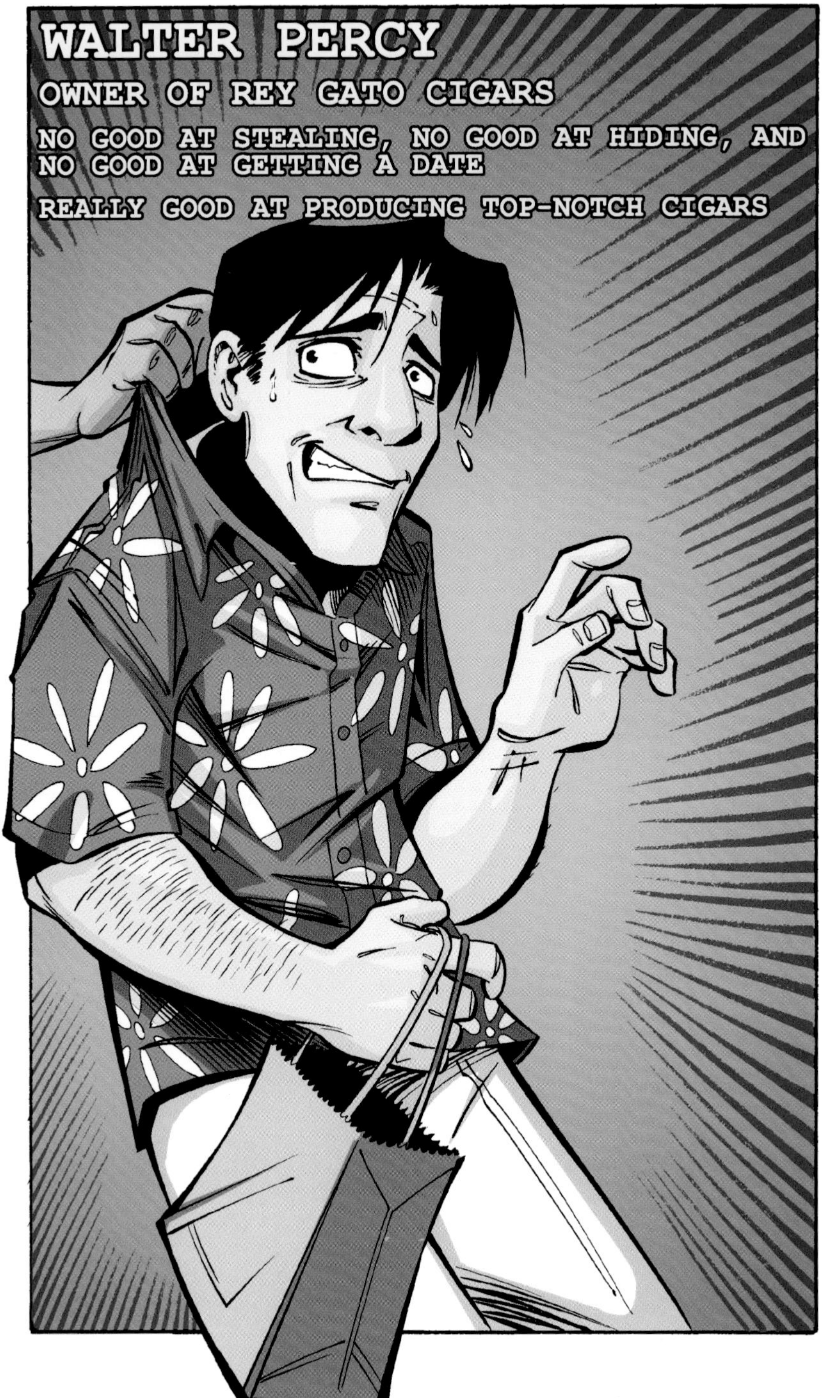
WALTER PERCY
OWNER OF REY GATO CIGARS
NO GOOD AT STEALING, NO GOOD AT HIDING, AND NO GOOD AT GETTING A DATE
REALLY GOOD AT PRODUCING TOP-NOTCH CIGARS

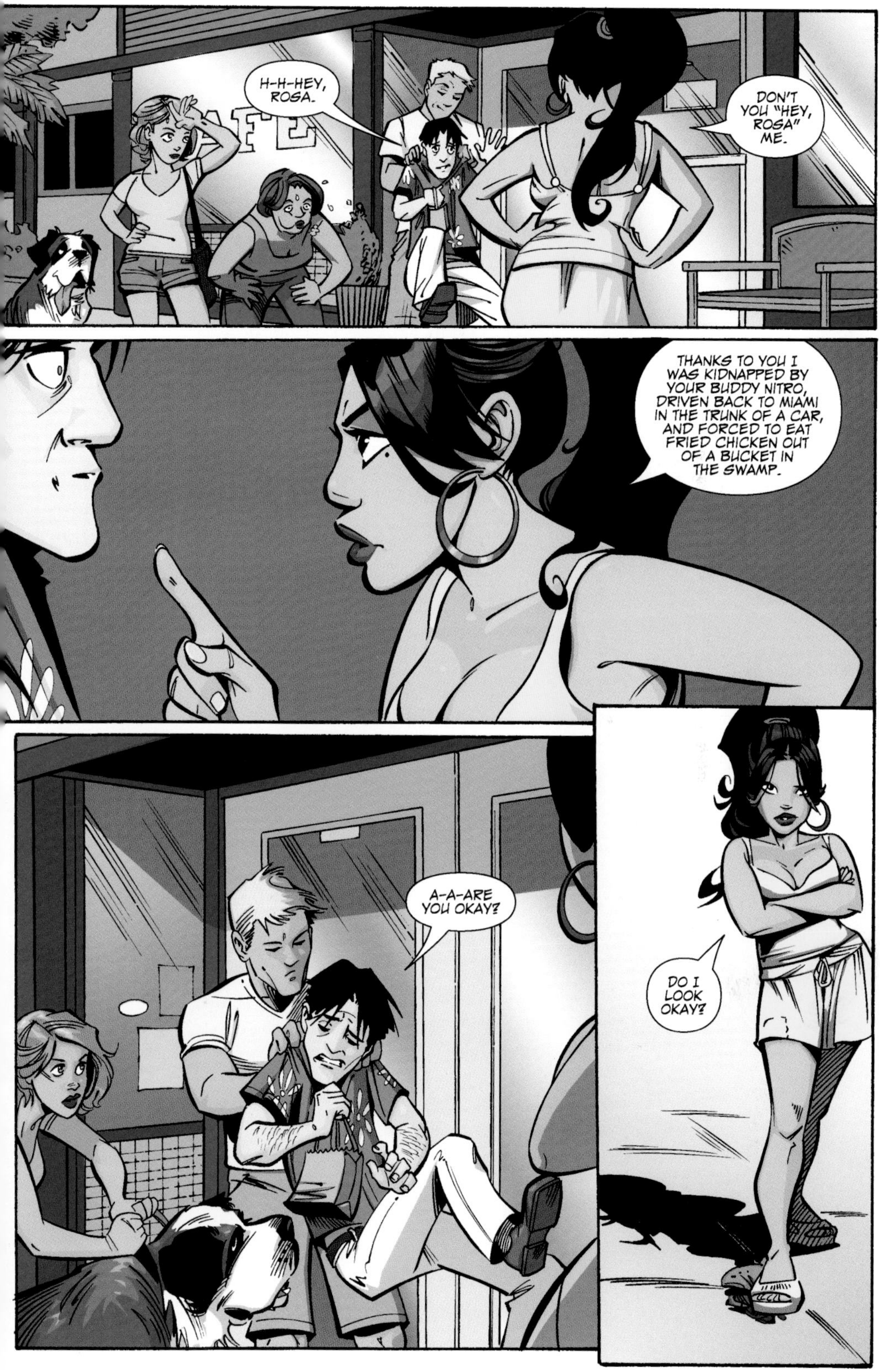
H-H-HEY, ROSA.
DON'T YOU "HEY, ROSA" ME.
THANKS TO YOU I WAS KIDNAPPED BY YOUR BUDDY NITRO, DRIVEN BACK TO MIAMI IN THE TRUNK OF A CAR, AND FORCED TO EAT FRIED CHICKEN OUT OF A BUCKET IN THE SWAMP.
A-A-ARE YOU OKAY?
DO I LOOK OKAY?

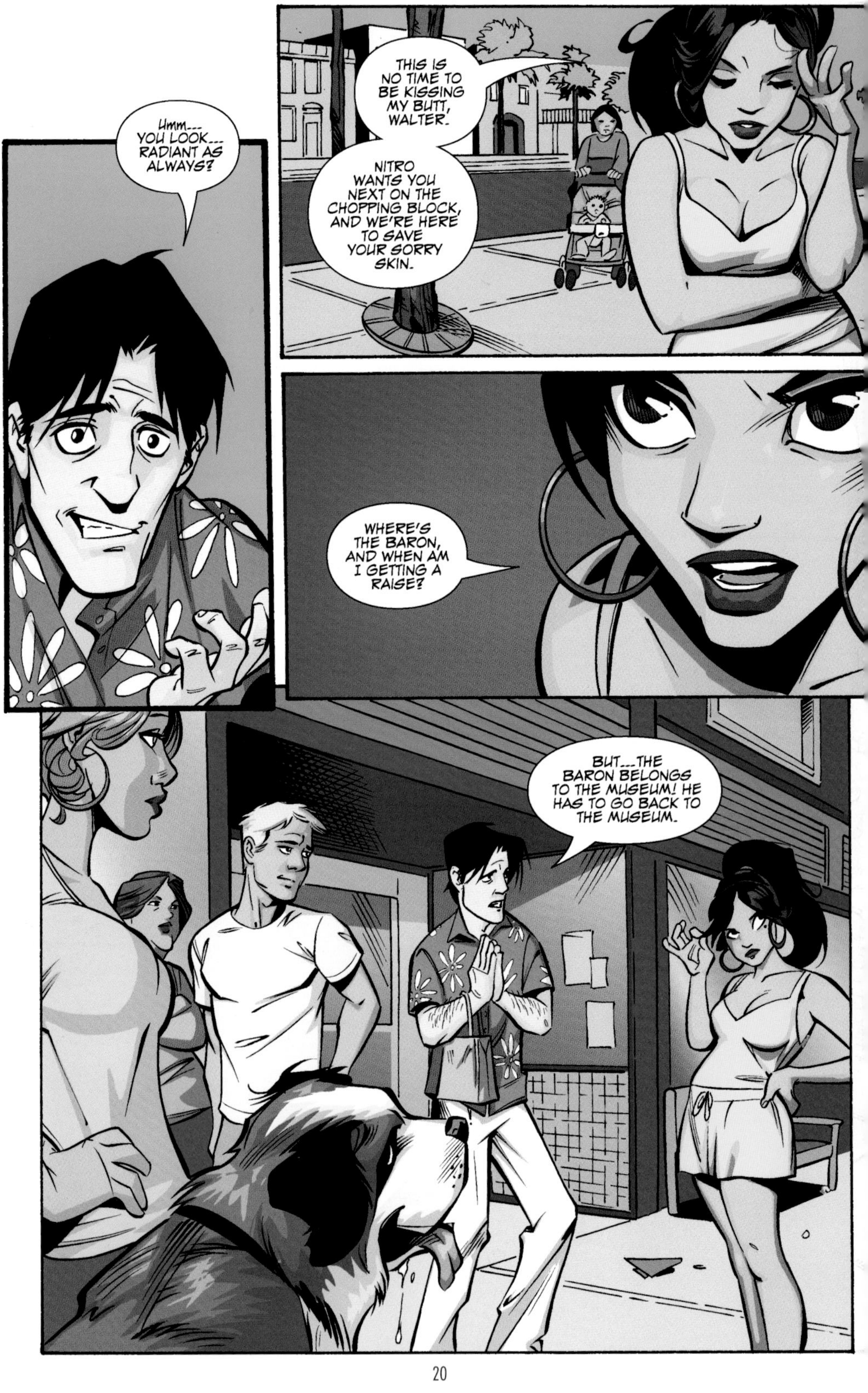
UMM... YOU LOOK... RADIANT AS ALWAYS?
THIS IS NO TIME TO BE KISSING MY BUTT, WALTER.
NITRO WANTS YOU NEXT ON THE CHOPPING BLOCK, AND WE'RE HERE TO SAVE YOUR SORRY SKIN.
WHERE'S THE BARON, AND WHEN AM I GETTING A RAISE?
BUT...THE BARON BELONGS TO THE MUSEUM! HE HAS TO GO BACK TO THE MUSEUM.

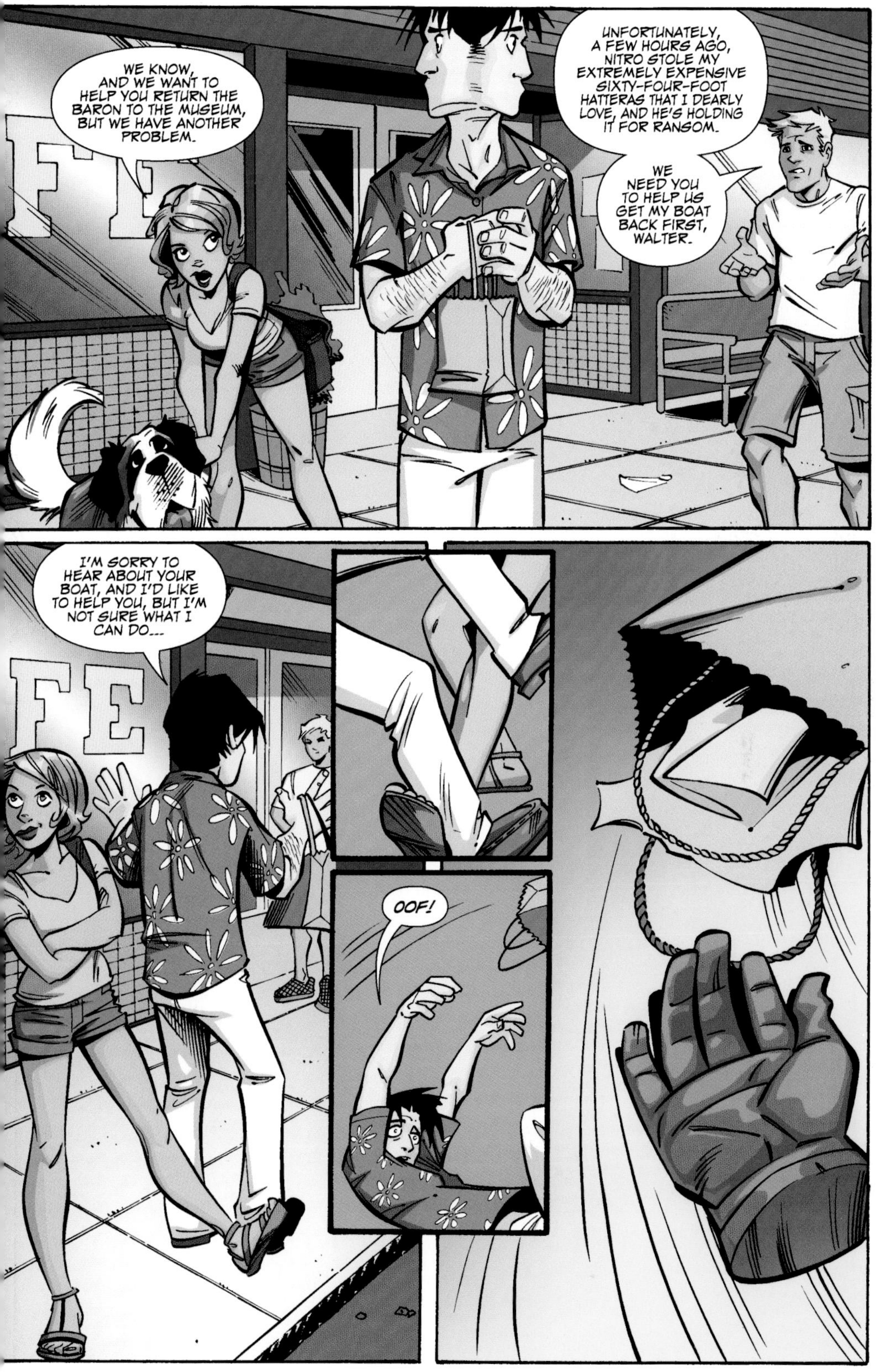
WE KNOW, AND WE WANT TO HELP YOU RETURN THE BARON TO THE MUSEUM, BUT WE HAVE ANOTHER PROBLEM.
UNFORTUNATELY, A FEW HOURS AGO, NITRO STOLE MY EXTREMELY EXPENSIVE SIXTY-FOUR-FOOT HATTERAS THAT I DEARLY LOVE, AND HE'S HOLDING IT FOR RANSOM.
WE NEED YOU TO HELP US GET MY BOAT BACK FIRST, WALTER.
I'M SORRY TO HEAR ABOUT YOUR BOAT, AND I'D LIKE TO HELP YOU, BUT I'M NOT SURE WHAT I CAN DO...
OOF!

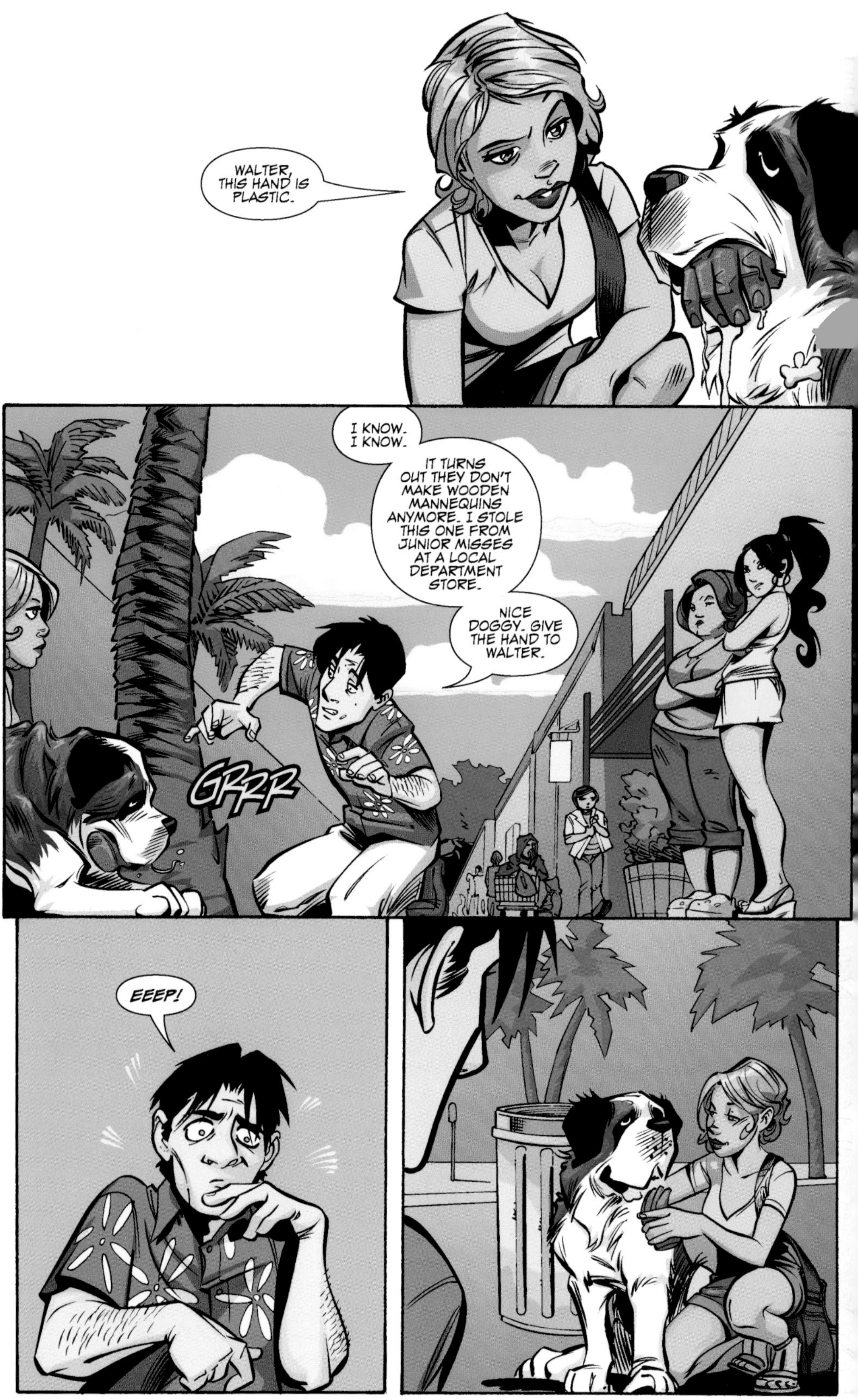

WALTER, THIS HAND IS PLASTIC.
I KNOW. I KNOW.
IT TURNS OUT THEY DON'T MAKE WOODEN MANNEQUINS ANYMORE. I STOLE THIS ONE FROM JUNIOR MISSES AT A LOCAL DEPARTMENT STORE.
NICE DOGGY. GIVE THE HAND TO WALTER.
GRRR
EEEP!

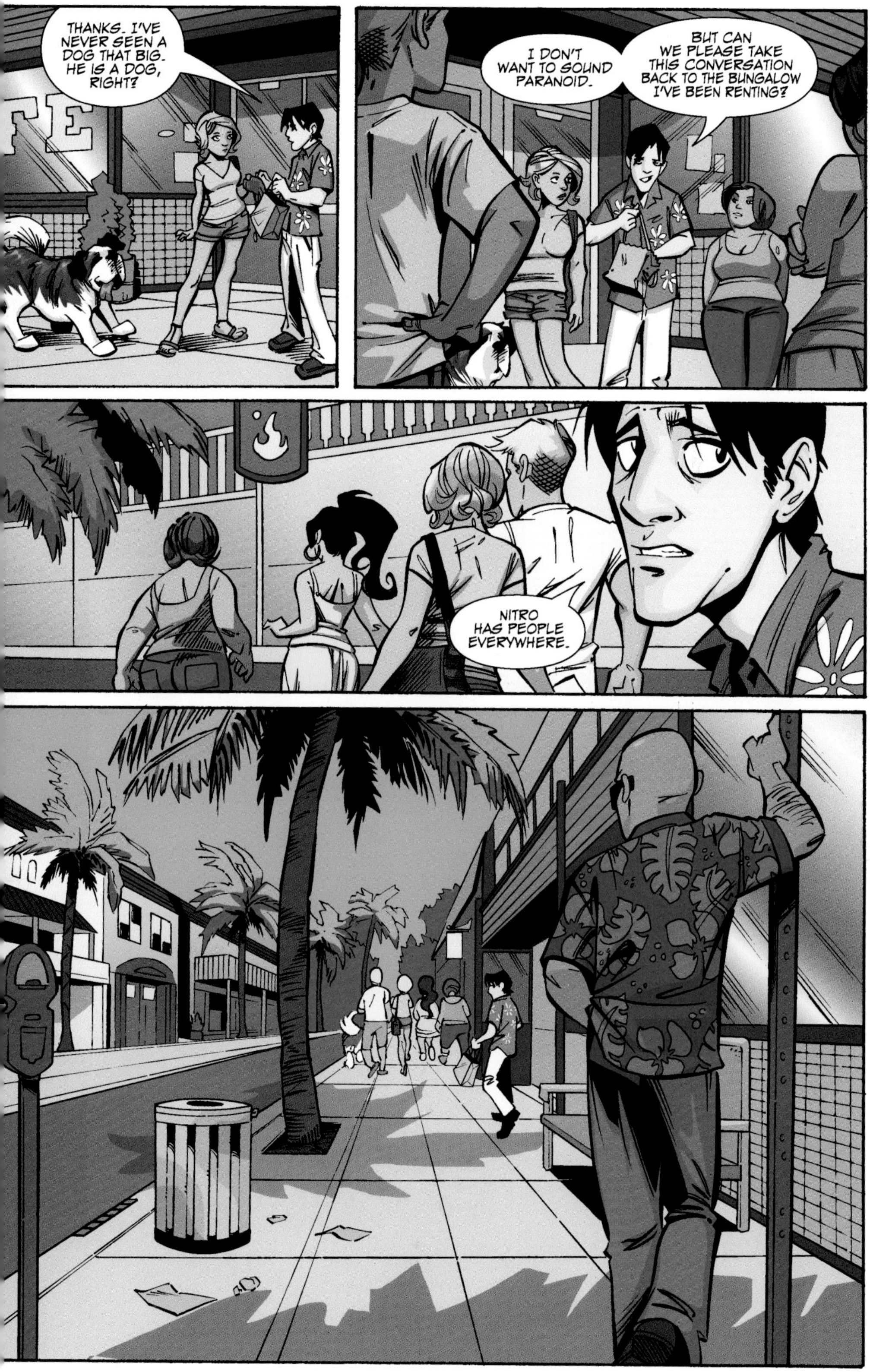

THANKS. I'VE NEVER SEEN A DOG THAT BIG. HE IS A DOG, RIGHT?
I DON'T WANT TO SOUND PARANOID.
BUT CAN WE PLEASE TAKE THIS CONVERSATION BACK TO THE BUNGALOW I'VE BEEN RENTING?
NITRO HAS PEOPLE EVERYWHERE.

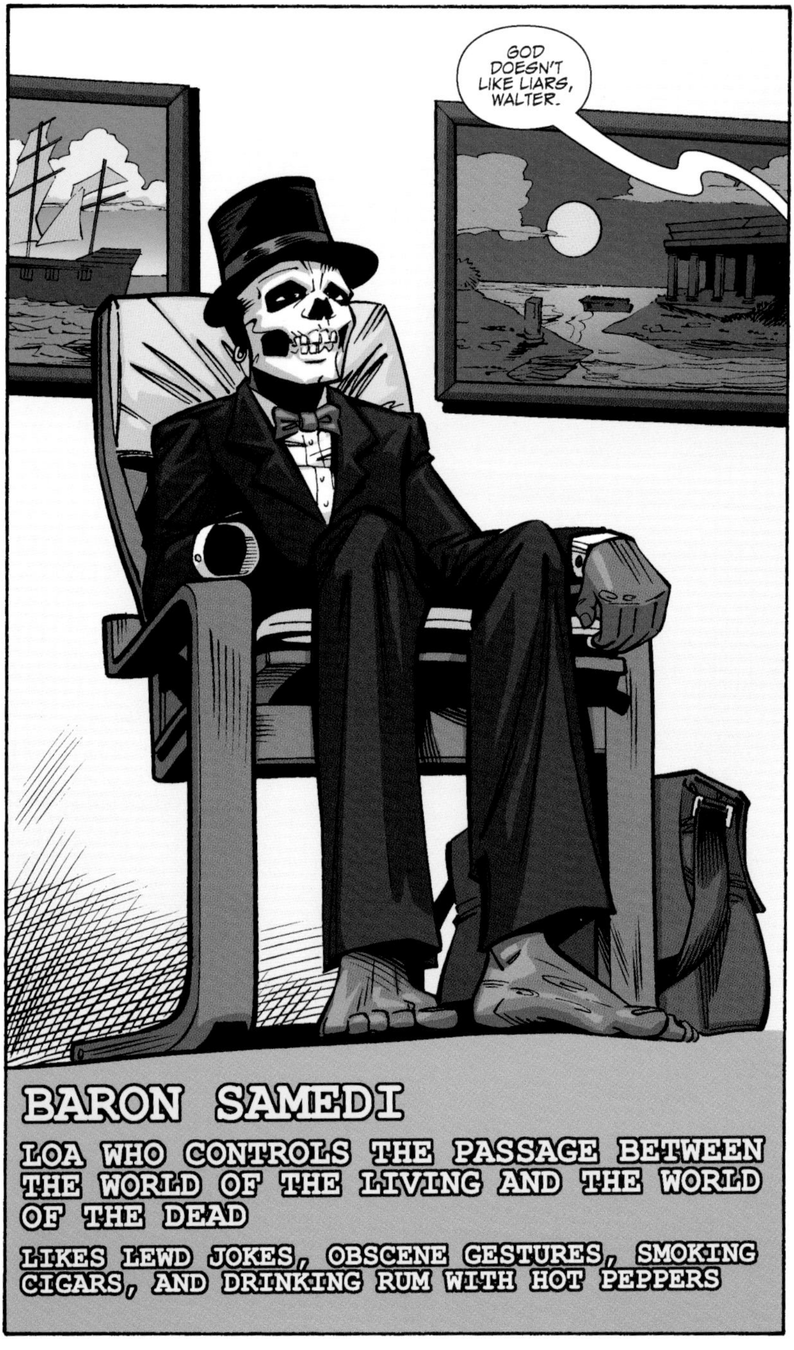
GOD DOESN'T LIKE LIARS, WALTER.
BARON SAMEDI
LOA WHO CONTROLS THE PASSAGE BETWEEN THE WORLD OF THE LIVING AND THE WORLD OF THE DEAD
LIKES LEWD JOKES, OBSCENE GESTURES, SMOKING CIGARS, AND DRINKING RUM WITH HOT PEPPERS

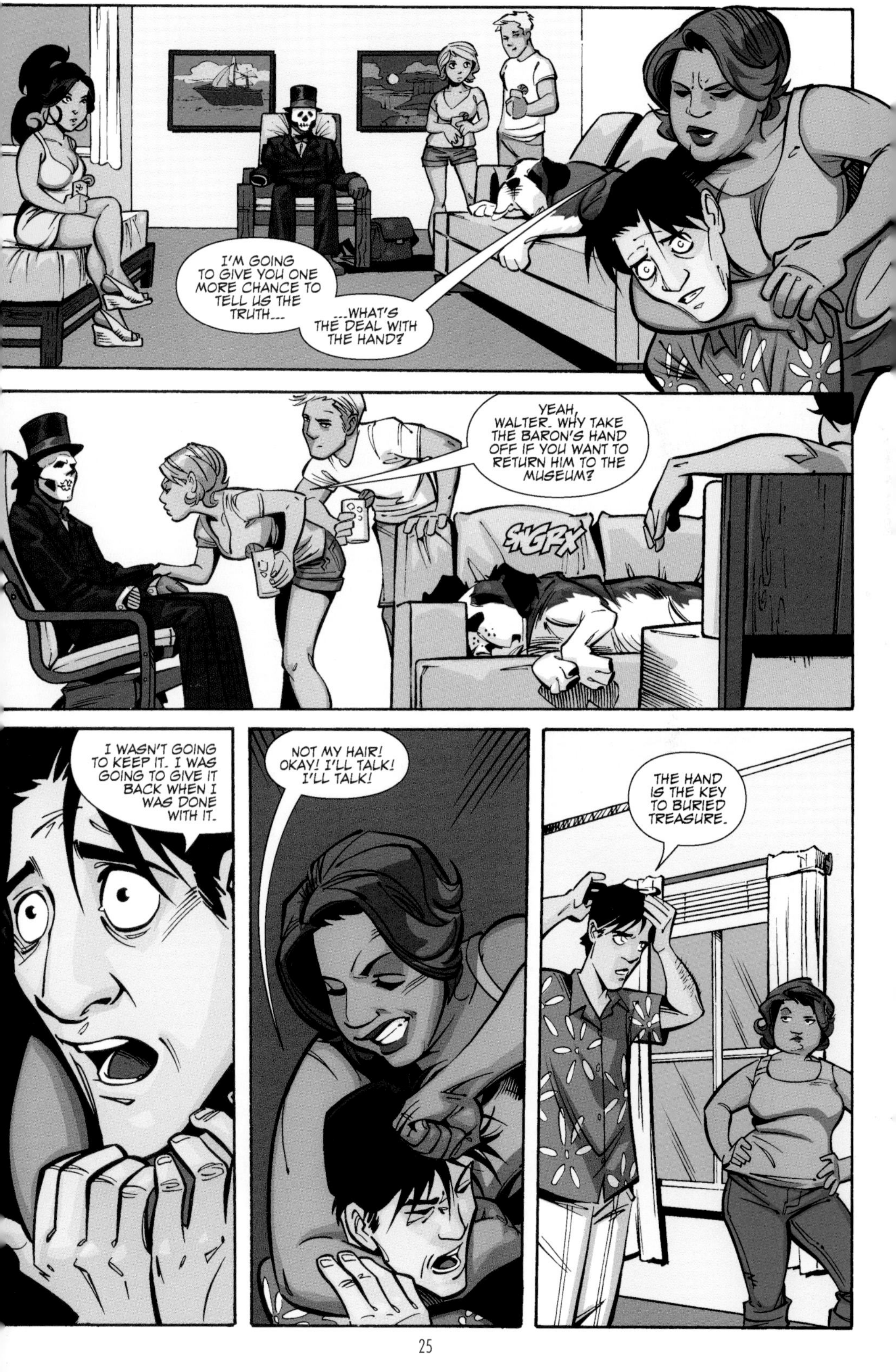
I'M GOING TO GIVE YOU ONE MORE CHANCE TO TELL US THE TRUTH...
...WHAT'S THE DEAL WITH THE HAND?
YEAH, WALTER. WHY TAKE THE BARON'S HAND OFF IF YOU WANT TO RETURN HIM TO THE MUSEUM?
SKGRX
I WASN'T GOING TO KEEP IT. I WAS GOING TO GIVE IT BACK WHEN I WAS DONE WITH IT.
NOT MY HAIR! OKAY! I'LL TALK! I'LL TALK!
THE HAND IS THE KEY TO BURIED TREASURE.

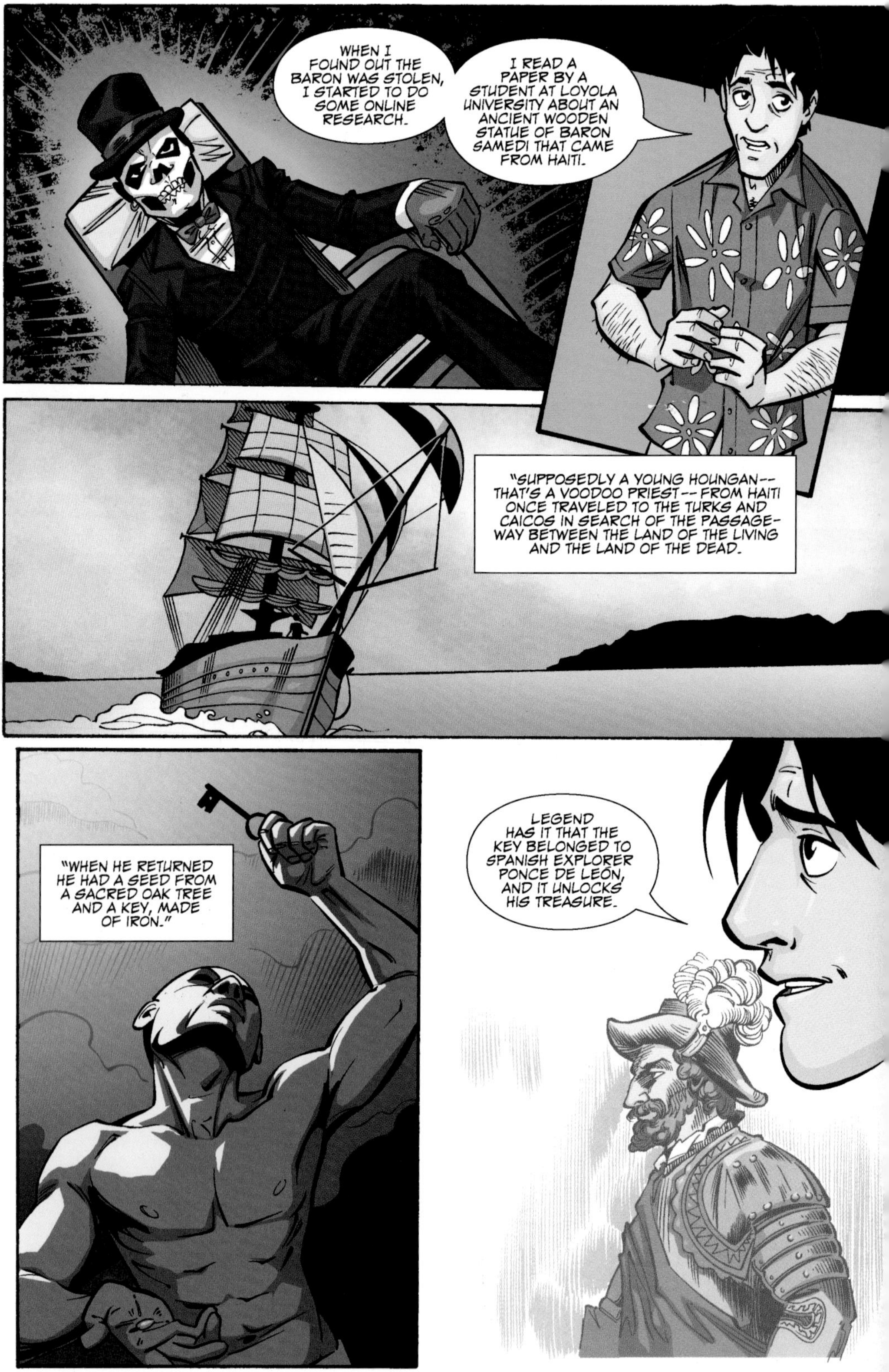
WHEN I FOUND OUT THE BARON WAS STOLEN, I STARTED TO DO SOME ONLINE RESEARCH.
I READ A PAPER BY A STUDENT AT LOYOLA UNIVERSITY ABOUT AN ANCIENT WOODEN STATUE OF BARON SAMEDI THAT CAME FROM HAITI.
"SUPPOSEDLY A YOUNG HOUNGAN--THAT'S A VOODOO PRIEST--FROM HAITI ONCE TRAVELED TO THE TURKS AND CAICOS IN SEARCH OF THE PASSAGE-WAY BETWEEN THE LAND OF THE LIVING AND THE LAND OF THE DEAD.
"WHEN HE RETURNED HE HAD A SEED FROM A SACRED OAK TREE AND A KEY, MADE OF IRON."
LEGEND HAS IT THAT THE KEY BELONGED TO SPANISH EXPLORER PONCE DE LEÓN, AND IT UNLOCKS HIS TREASURE.

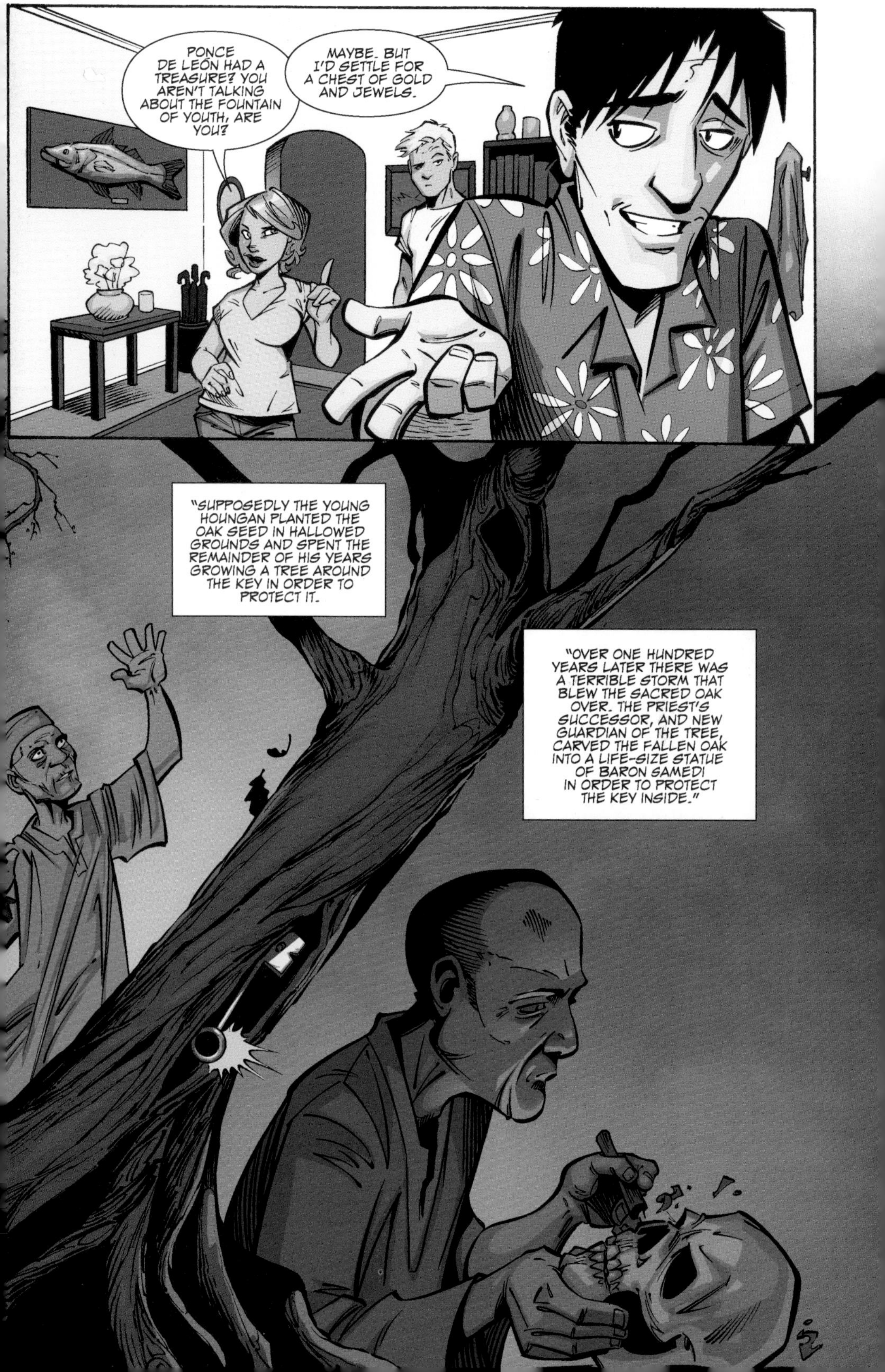
PONCE DE LEÓN HAD A TREASURE? YOU AREN'T TALKING ABOUT THE FOUNTAIN OF YOUTH, ARE YOU?
MAYBE. BUT I'D SETTLE FOR A CHEST OF GOLD AND JEWELS.
"SUPPOSEDLY THE YOUNG HOUNGAN PLANTED THE OAK SEED IN HALLOWED GROUNDS AND SPENT THE REMAINDER OF HIS YEARS GROWING A TREE AROUND THE KEY IN ORDER TO PROTECT IT.
"OVER ONE HUNDRED YEARS LATER THERE WAS A TERRIBLE STORM THAT BLEW THE SACRED OAK OVER. THE PRIEST'S SUCCESSOR, AND NEW GUARDIAN OF THE TREE, CARVED THE FALLEN OAK INTO A LIFE-SIZE STATUE OF BARON SAMEDI IN ORDER TO PROTECT THE KEY INSIDE."

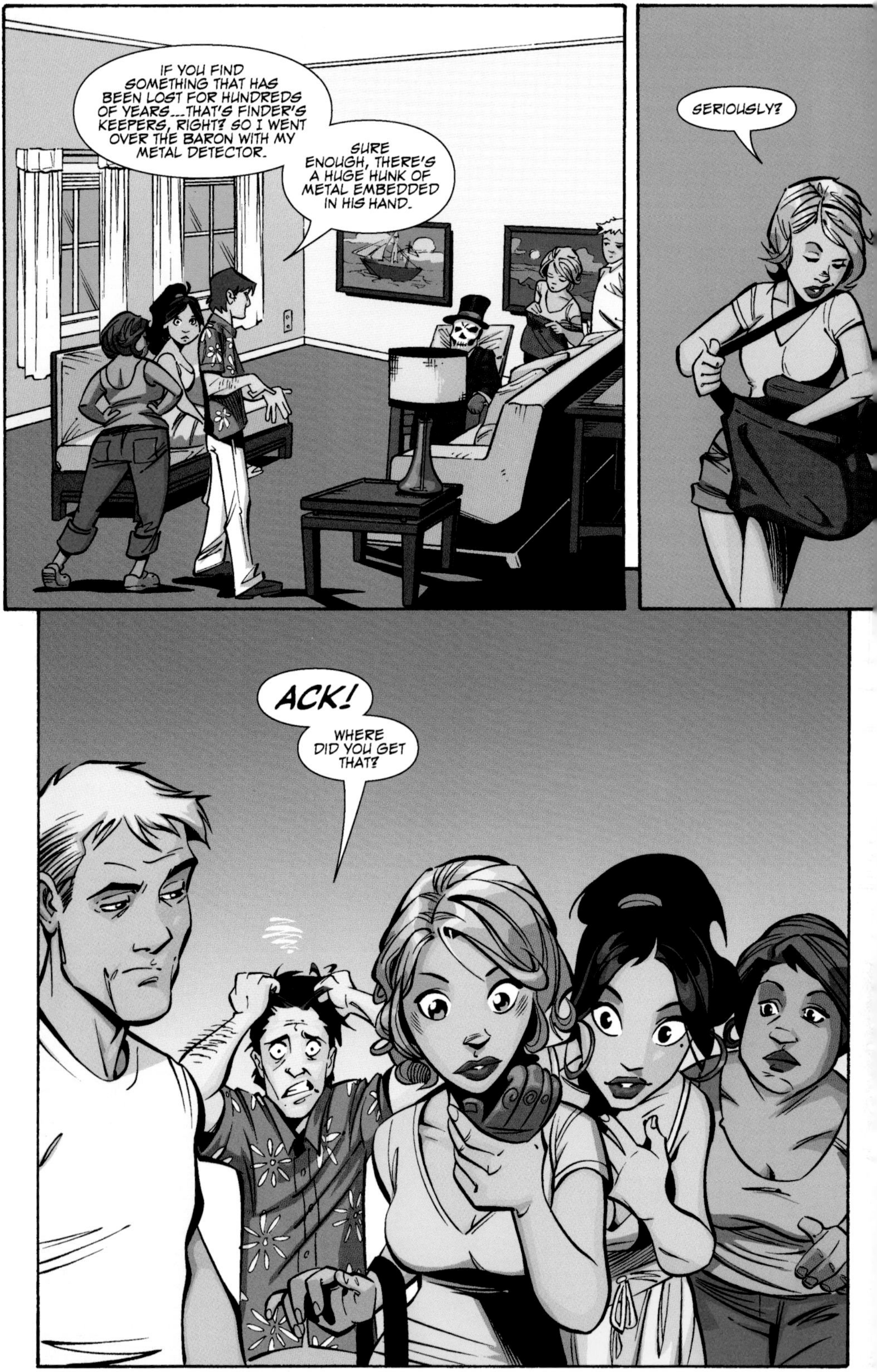
IF YOU FIND SOMETHING THAT HAS BEEN LOST FOR HUNDREDS OF YEARS...THAT'S FINDER'S KEEPERS, RIGHT? SO I WENT OVER THE BARON WITH MY METAL DETECTOR.
SURE ENOUGH, THERE'S A HUGE HUNK OF METAL EMBEDDED IN HIS HAND.
SERIOUSLY?
ACK!
WHERE DID YOU GET THAT?

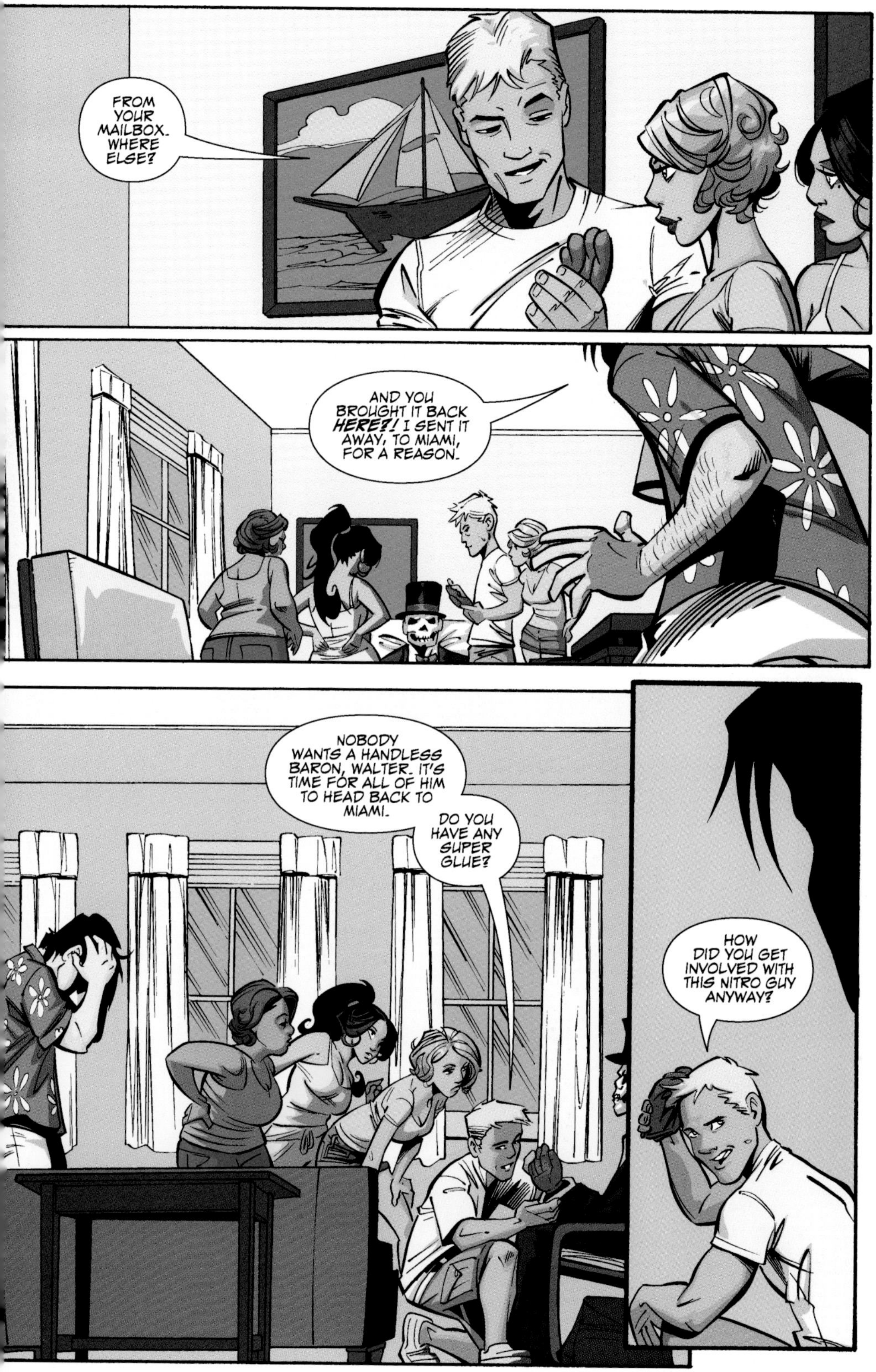
FROM YOUR MAILBOX. WHERE ELSE?
AND YOU BROUGHT IT BACK HERE?! I SENT IT AWAY, TO MIAMI, FOR A REASON.
NOBODY WANTS A HANDLESS BARON, WALTER. IT'S TIME FOR ALL OF HIM TO HEAD BACK TO MIAMI.
DO YOU HAVE ANY SUPER GLUE?
HOW DID YOU GET INVOLVED WITH THIS NITRO GUY ANYWAY?

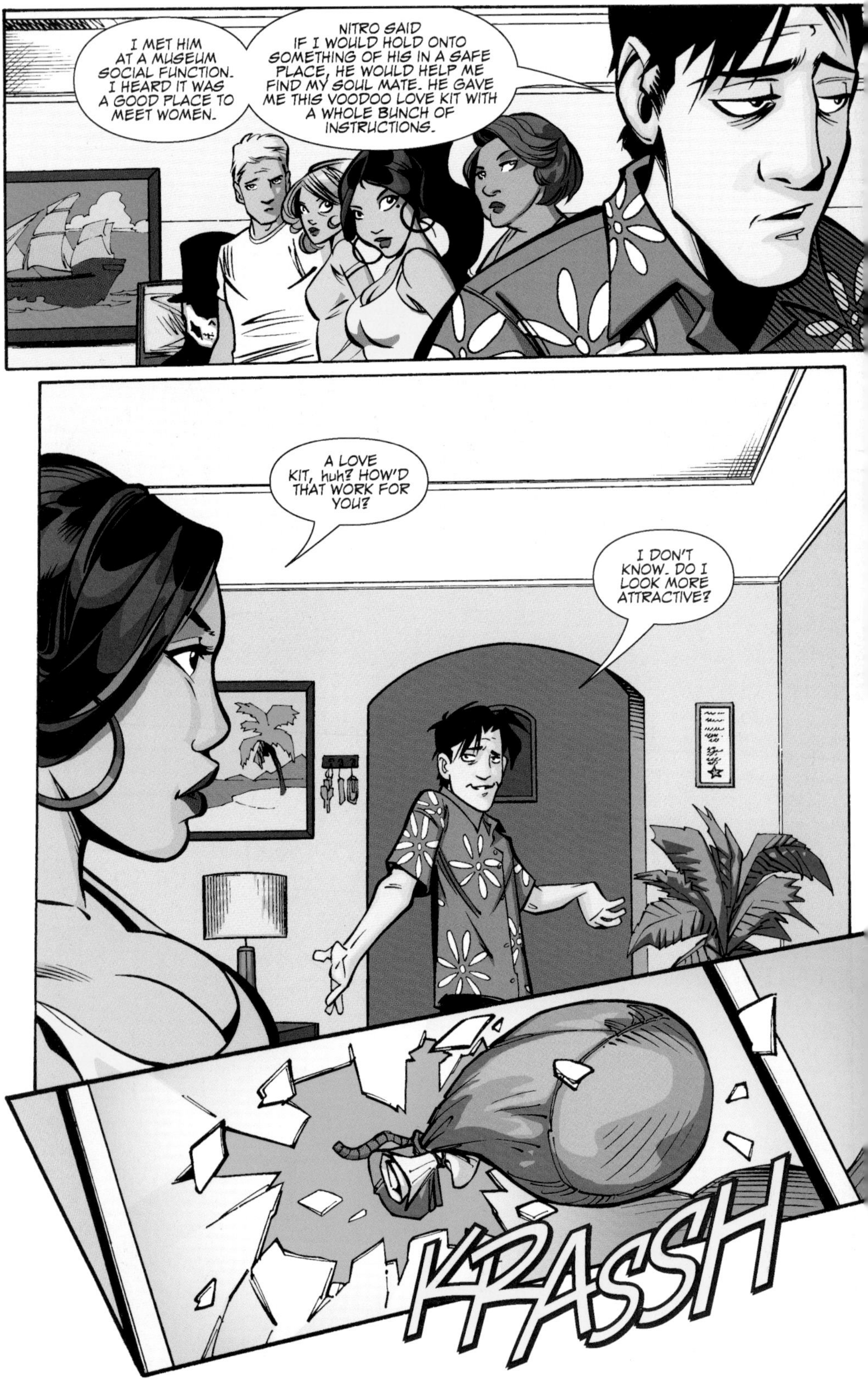
I MET HIM AT A MUSEUM SOCIAL FUNCTION. I HEARD IT WAS A GOOD PLACE TO MEET WOMEN.
NITRO SAID IF I WOULD HOLD ONTO SOMETHING OF HIS IN A SAFE PLACE, HE WOULD HELP ME FIND MY SOUL MATE. HE GAVE ME THIS VOODOO LOVE KIT WITH A WHOLE BUNCH OF INSTRUCTIONS.
A LOVE KIT, huh? HOW'D THAT WORK FOR YOU?
I DON'T KNOW. DO I LOOK MORE ATTRACTIVE?
KRASSH

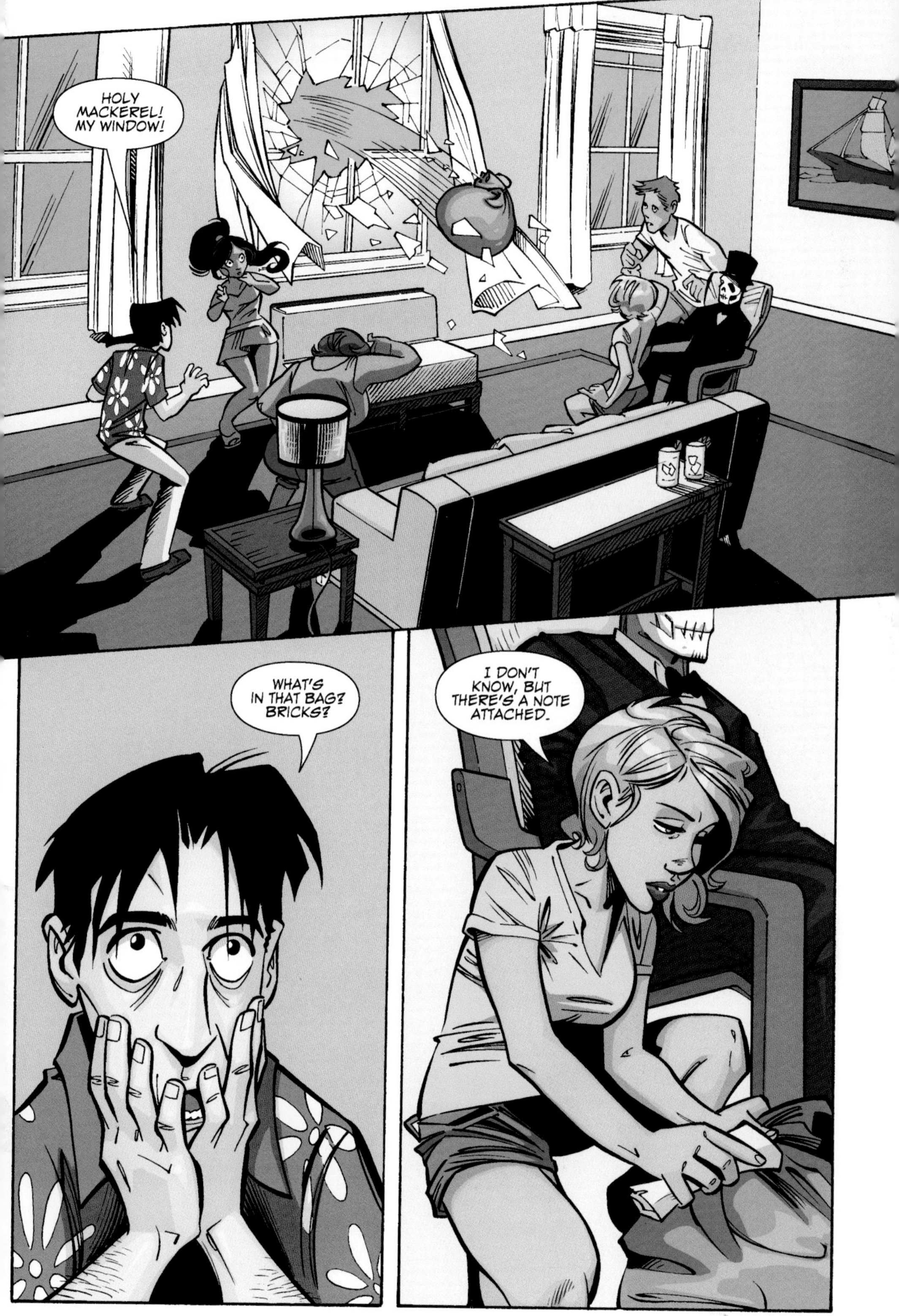
HOLY MACKEREL! MY WINDOW!
WHAT'S IN THAT BAG? BRICKS?
I DON'T KNOW, BUT THERE'S A NOTE ATTACHED.

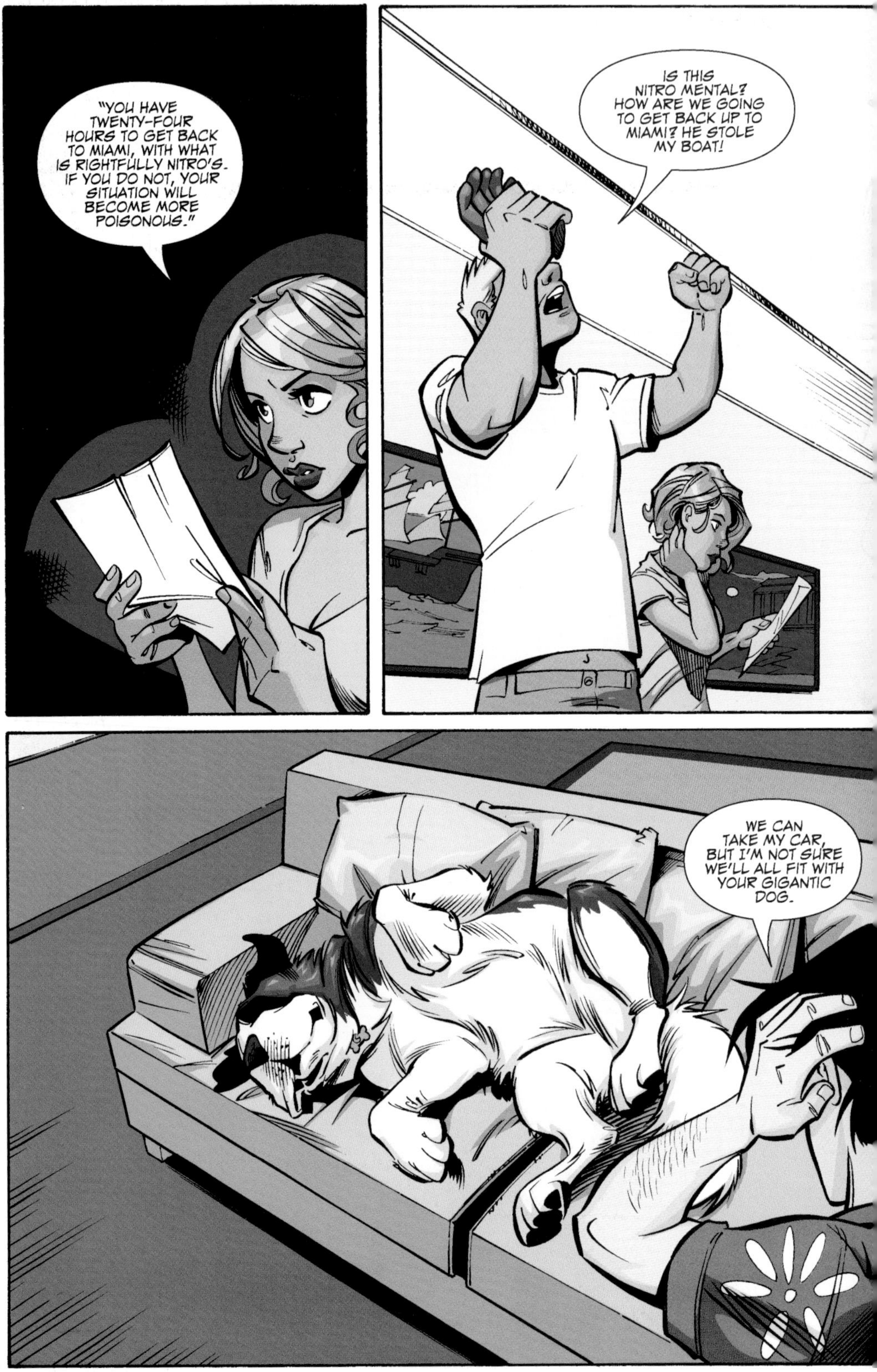
"YOU HAVE TWENTY-FOUR HOURS TO GET BACK TO MIAMI, WITH WHAT IS RIGHTFULLY NITRO'S. IF YOU DO NOT, YOUR SITUATION WILL BECOME MORE POISONOUS."
IS THIS NITRO MENTAL? HOW ARE WE GOING TO GET BACK UP TO MIAMI? HE STOLE MY BOAT!
WE CAN TAKE MY CAR, BUT I'M NOT SURE WE'LL ALL FIT WITH YOUR GIGANTIC DOG.

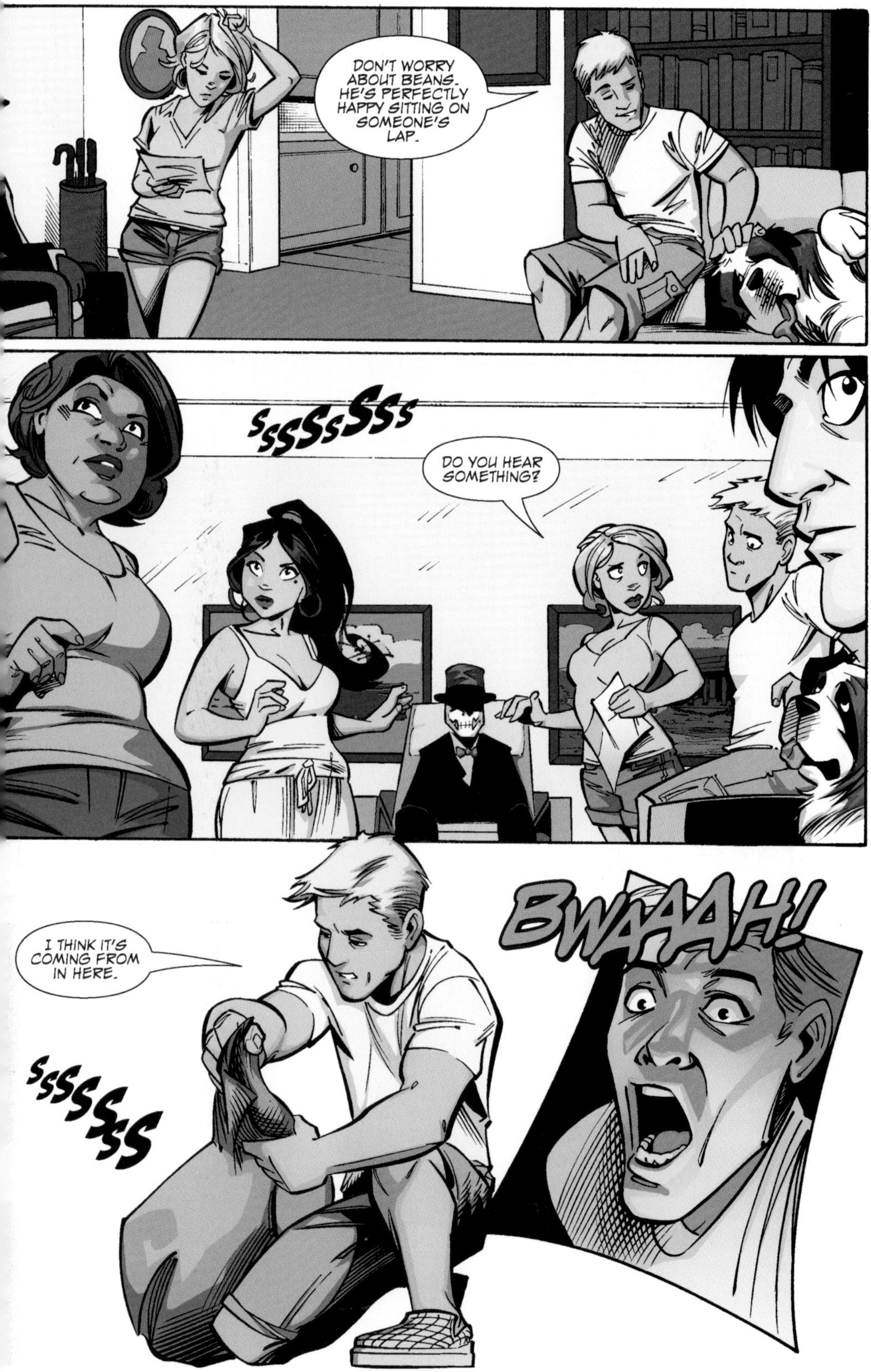
DON'T WORRY ABOUT BEANS. HE'S PERFECTLY HAPPY SITTING ON SOMEONE'S LAP.
sssSsSSs
DO YOU HEAR SOMETHING?
I THINK IT'S COMING FROM IN HERE.
ssssSss
BWAAAH!

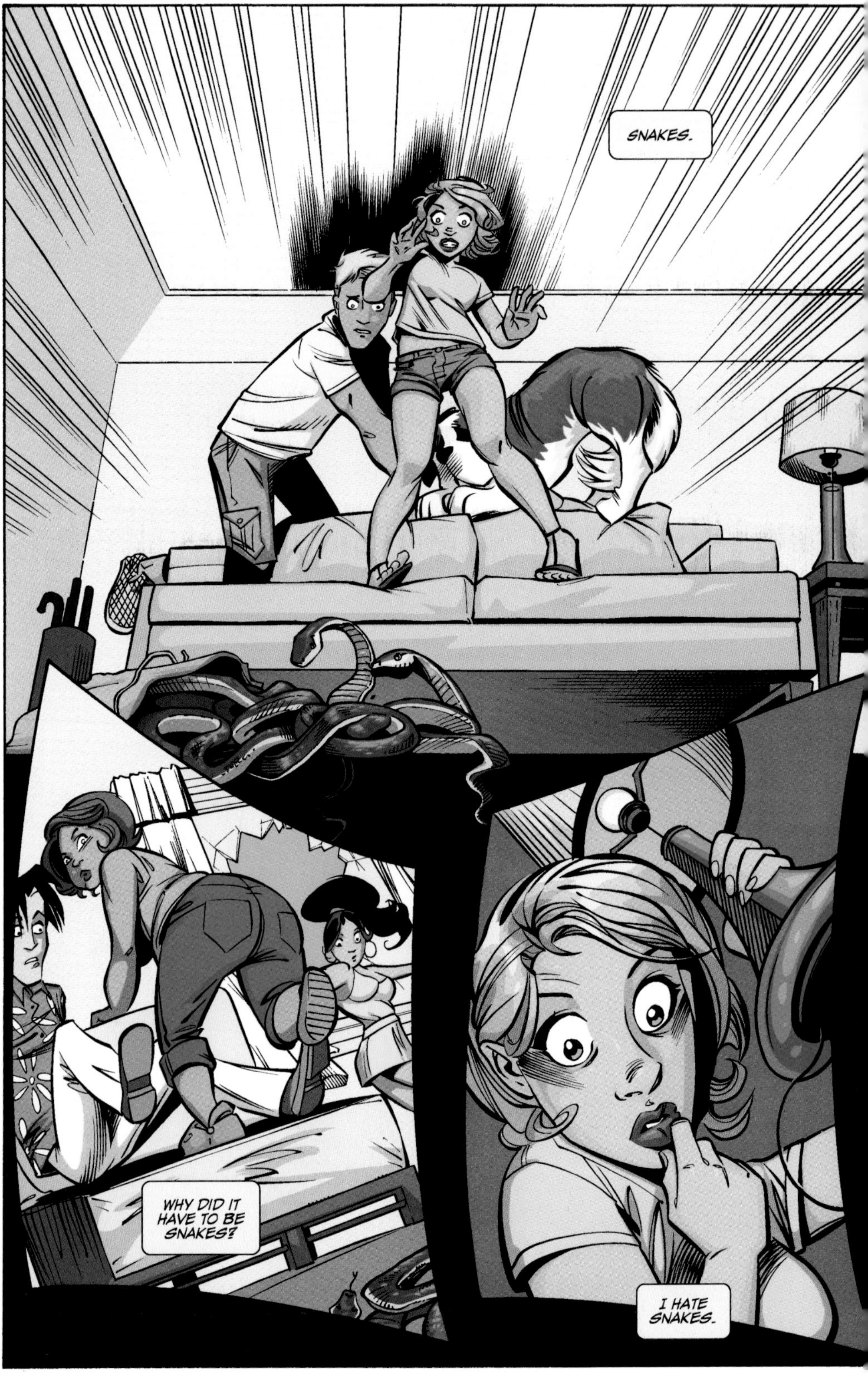
SNAKES.
WHY DID IT HAVE TO BE SNAKES?
I HATE SNAKES.

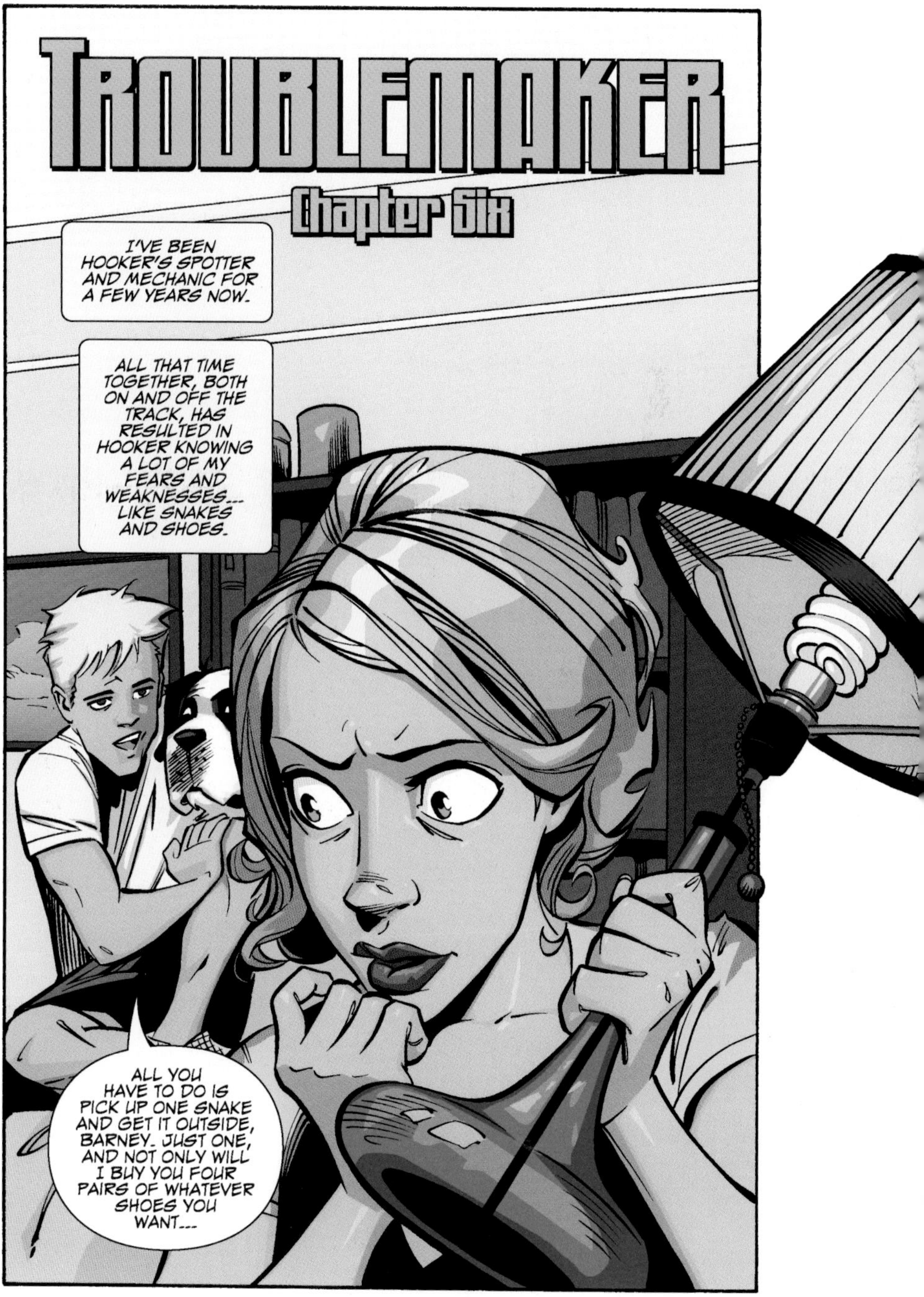
TROUBLEMAKER
Chapter Six
I'VE BEEN HOOKER'S SPOTTER AND MECHANIC FOR A FEW YEARS NOW.
ALL THAT TIME TOGETHER, BOTH ON AND OFF THE TRACK, HAS RESULTED IN HOOKER KNOWING A LOT OF MY FEARS AND WEAKNESSES... LIKE SNAKES AND SHOES.
ALL YOU HAVE TO DO IS PICK UP ONE SNAKE AND GET IT OUTSIDE, BARNEY. JUST ONE, AND NOT ONLY WILL I BUY YOU FOUR PAIRS OF WHATEVER SHOES YOU WANT...

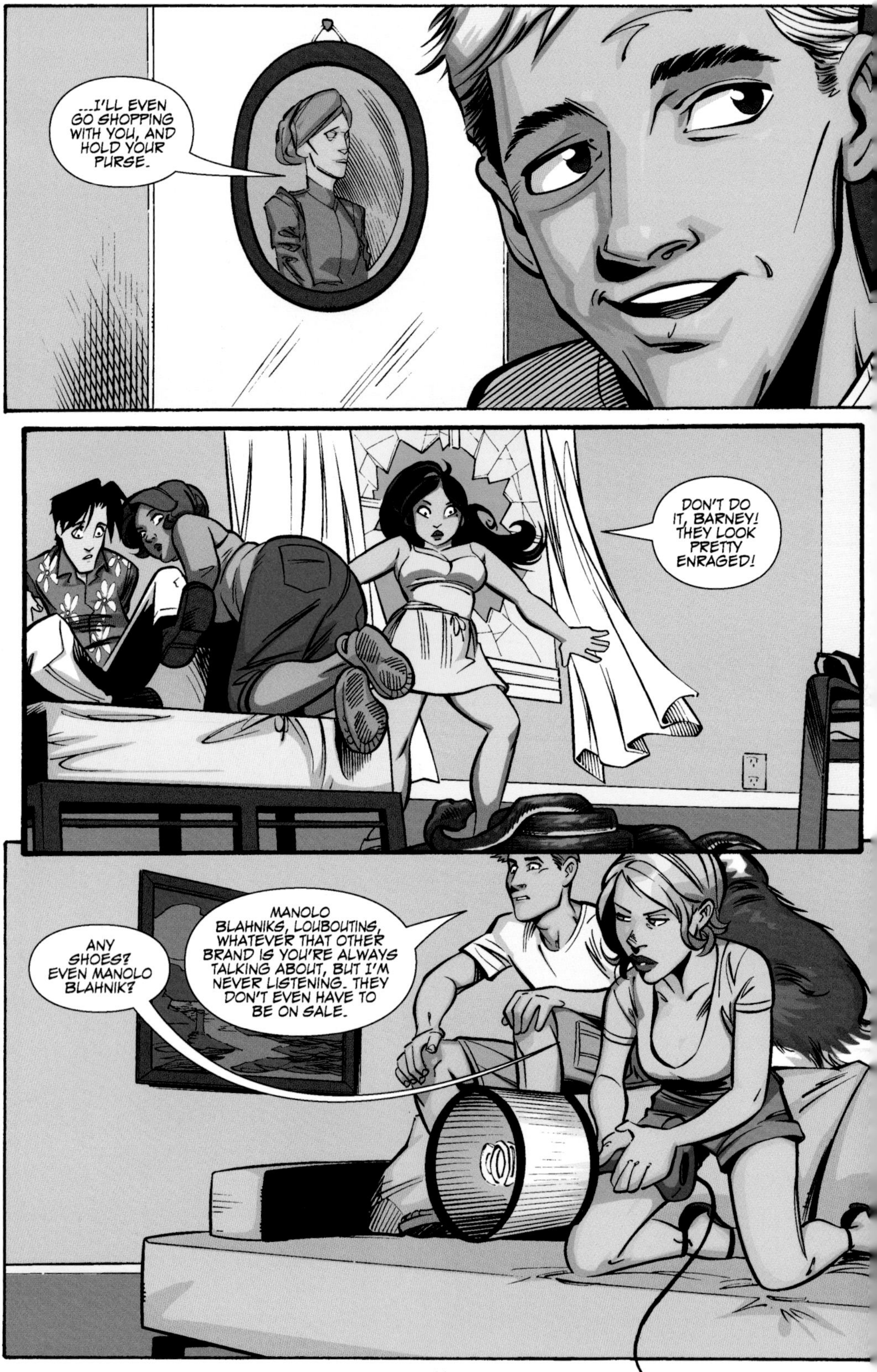
...I'LL EVEN GO SHOPPING WITH YOU, AND HOLD YOUR PURSE.
DON'T DO IT, BARNEY! THEY LOOK PRETTY ENRAGED!
ANY SHOES? EVEN MANOLO BLAHNIK?
MANOLO BLAHNIKS, LOUBOUTINS, WHATEVER THAT OTHER BRAND IS YOU'RE ALWAYS TALKING ABOUT, BUT I'M NEVER LISTENING. THEY DON'T EVEN HAVE TO BE ON SALE.

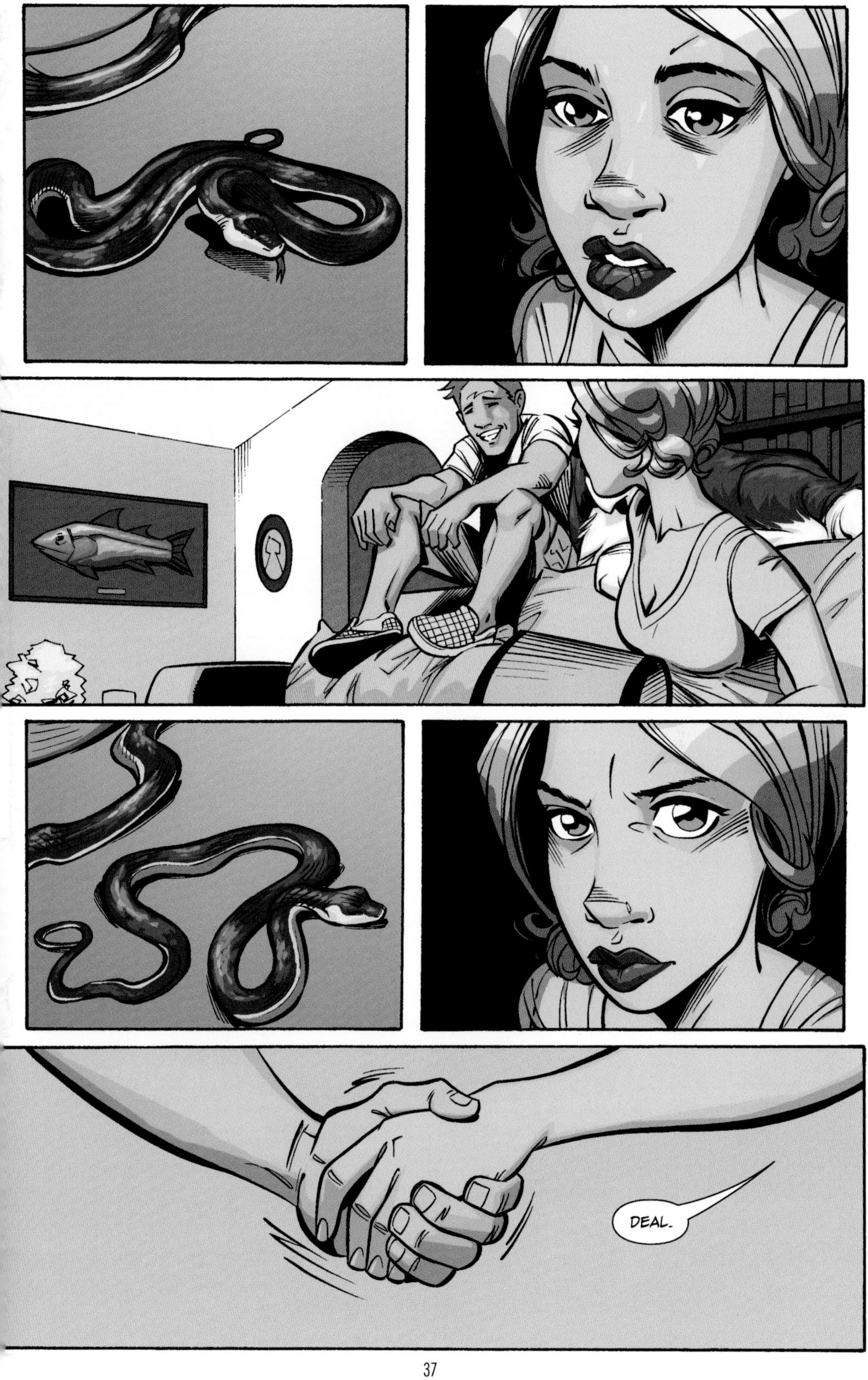
DEAL.

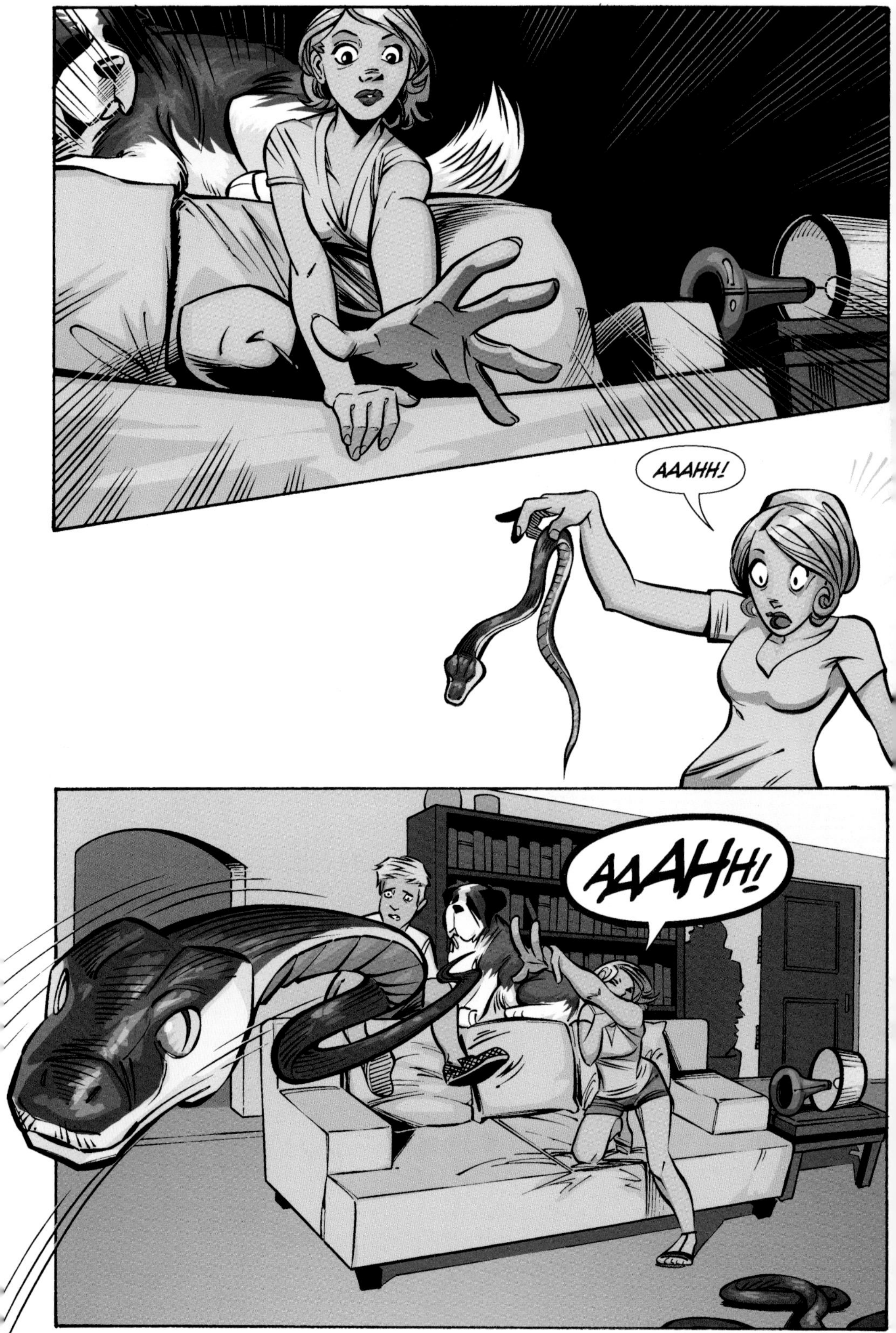
AAAHH!
AAAHH!

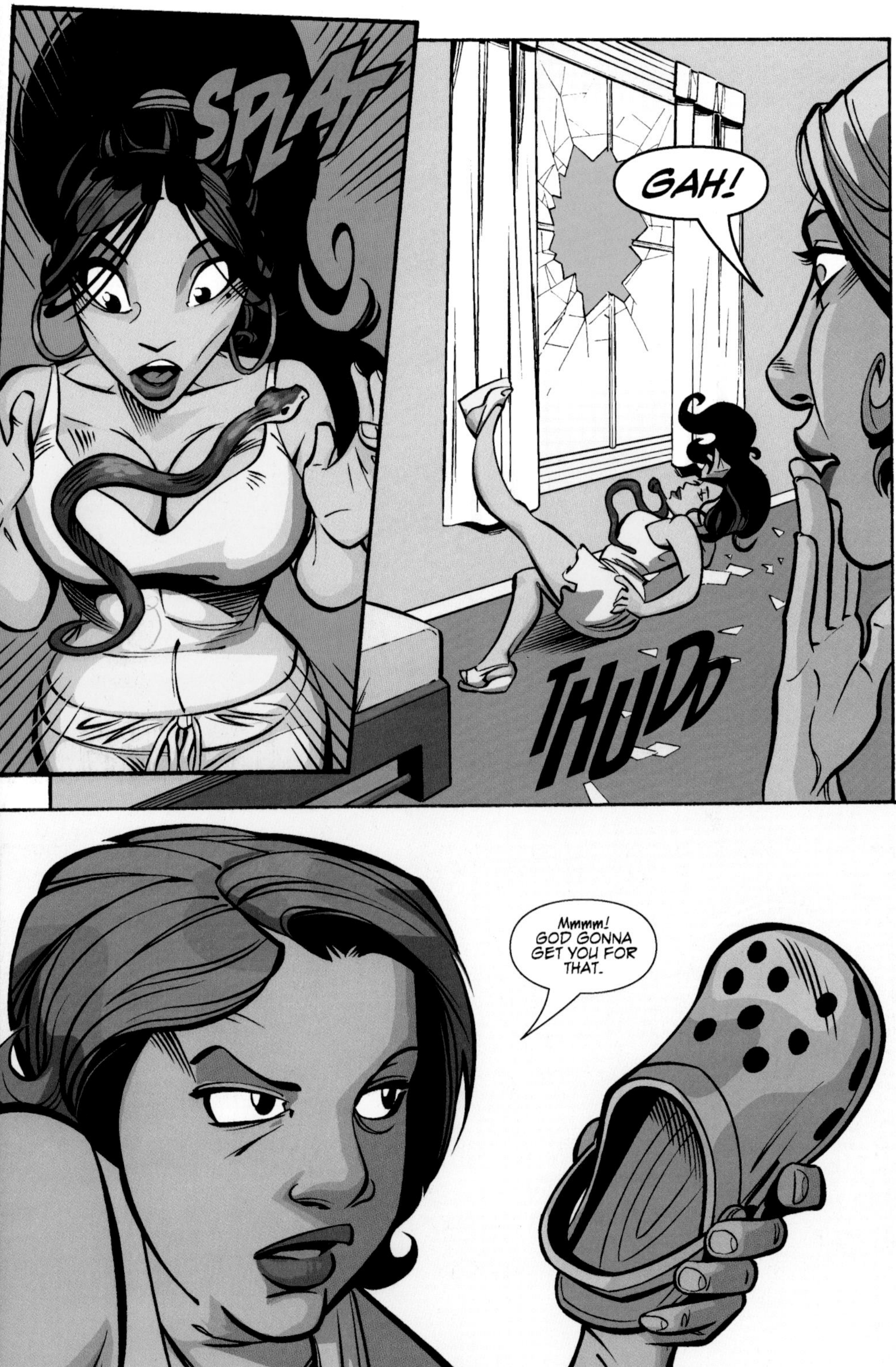
SPLAT
GAH!
THUDD
Mmmm!
GOD GONNA
GET YOU FOR
THAT.

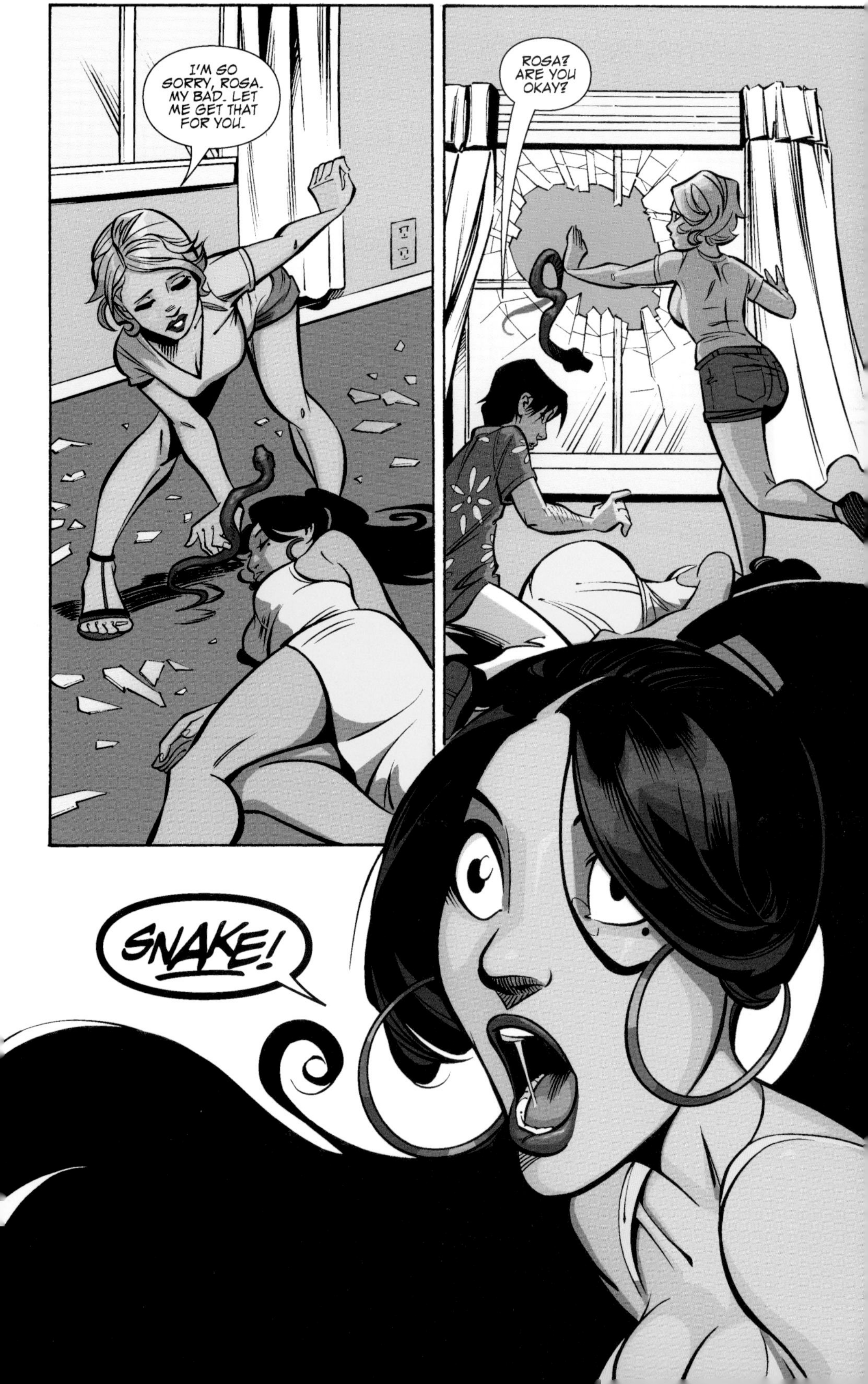
I'M SO SORRY, ROSA. MY BAD. LET ME GET THAT FOR YOU.
ROSA? ARE YOU OKAY?
SNAKE!

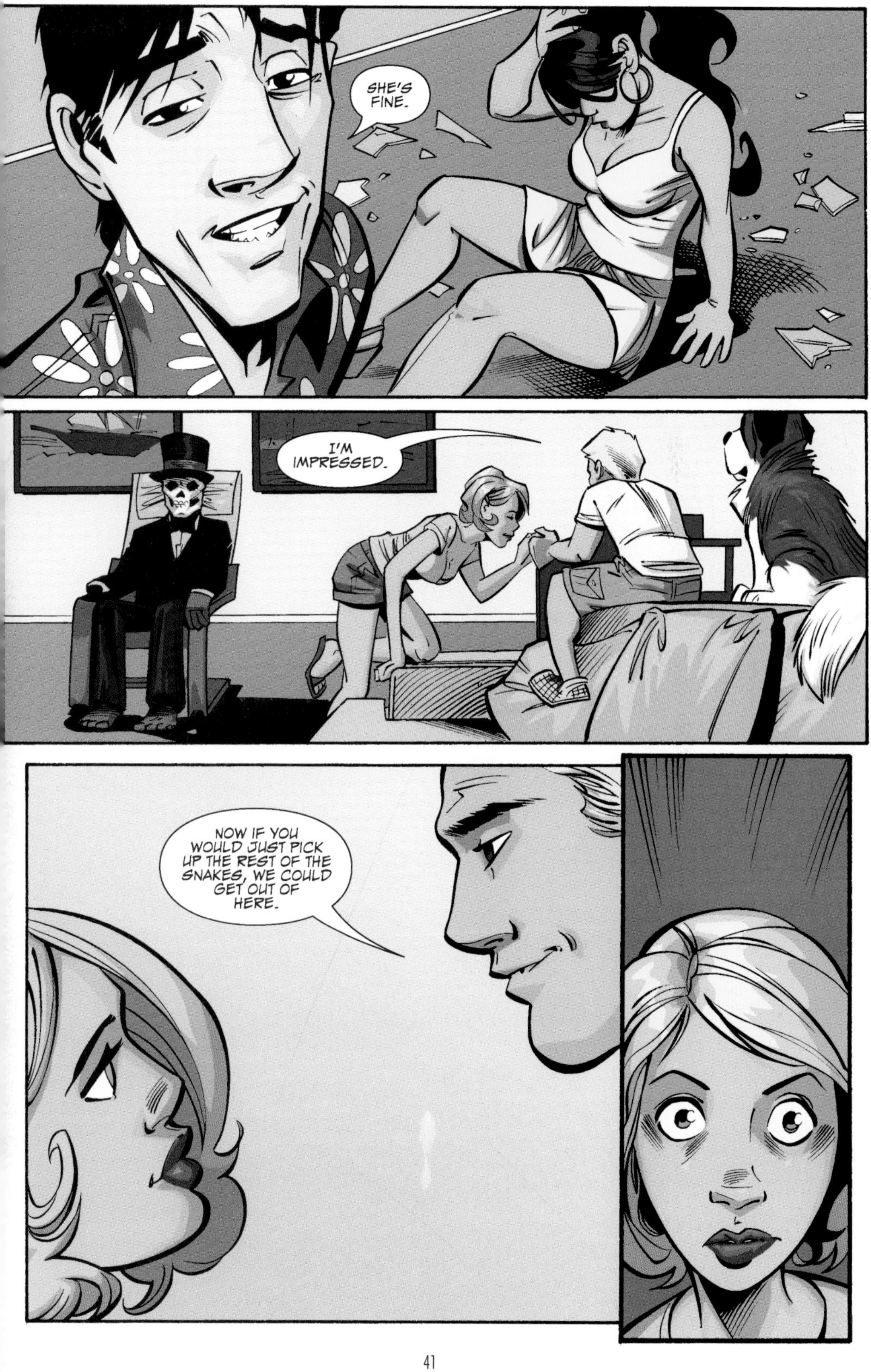
SHE'S FINE.
I'M IMPRESSED.
NOW IF YOU WOULD JUST PICK UP THE REST OF THE SNAKES, WE COULD GET OUT OF HERE.

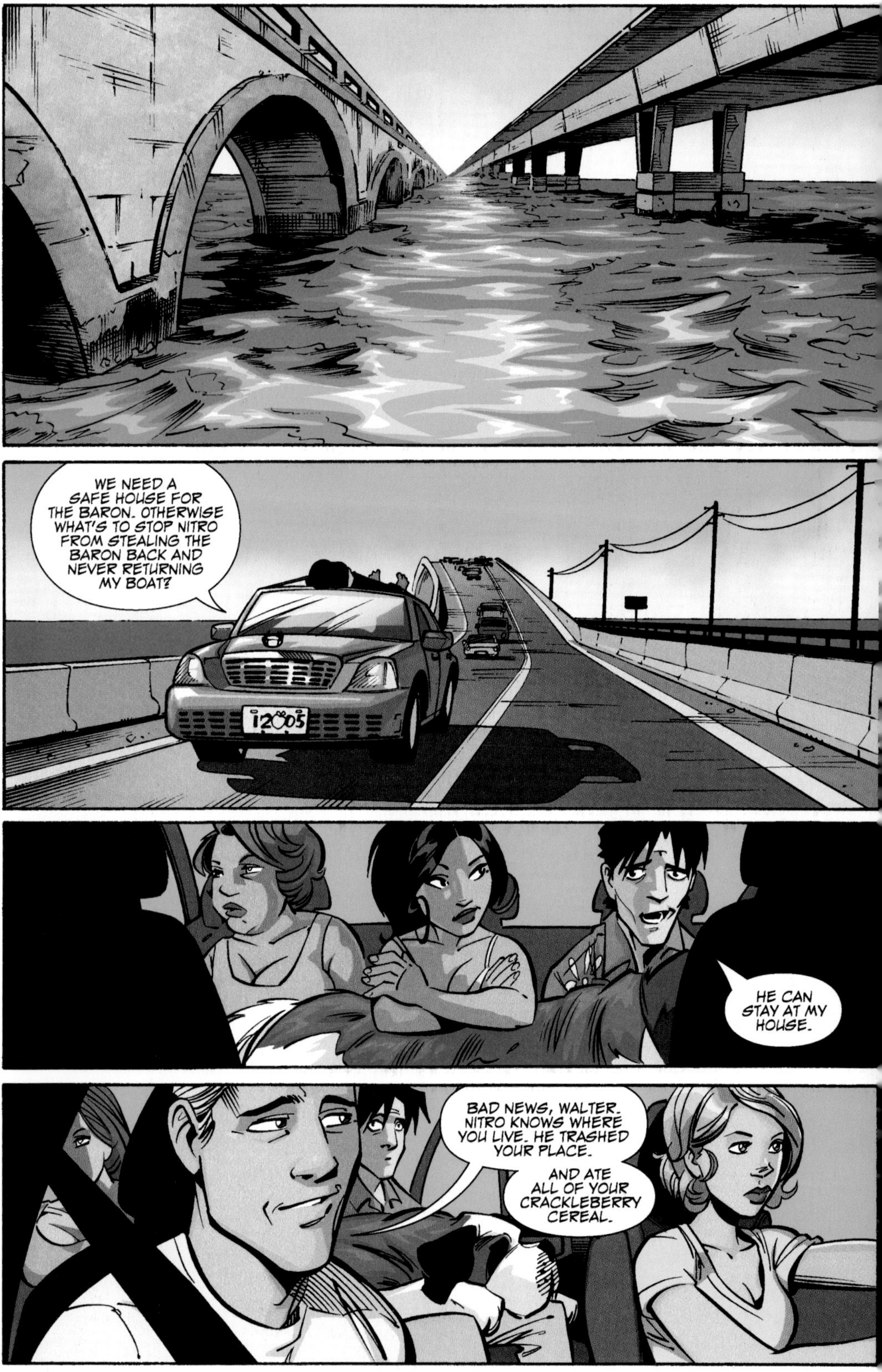
WE NEED A SAFE HOUSE FOR THE BARON. OTHERWISE WHAT'S TO STOP NITRO FROM STEALING THE BARON BACK AND NEVER RETURNING MY BOAT?
12005
HE CAN STAY AT MY HOUSE.
BAD NEWS, WALTER. NITRO KNOWS WHERE YOU LIVE. HE TRASHED YOUR PLACE.
AND ATE ALL OF YOUR CRACKLEBERRY CEREAL.

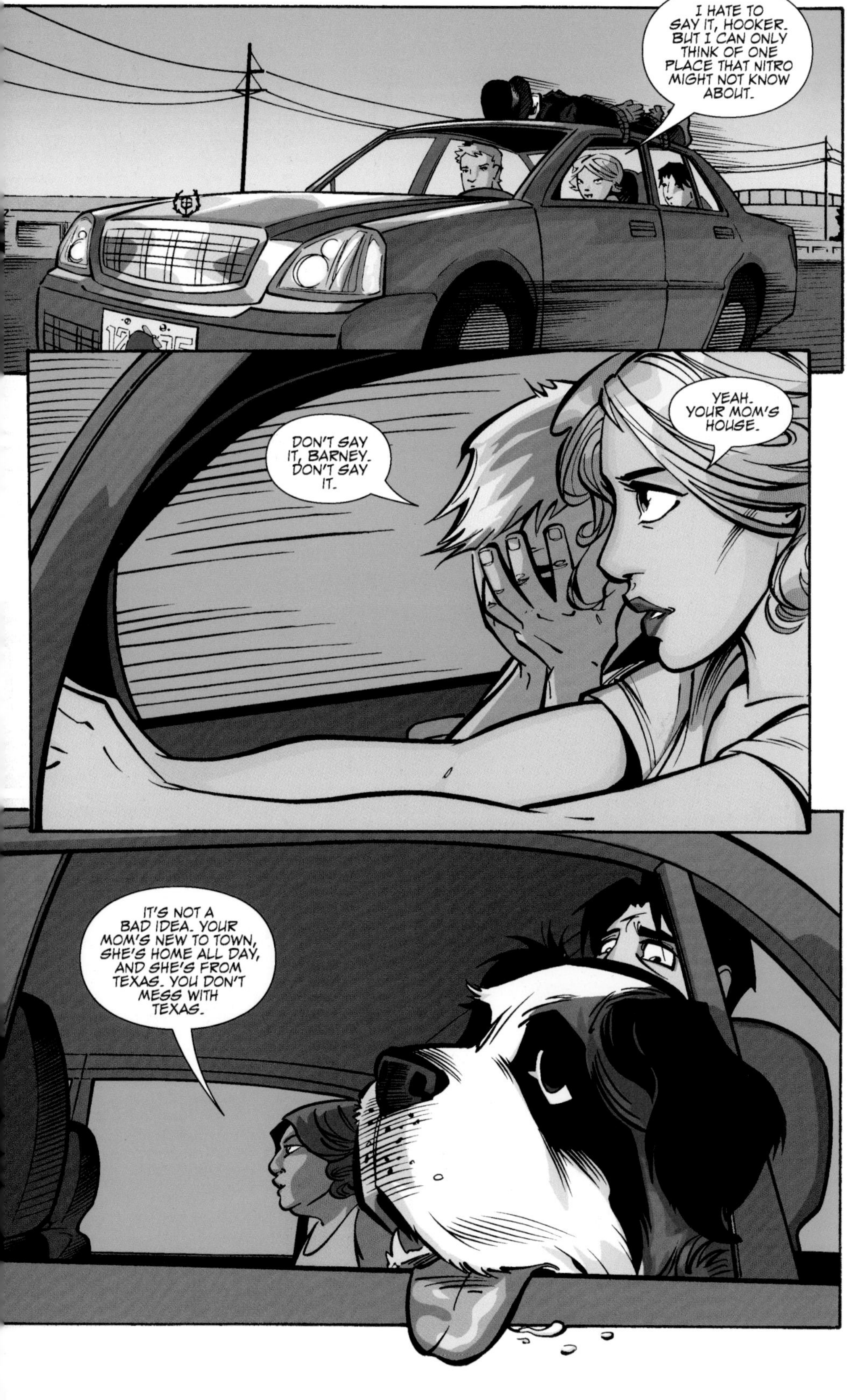
I HATE TO SAY IT, HOOKER. BUT I CAN ONLY THINK OF ONE PLACE THAT NITRO MIGHT NOT KNOW ABOUT.
YEAH. YOUR MOM'S HOUSE.
DON'T SAY IT, BARNEY. DON'T SAY IT.
IT'S NOT A BAD IDEA. YOUR MOM'S NEW TO TOWN, SHE'S HOME ALL DAY, AND SHE'S FROM TEXAS. YOU DON'T MESS WITH TEXAS.

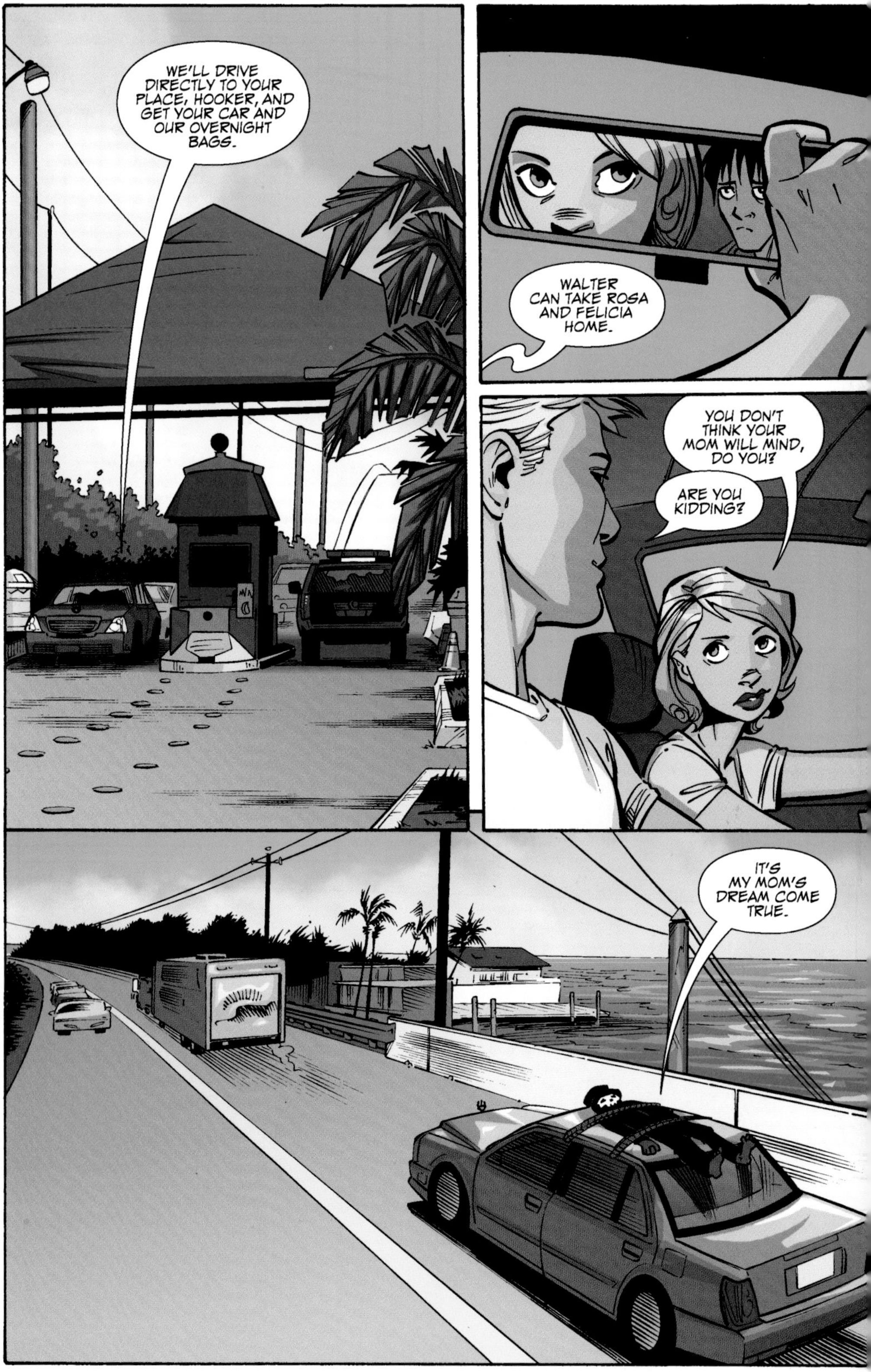
WE'LL DRIVE DIRECTLY TO YOUR PLACE, HOOKER, AND GET YOUR CAR AND OUR OVERNIGHT BAGS.
WALTER CAN TAKE ROSA AND FELICIA HOME.
YOU DON'T THINK YOUR MOM WILL MIND, DO YOU?
ARE YOU KIDDING?
IT'S MY MOM'S DREAM COME TRUE.

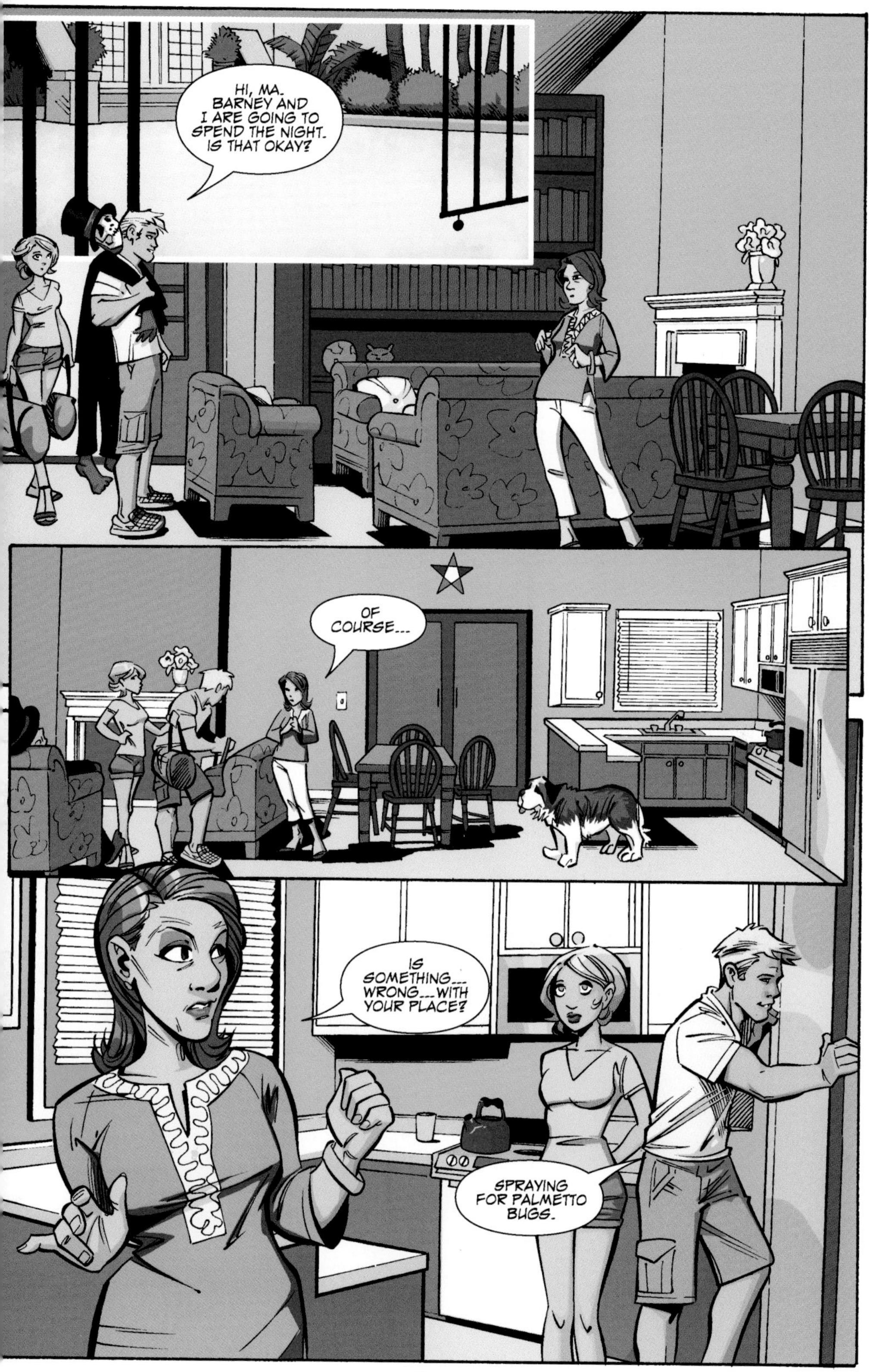
HI, MA. BARNEY AND I ARE GOING TO SPEND THE NIGHT. IS THAT OKAY?
OF COURSE...
IS SOMETHING... WRONG... WITH YOUR PLACE?
SPRAYING FOR PALMETTO BUGS.

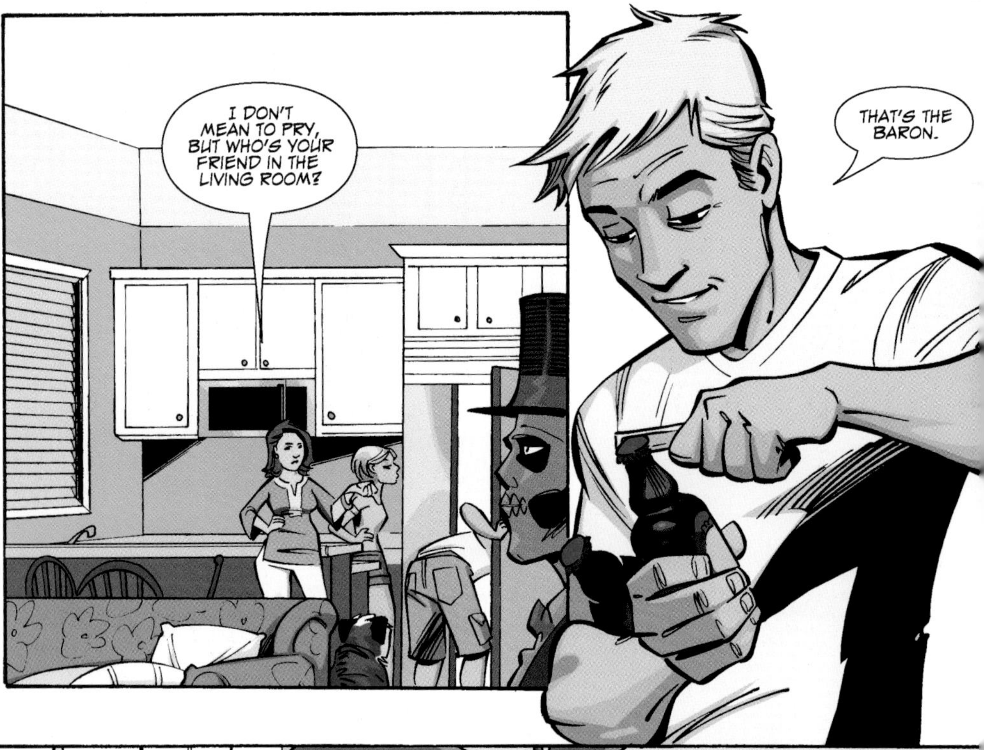
I DON'T MEAN TO PRY, BUT WHO'S YOUR FRIEND IN THE LIVING ROOM?
THAT'S THE BARON.

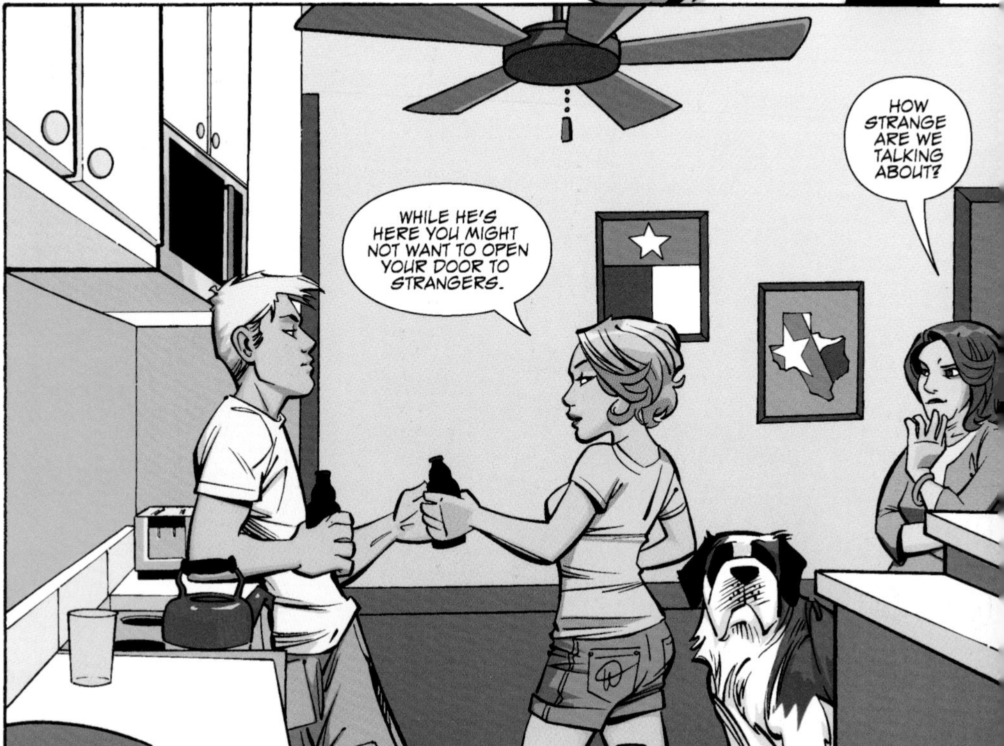
HOW STRANGE ARE WE TALKING ABOUT?
WHILE HE'S HERE YOU MIGHT NOT WANT TO OPEN YOUR DOOR TO STRANGERS.

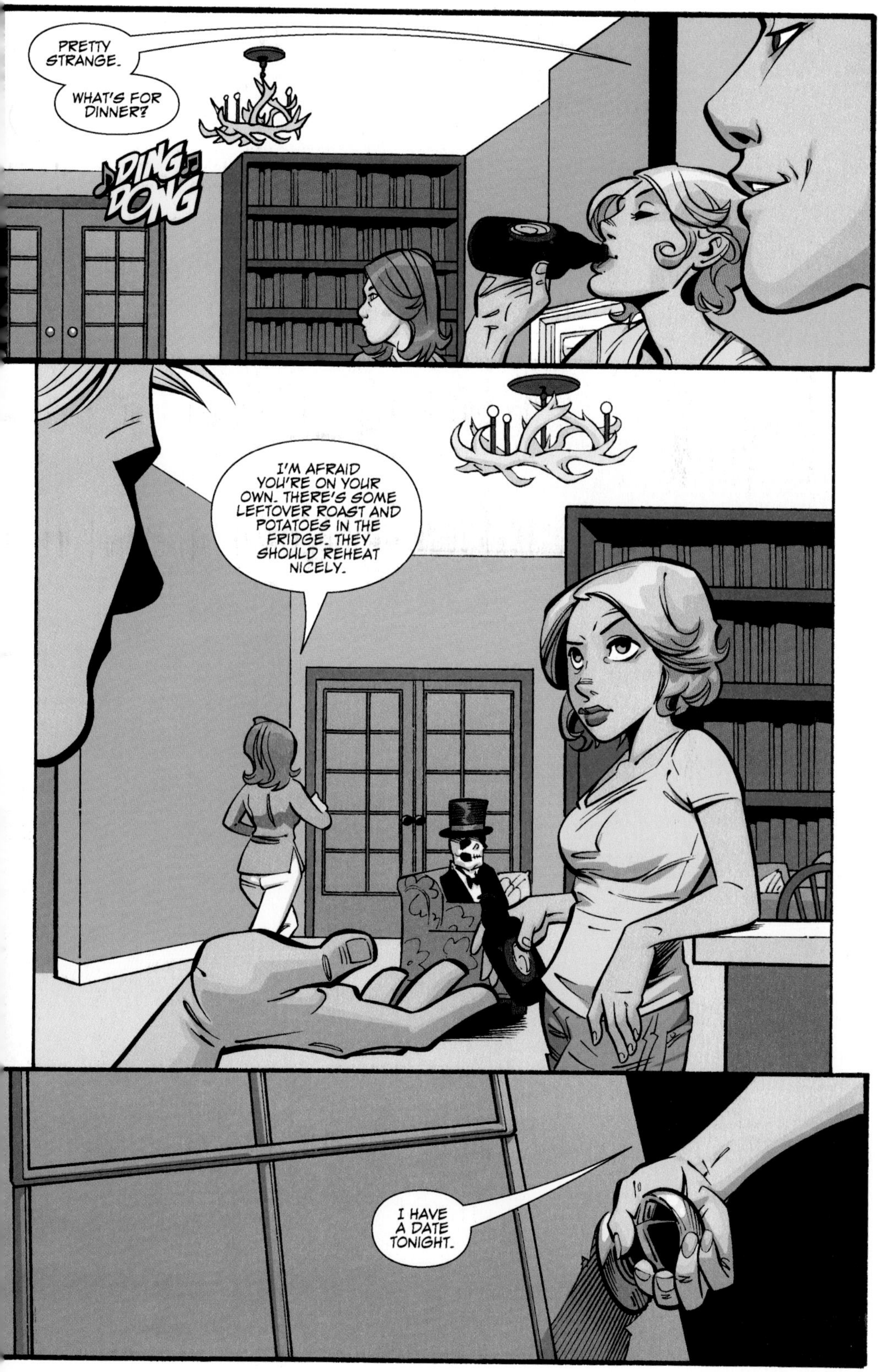
PRETTY STRANGE.
WHAT'S FOR DINNER?
DING DONG
I'M AFRAID YOU'RE ON YOUR OWN. THERE'S SOME LEFTOVER ROAST AND POTATOES IN THE FRIDGE. THEY SHOULD REHEAT NICELY.
I HAVE A DATE TONIGHT.

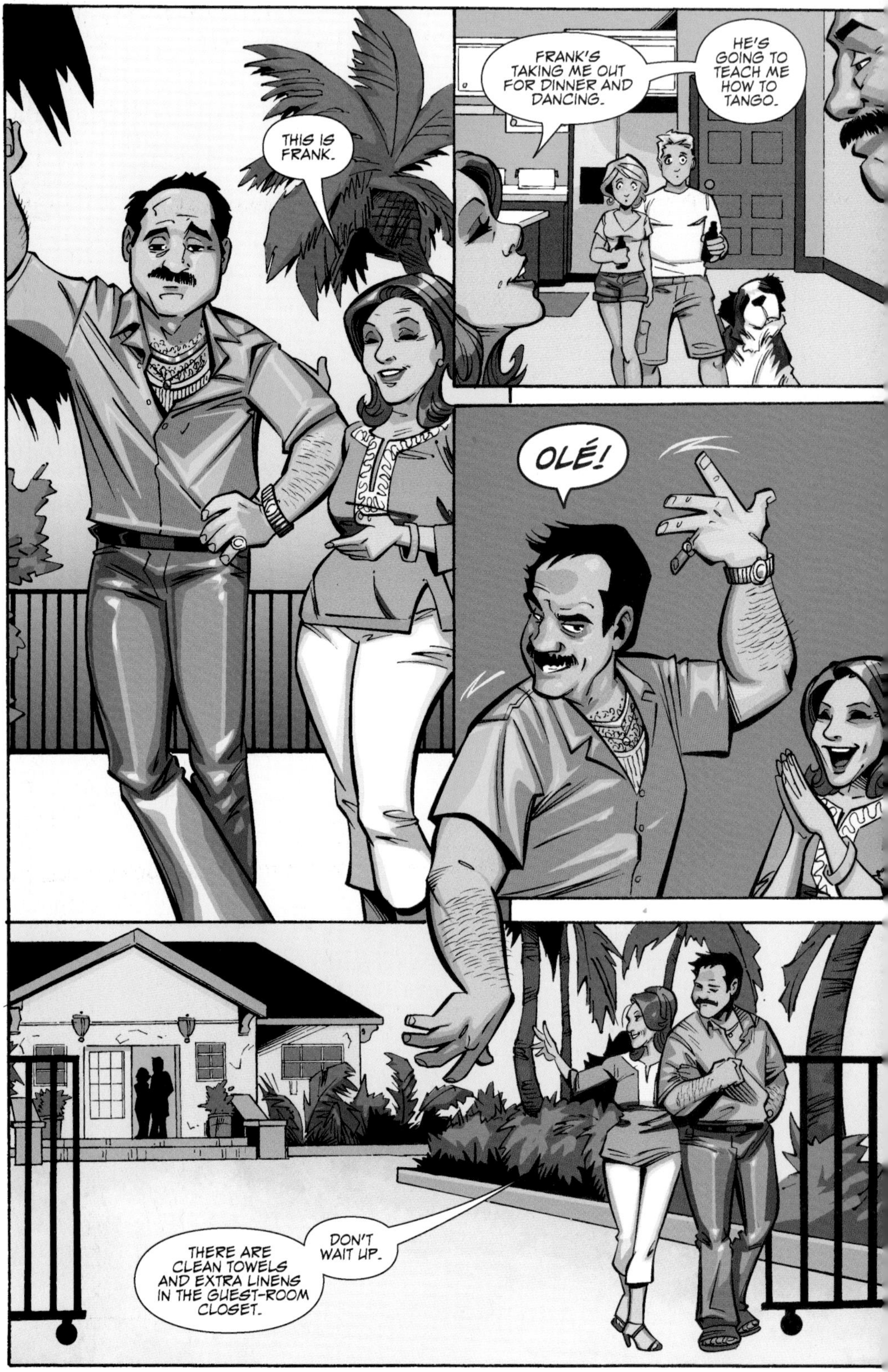
THIS IS FRANK.
FRANK'S TAKING ME OUT FOR DINNER AND DANCING.
HE'S GOING TO TEACH ME HOW TO TANGO.
OLÉ!
DON'T WAIT UP.
THERE ARE CLEAN TOWELS AND EXTRA LINENS IN THE GUEST-ROOM CLOSET.

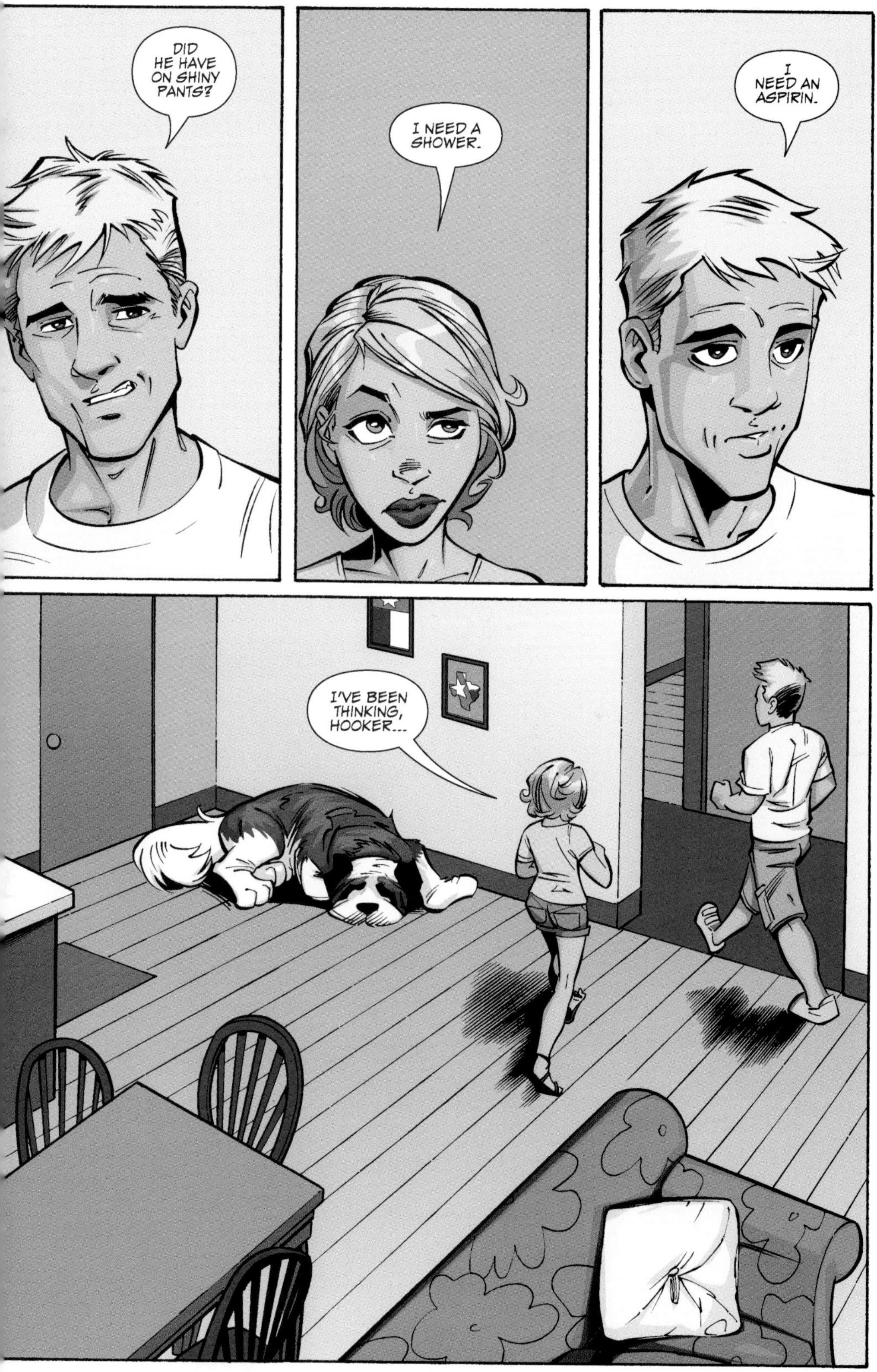
DID HE HAVE ON SHINY PANTS?
I NEED A SHOWER.
I NEED AN ASPIRIN.
I'VE BEEN THINKING, HOOKER...

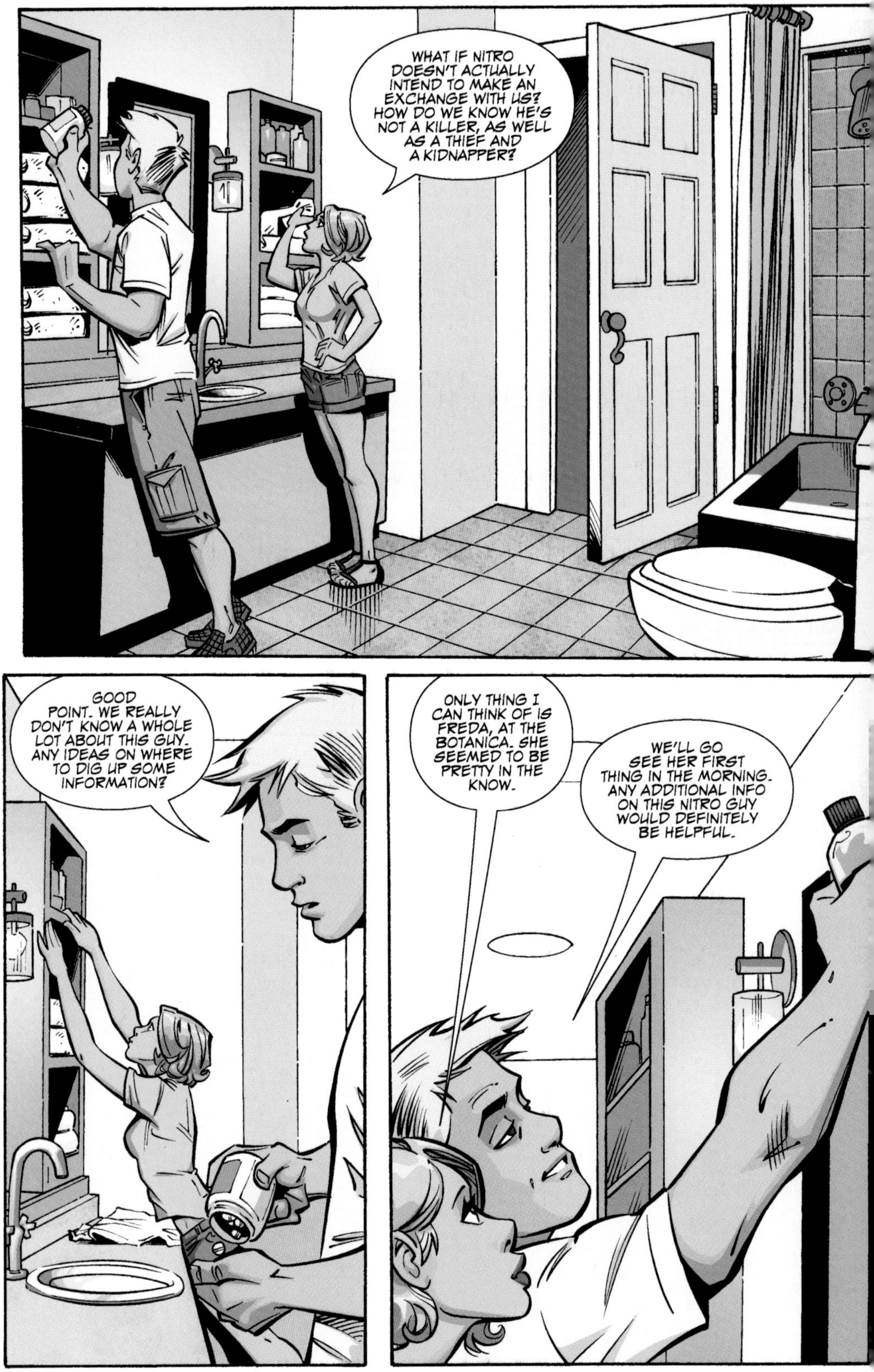
WHAT IF NITRO DOESN'T ACTUALLY INTEND TO MAKE AN EXCHANGE WITH US? HOW DO WE KNOW HE'S NOT A KILLER, AS WELL AS A THIEF AND A KIDNAPPER?
GOOD POINT. WE REALLY DON'T KNOW A WHOLE LOT ABOUT THIS GUY. ANY IDEAS ON WHERE TO DIG UP SOME INFORMATION?
ONLY THING I CAN THINK OF IS FREDA, AT THE BOTANICA. SHE SEEMED TO BE PRETTY IN THE KNOW.
WE'LL GO SEE HER FIRST THING IN THE MORNING. ANY ADDITIONAL INFO ON THIS NITRO GUY WOULD DEFINITELY BE HELPFUL.

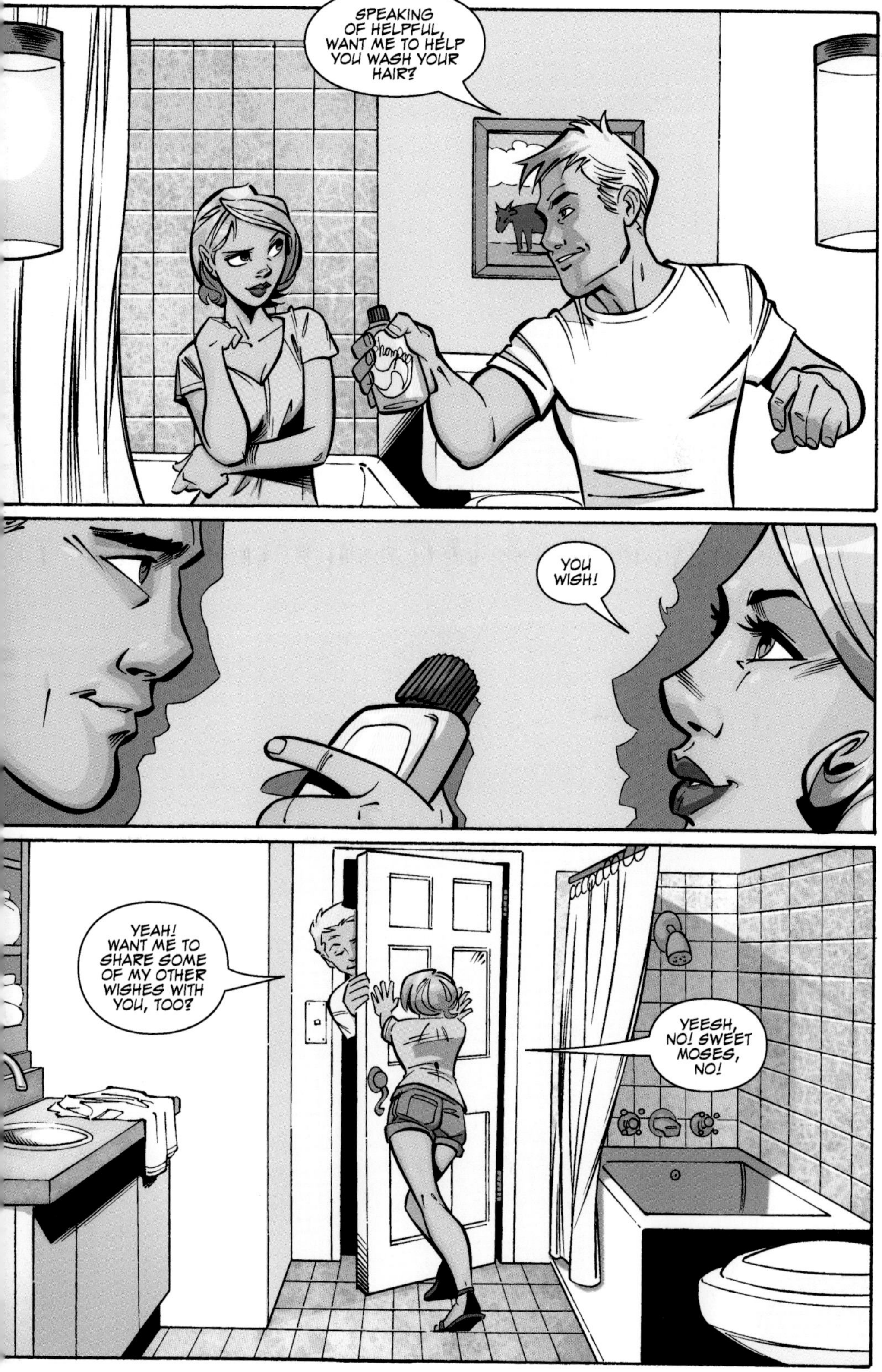
SPEAKING OF HELPFUL, WANT ME TO HELP YOU WASH YOUR HAIR?
YOU WISH!
YEAH! WANT ME TO SHARE SOME OF MY OTHER WISHES WITH YOU, TOO?
YEESH, NO! SWEET MOSES, NO!

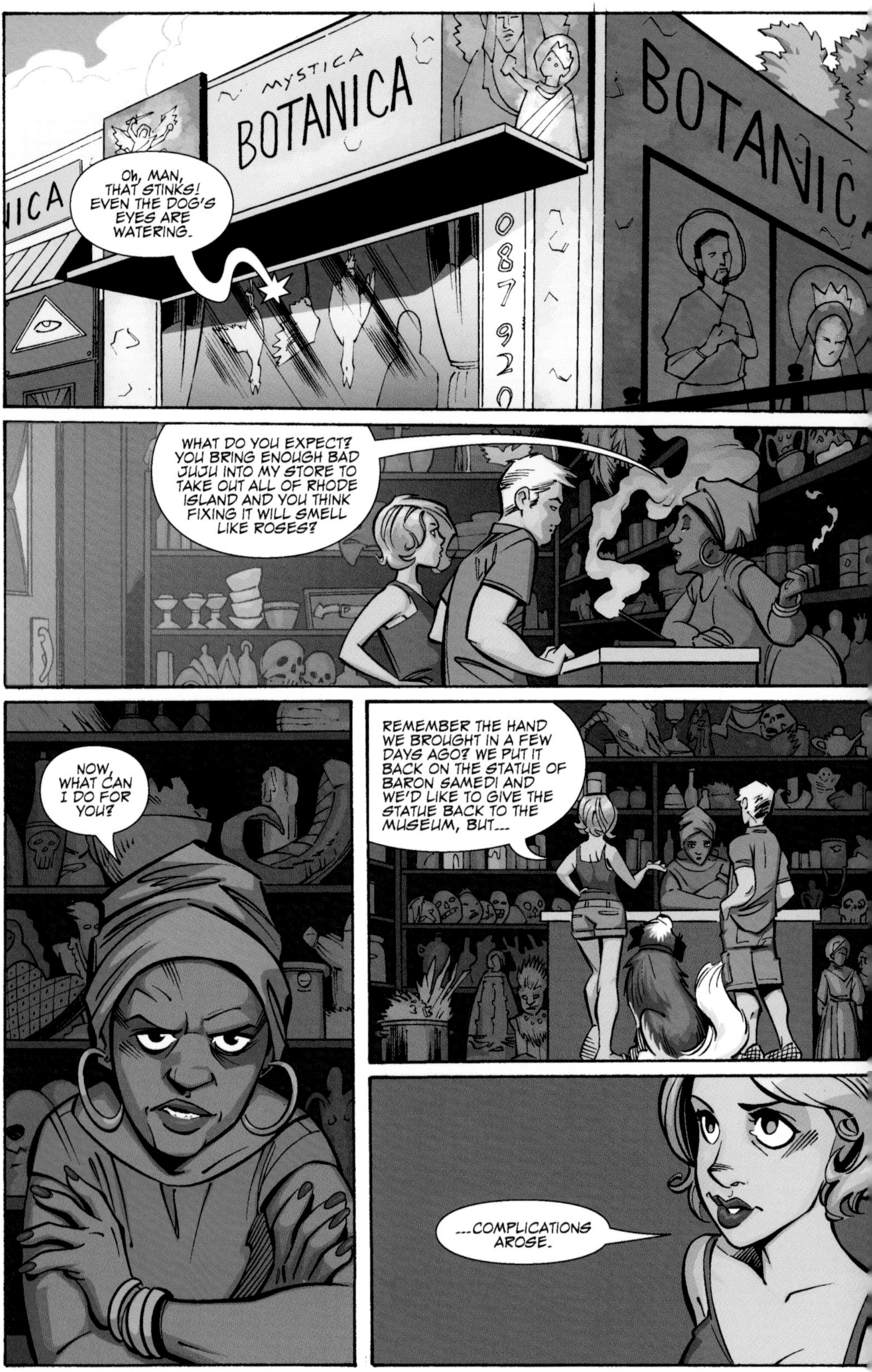
MYSTICA
BOTANICA
ICA
Oh, MAN, THAT STINKS! EVEN THE DOG'S EYES ARE WATERING.
087920
BOTANICA
WHAT DO YOU EXPECT? YOU BRING ENOUGH BAD JUJU INTO MY STORE TO TAKE OUT ALL OF RHODE ISLAND AND YOU THINK FIXING IT WILL SMELL LIKE ROSES?
NOW, WHAT CAN I DO FOR YOU?
REMEMBER THE HAND WE BROUGHT IN A FEW DAYS AGO? WE PUT IT BACK ON THE STATUE OF BARON SAMEDI AND WE'D LIKE TO GIVE THE STATUE BACK TO THE MUSEUM, BUT...
...COMPLICATIONS AROSE.

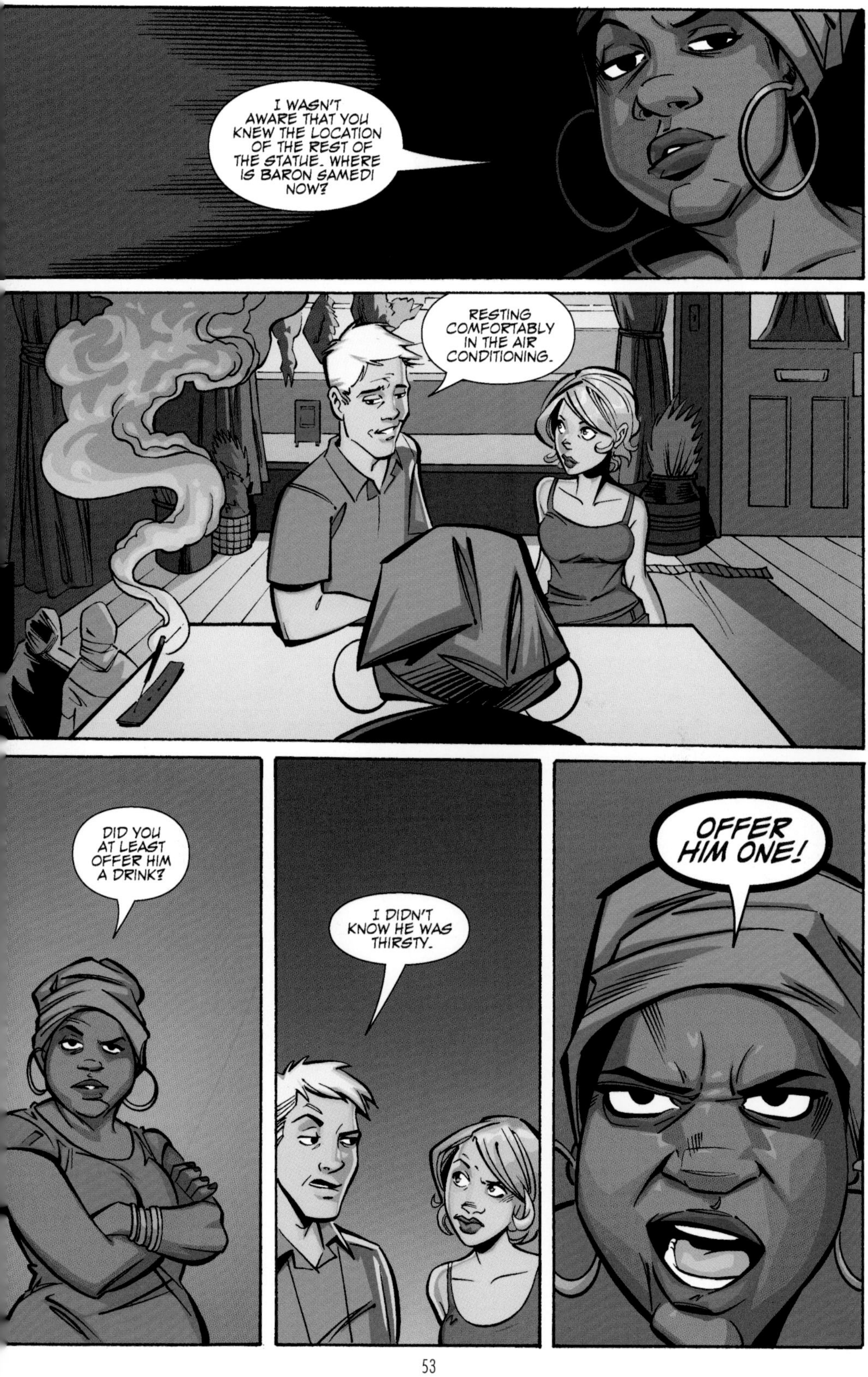
I WASN'T AWARE THAT YOU KNEW THE LOCATION OF THE REST OF THE STATUE. WHERE IS BARON SAMEDI NOW?
RESTING COMFORTABLY IN THE AIR CONDITIONING.
DID YOU AT LEAST OFFER HIM A DRINK?
I DIDN'T KNOW HE WAS THIRSTY.
OFFER HIM ONE!

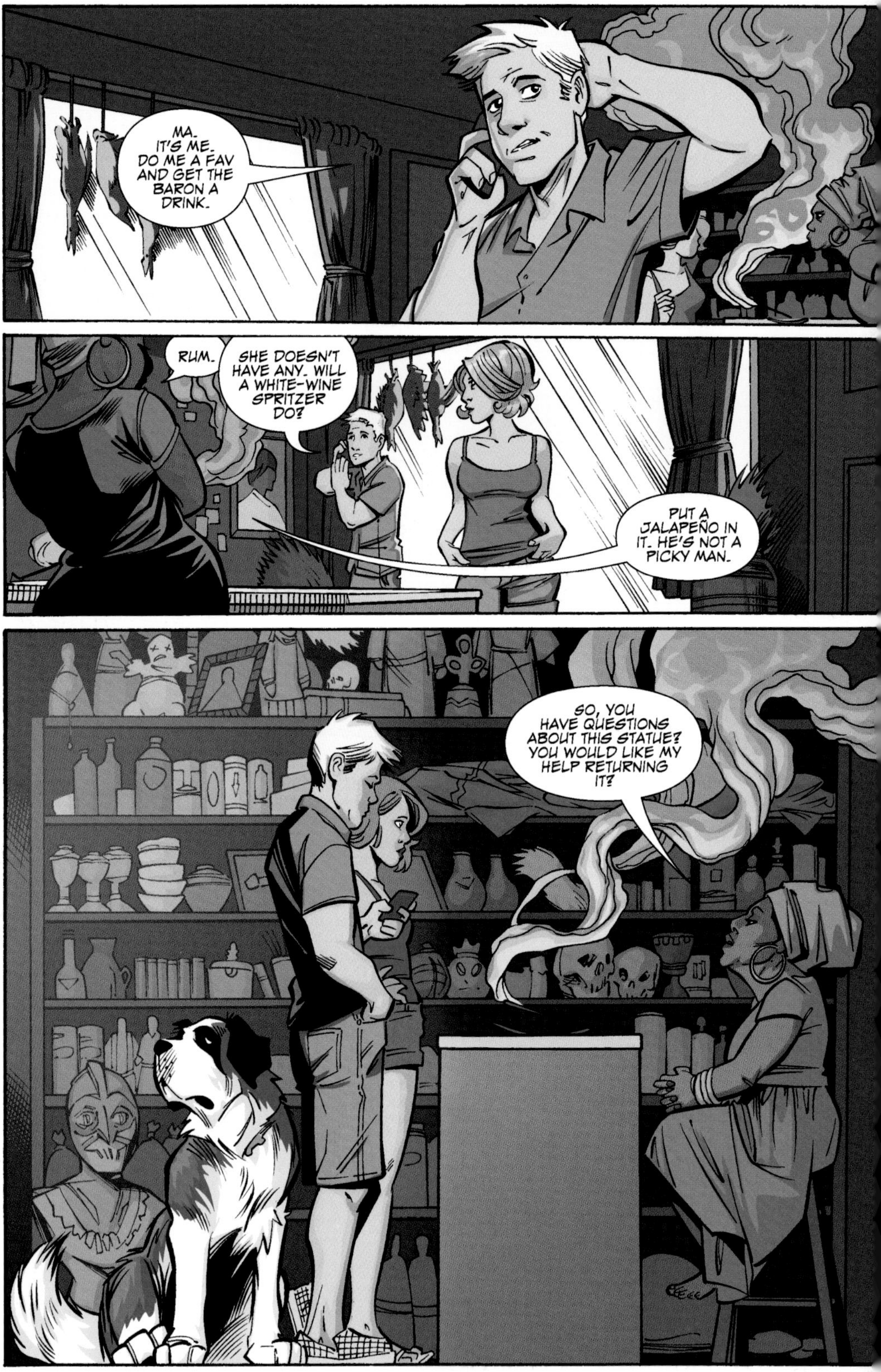
MA. IT'S ME. DO ME A FAV AND GET THE BARON A DRINK.
RUM.
SHE DOESN'T HAVE ANY. WILL A WHITE-WINE SPRITZER DO?
PUT A JALAPEÑO IN IT. HE'S NOT A PICKY MAN.
SO, YOU HAVE QUESTIONS ABOUT THIS STATUE? YOU WOULD LIKE MY HELP RETURNING IT?

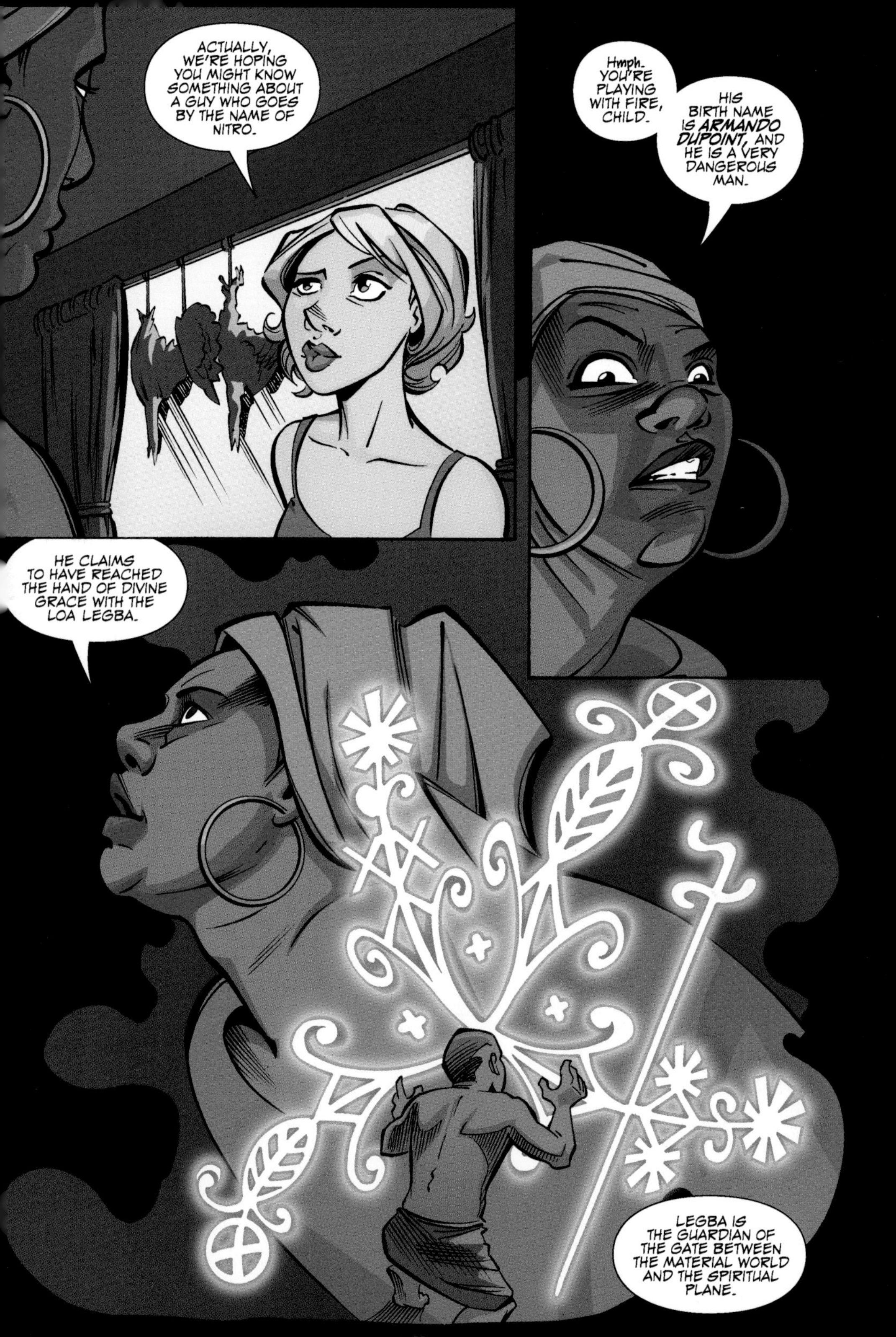
ACTUALLY, WE'RE HOPING YOU MIGHT KNOW SOMETHING ABOUT A GUY WHO GOES BY THE NAME OF NITRO.
Hmph. YOU'RE PLAYING WITH FIRE, CHILD.
HIS BIRTH NAME IS ARMANDO DUPOINT, AND HE IS A VERY DANGEROUS MAN.
HE CLAIMS TO HAVE REACHED THE HAND OF DIVINE GRACE WITH THE LOA LEGBA.
LEGBA IS THE GUARDIAN OF THE GATE BETWEEN THE MATERIAL WORLD AND THE SPIRITUAL PLANE.

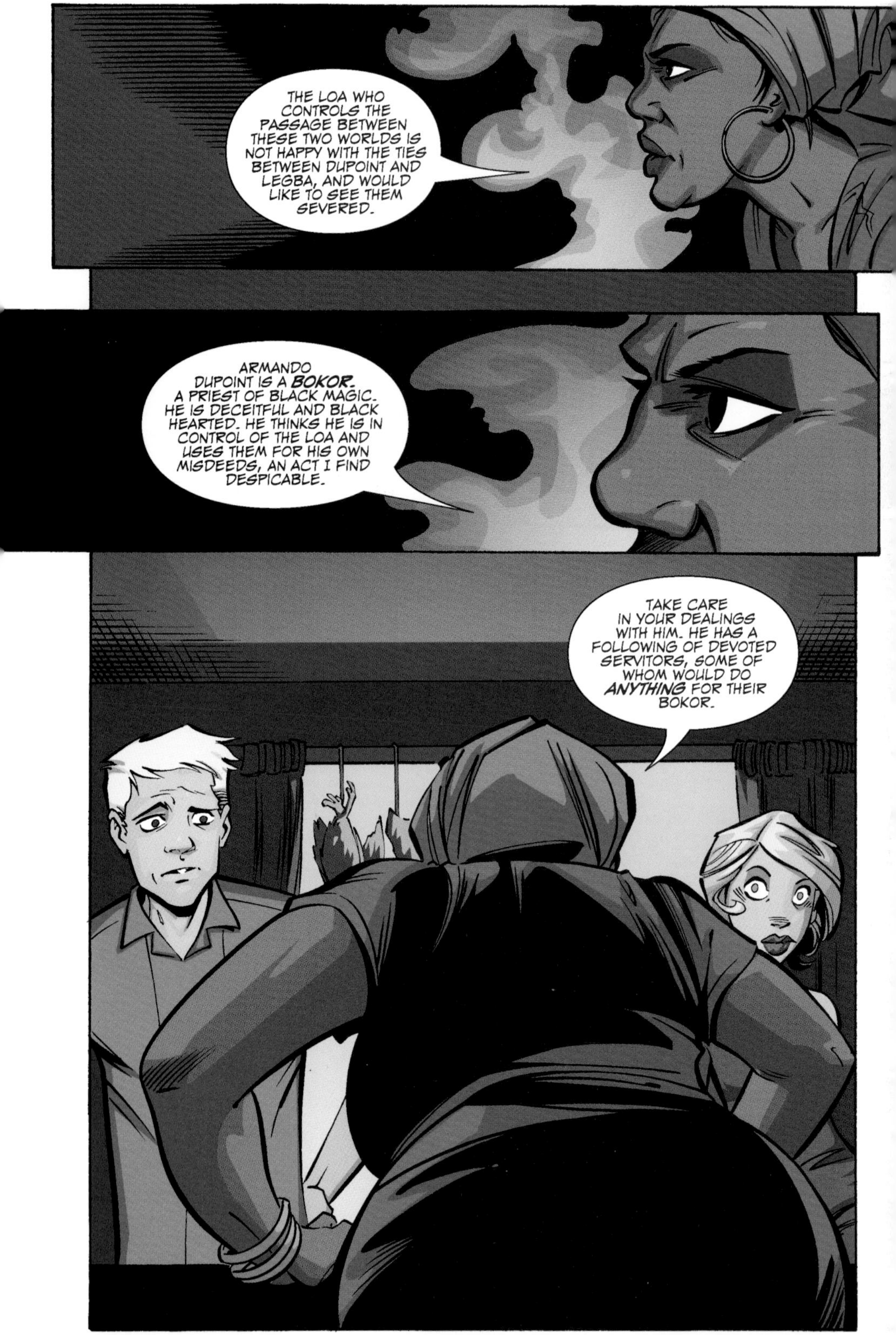
THE LOA WHO CONTROLS THE PASSAGE BETWEEN THESE TWO WORLDS IS NOT HAPPY WITH THE TIES BETWEEN DUPOINT AND LEGBA, AND WOULD LIKE TO SEE THEM SEVERED.
ARMANDO DUPOINT IS A BOKOR. A PRIEST OF BLACK MAGIC. HE IS DECEITFUL AND BLACK HEARTED. HE THINKS HE IS IN CONTROL OF THE LOA AND USES THEM FOR HIS OWN MISDEEDS, AN ACT I FIND DESPICABLE.
TAKE CARE IN YOUR DEALINGS WITH HIM. HE HAS A FOLLOWING OF DEVOTED SERVITORS, SOME OF WHOM WOULD DO ANYTHING FOR THEIR BOKOR.

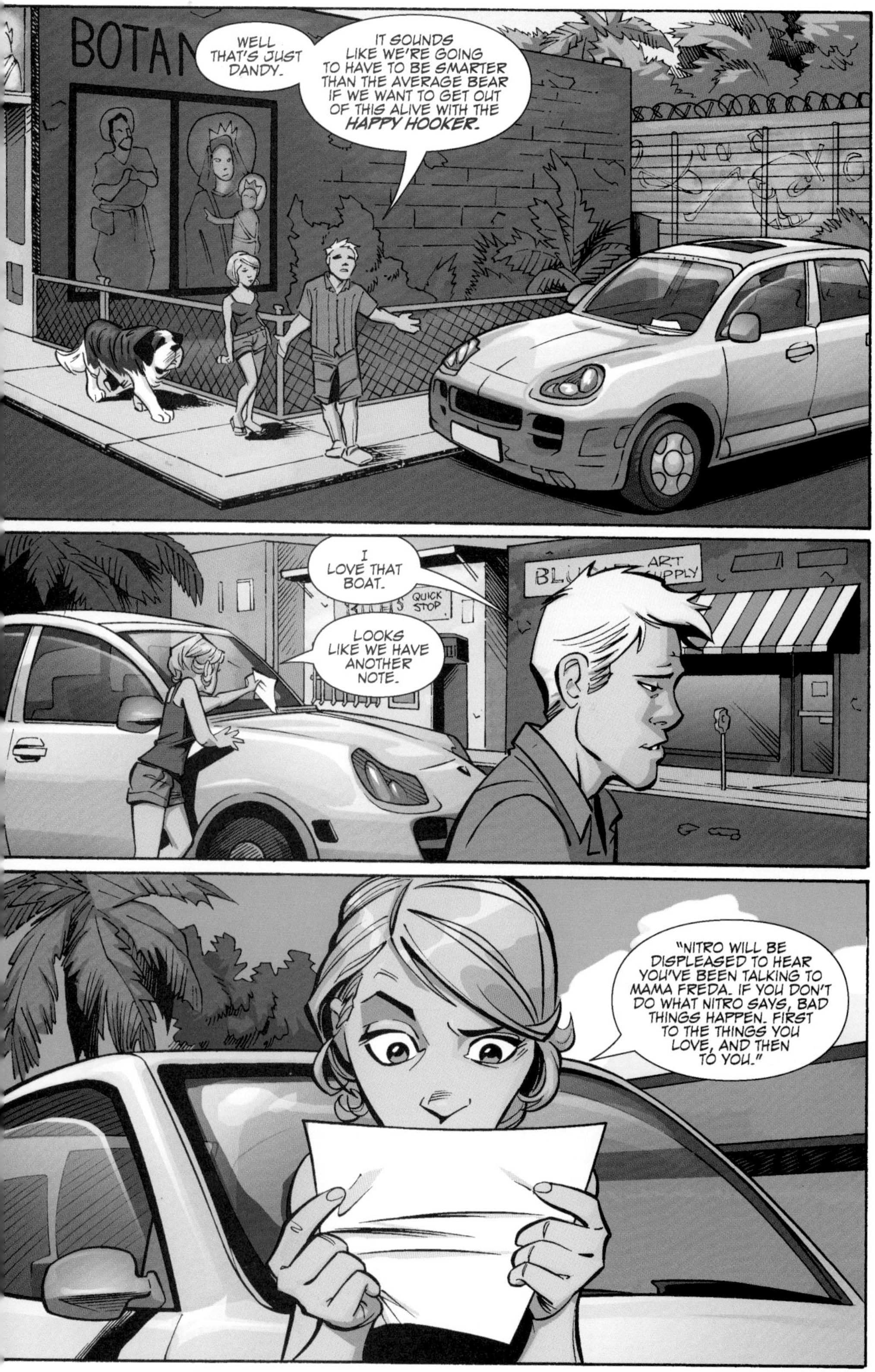
BOTAN
WELL THAT'S JUST DANDY.
IT SOUNDS LIKE WE'RE GOING TO HAVE TO BE SMARTER THAN THE AVERAGE BEAR IF WE WANT TO GET OUT OF THIS ALIVE WITH THE HAPPY HOOKER.
ART SUPPLY
QUICK STOP
I LOVE THAT BOAT.
LOOKS LIKE WE HAVE ANOTHER NOTE.
"NITRO WILL BE DISPLEASED TO HEAR YOU'VE BEEN TALKING TO MAMA FREDA. IF YOU DON'T DO WHAT NITRO SAYS, BAD THINGS HAPPEN. FIRST TO THE THINGS YOU LOVE, AND THEN TO YOU."

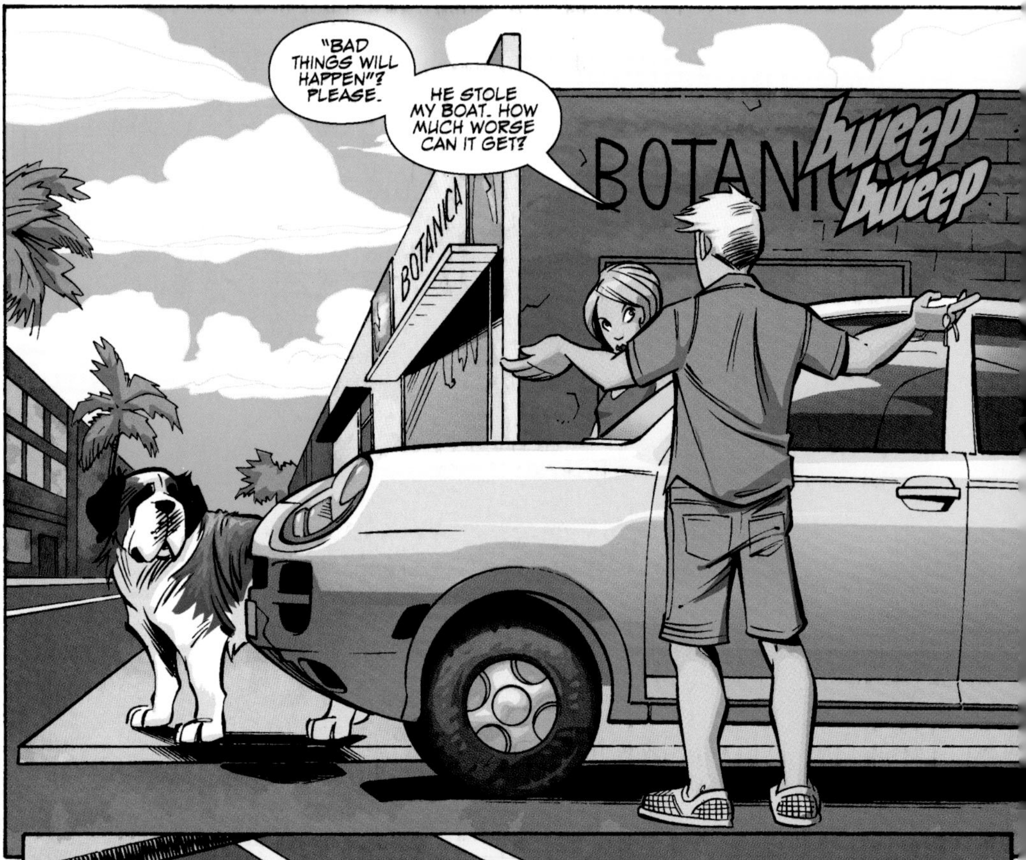
"BAD THINGS WILL HAPPEN"? PLEASE.
HE STOLE MY BOAT. HOW MUCH WORSE CAN IT GET?
BOTANICA
BOTANICA
bweep bweep

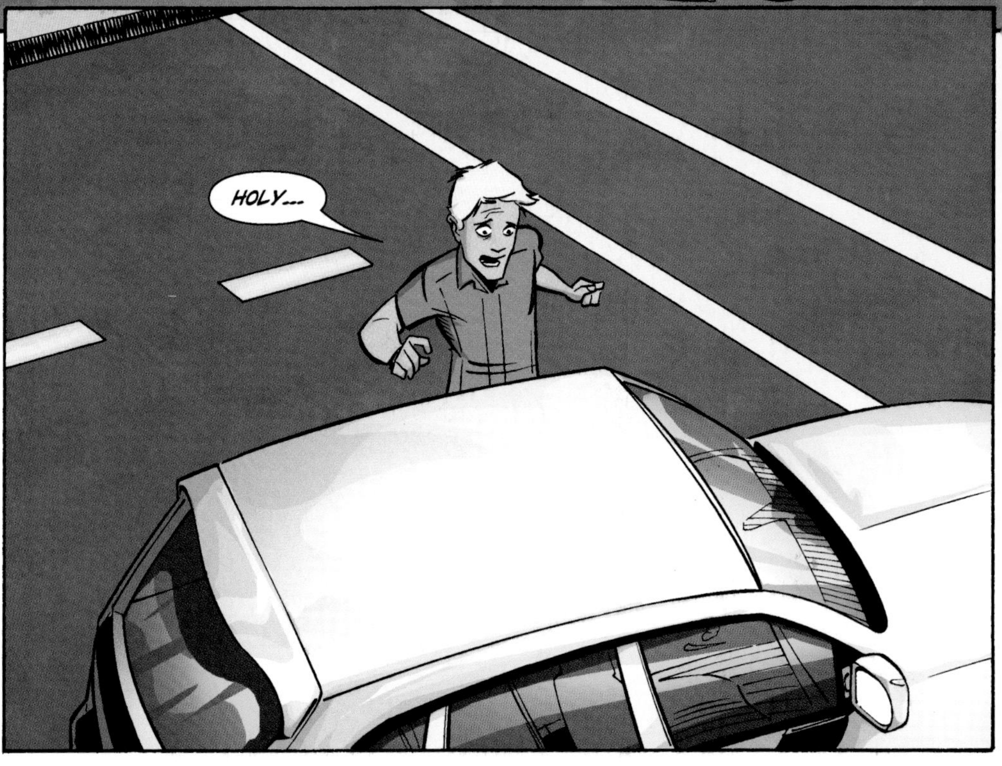
HOLY...

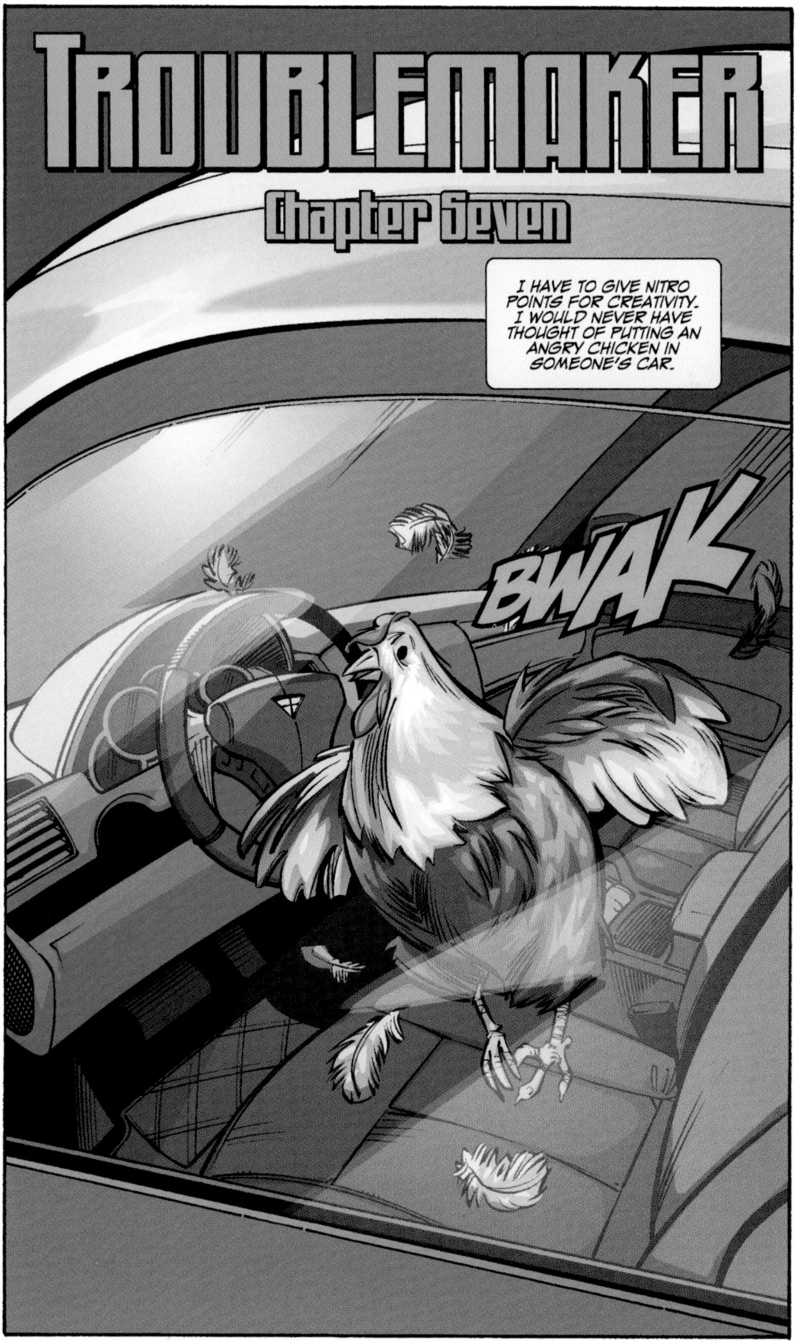
TROUBLEMAKER
Chapter Seven
I HAVE TO GIVE NITRO POINTS FOR CREATIVITY. I WOULD NEVER HAVE THOUGHT OF PUTTING AN ANGRY CHICKEN IN SOMEONE'S CAR.
BWAK

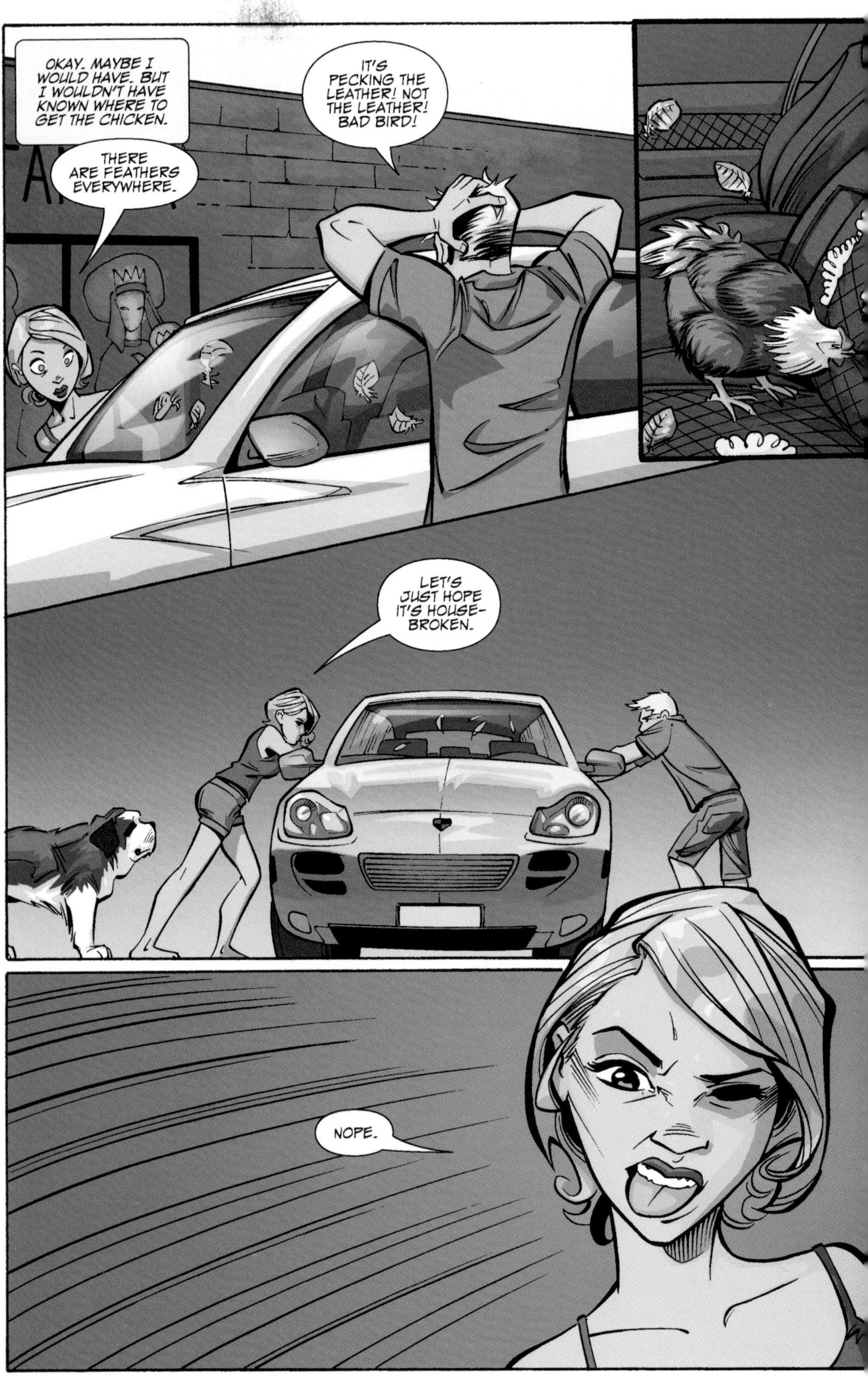
OKAY. MAYBE I WOULD HAVE. BUT I WOULDN'T HAVE KNOWN WHERE TO GET THE CHICKEN.
THERE ARE FEATHERS EVERYWHERE.
IT'S PECKING THE LEATHER! NOT THE LEATHER! BAD BIRD!
LET'S JUST HOPE IT'S HOUSE-BROKEN.
NOPE.

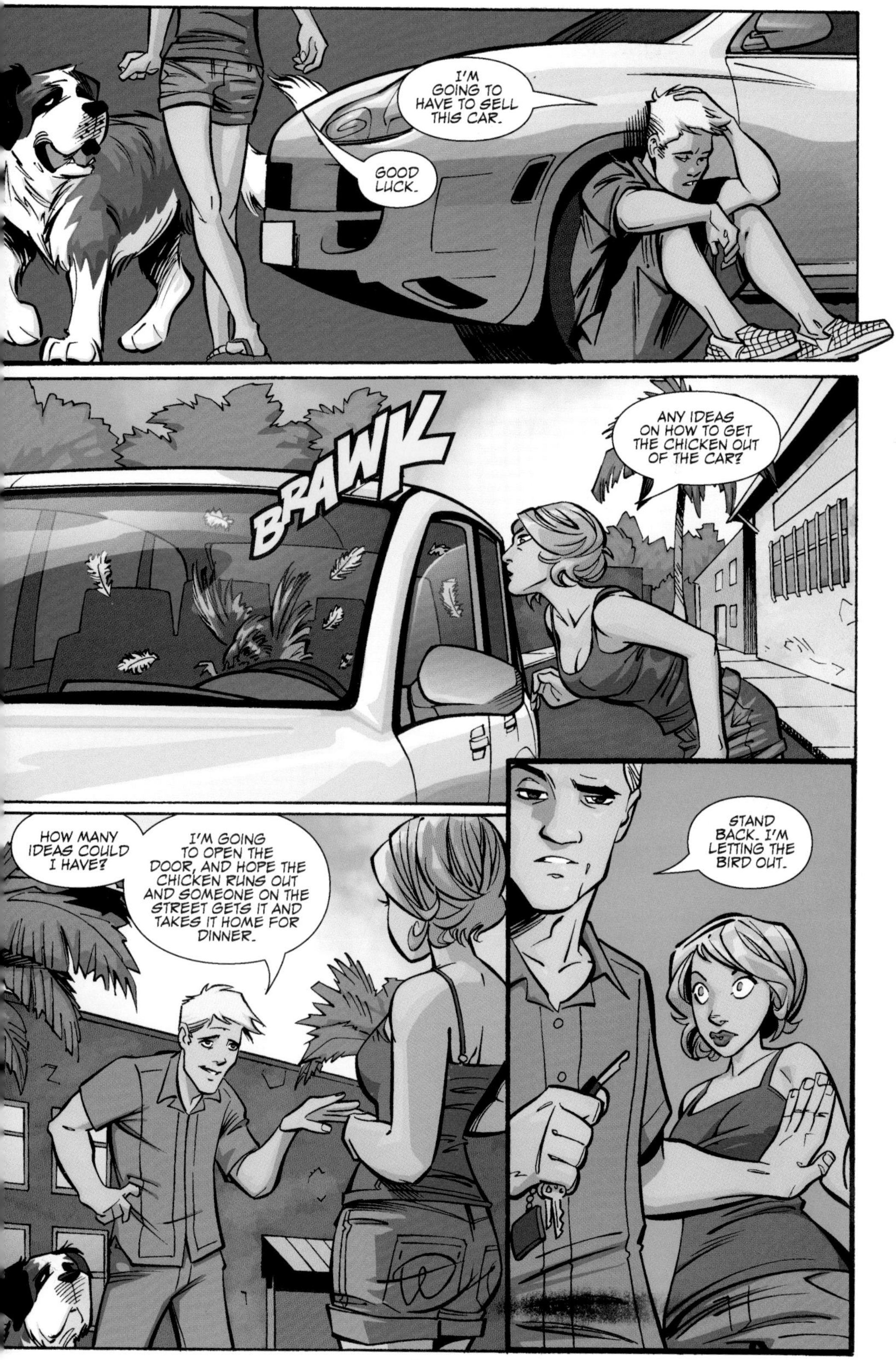
I'M GOING TO HAVE TO SELL THIS CAR.
GOOD LUCK.
BRAWK
ANY IDEAS ON HOW TO GET THE CHICKEN OUT OF THE CAR?
HOW MANY IDEAS COULD I HAVE?
I'M GOING TO OPEN THE DOOR, AND HOPE THE CHICKEN RUNS OUT AND SOMEONE ON THE STREET GETS IT AND TAKES IT HOME FOR DINNER.
STAND BACK. I'M LETTING THE BIRD OUT.

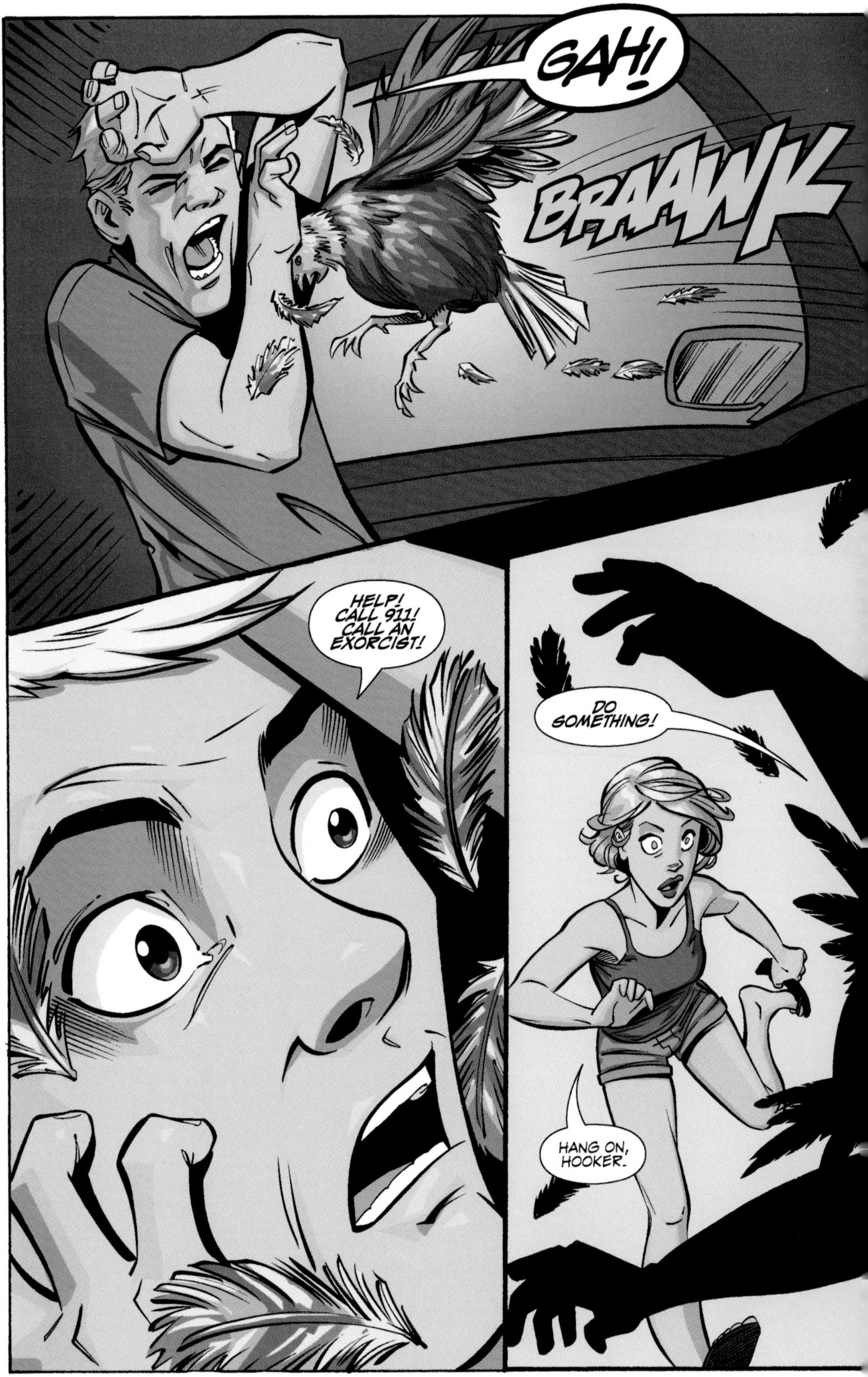
GAH!
BRAAWK
HELP! CALL 911! CALL AN EXORCIST!
DO SOMETHING!
HANG ON, HOOKER.

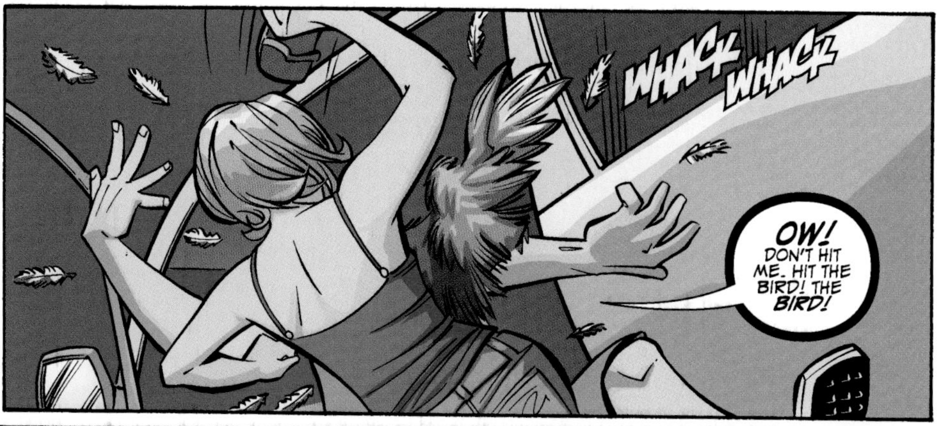
WHACK WHACK
OW! DON'T HIT ME. HIT THE BIRD! THE BIRD!

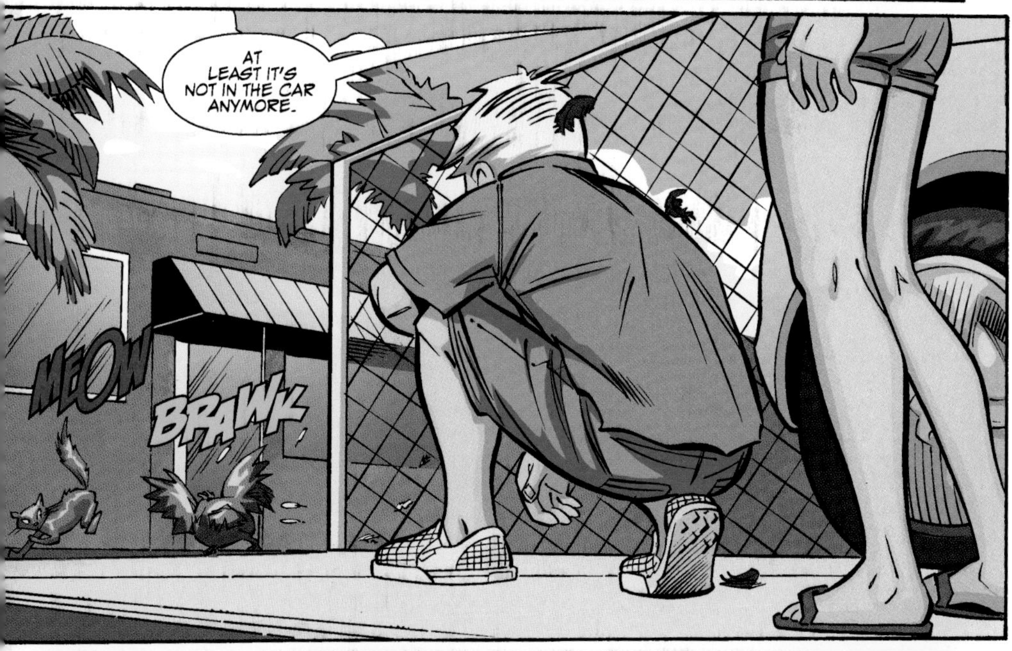
AT LEAST IT'S NOT IN THE CAR ANYMORE.
MEOW
BRAWK

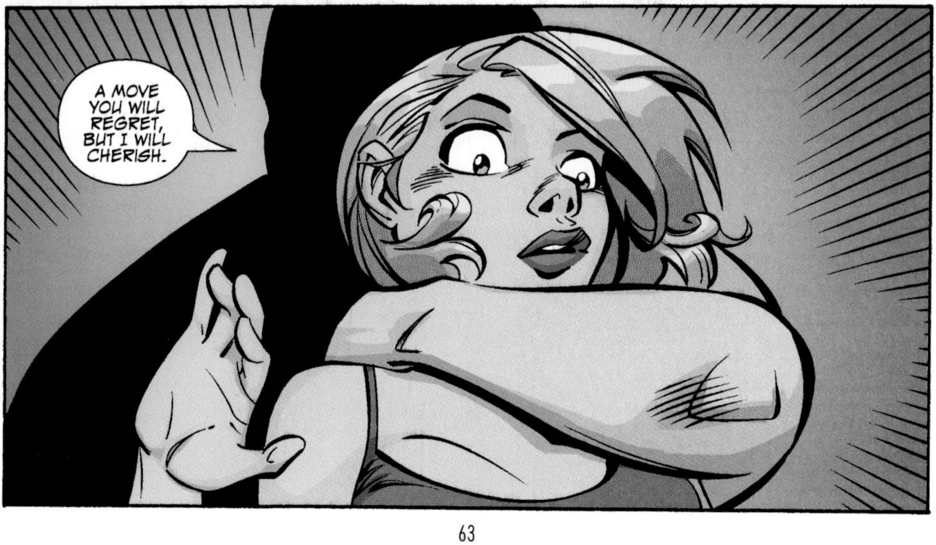
A MOVE YOU WILL REGRET, BUT I WILL CHERISH.

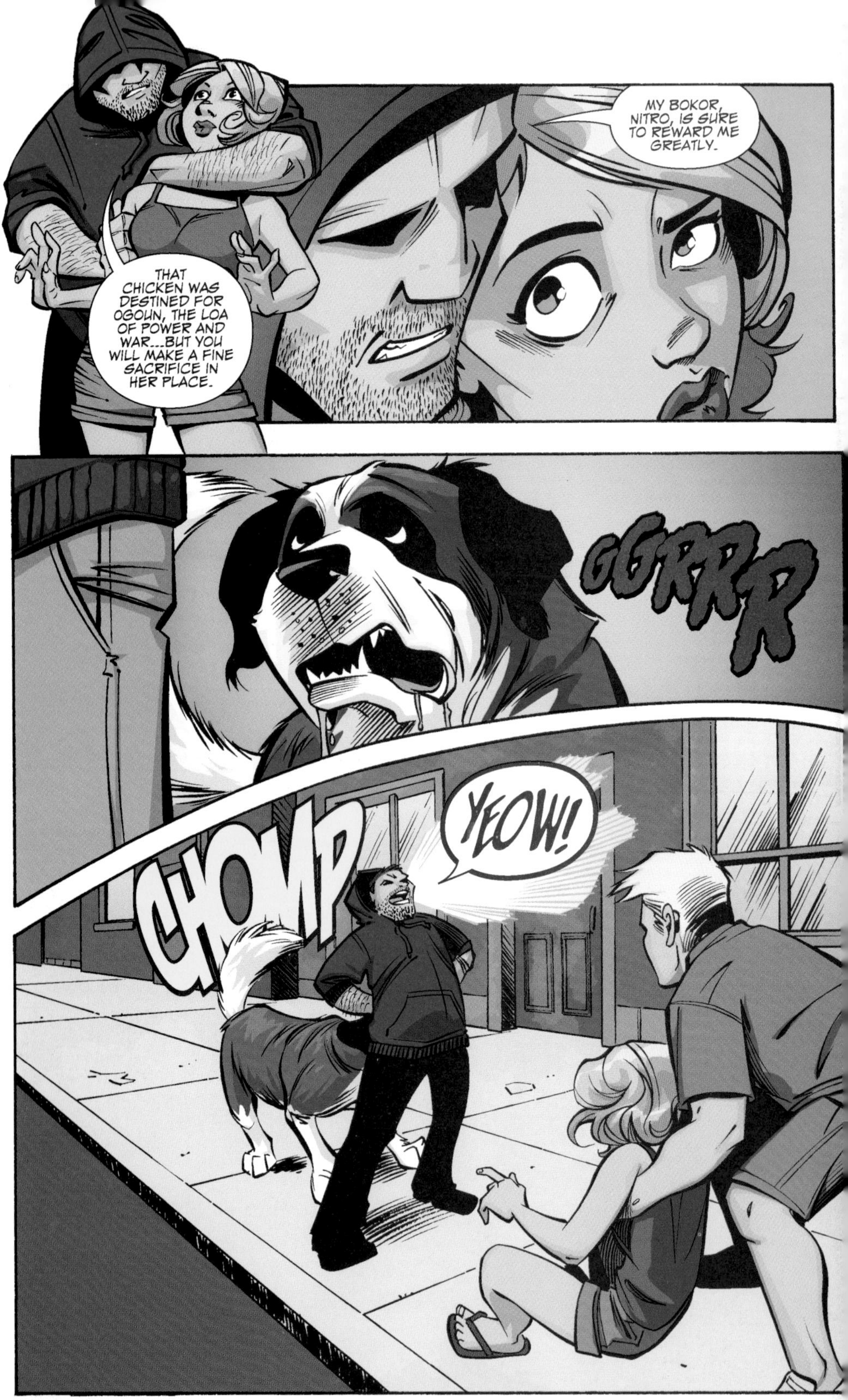
THAT CHICKEN WAS DESTINED FOR OGOUN, THE LOA OF POWER AND WAR...BUT YOU WILL MAKE A FINE SACRIFICE IN HER PLACE.
MY BOKOR, NITRO, IS SURE TO REWARD ME GREATLY.
GGRRRR
CHOMP
YEOW!

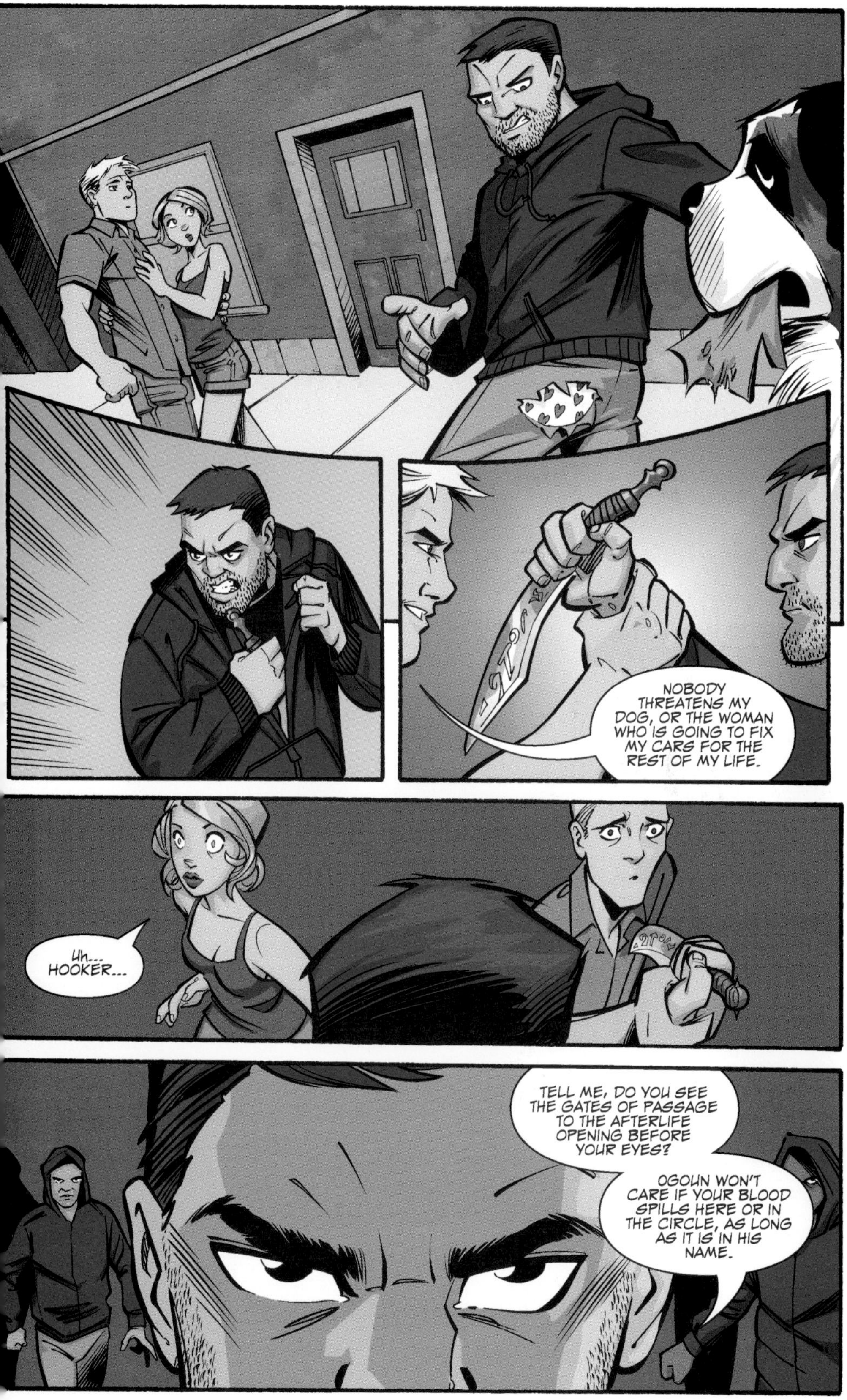
NOBODY THREATENS MY DOG, OR THE WOMAN WHO IS GOING TO FIX MY CARS FOR THE REST OF MY LIFE.
UH... HOOKER...
TELL ME, DO YOU SEE THE GATES OF PASSAGE TO THE AFTERLIFE OPENING BEFORE YOUR EYES?
OGOUN WON'T CARE IF YOUR BLOOD SPILLS HERE OR IN THE CIRCLE, AS LONG AS IT IS IN HIS NAME.

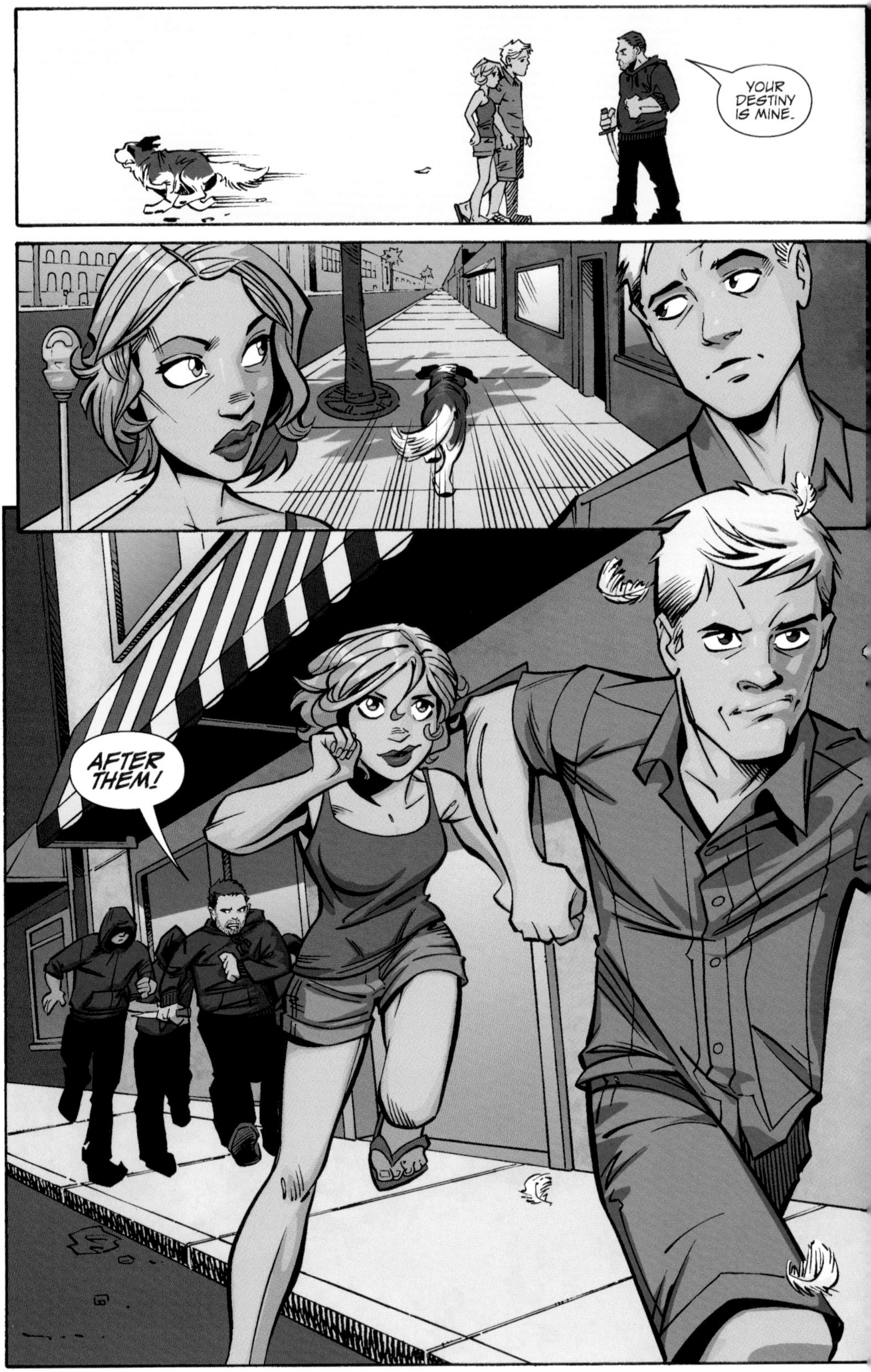

YOUR DESTINY IS MINE.
AFTER THEM!

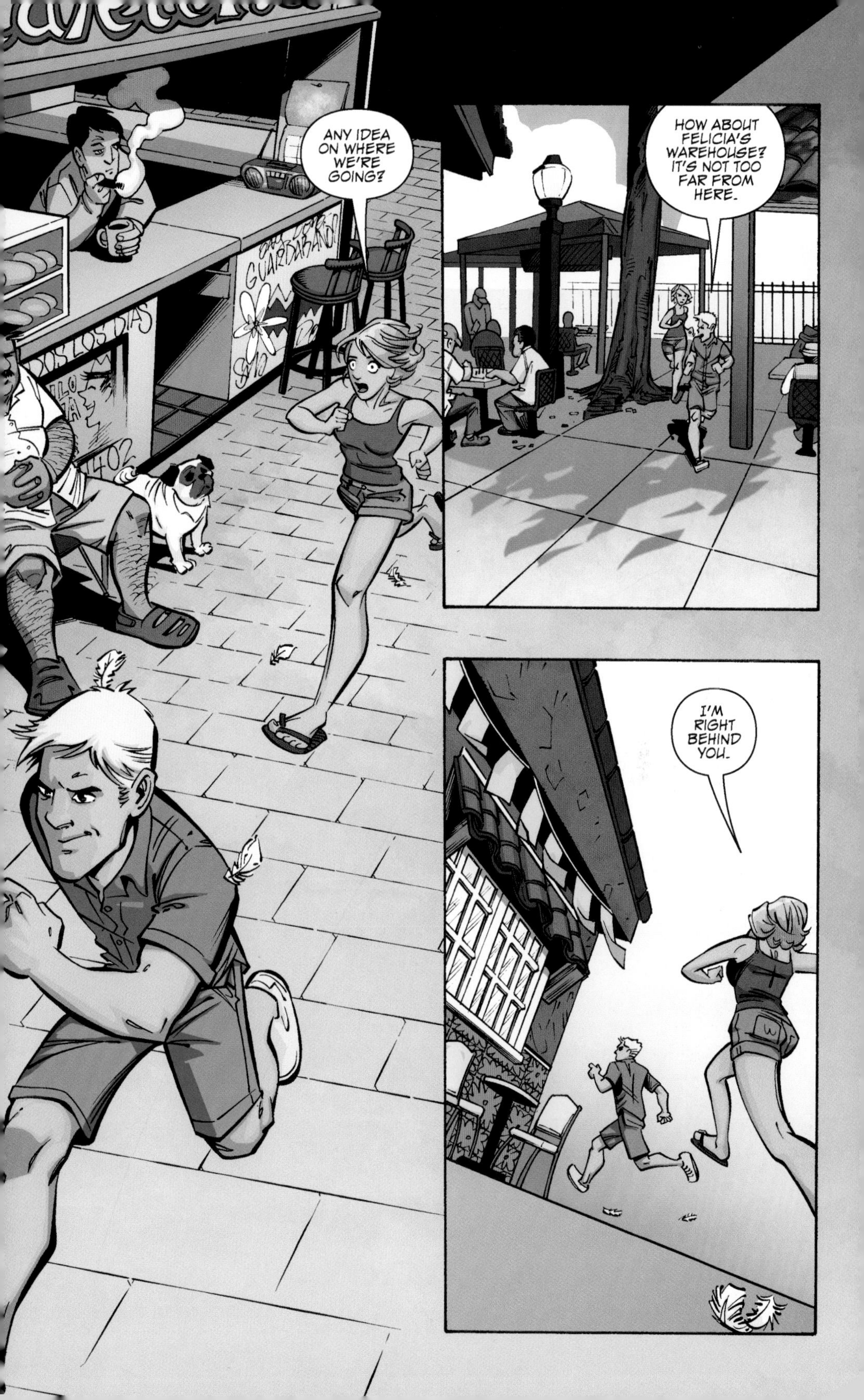
ANY IDEA ON WHERE WE'RE GOING?
HOW ABOUT FELICIA'S WAREHOUSE? IT'S NOT TOO FAR FROM HERE.
I'M RIGHT BEHIND YOU.

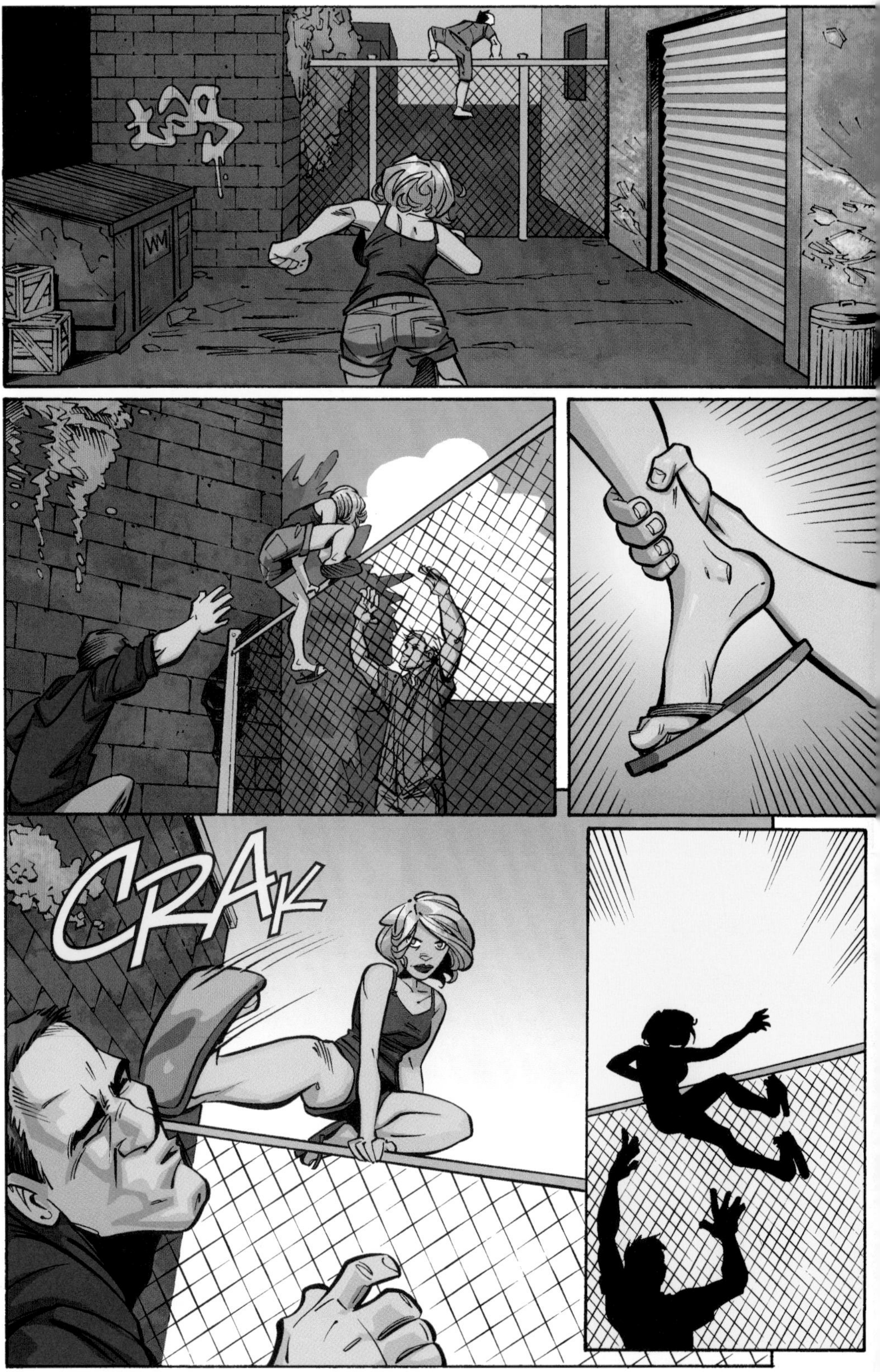
CRAK

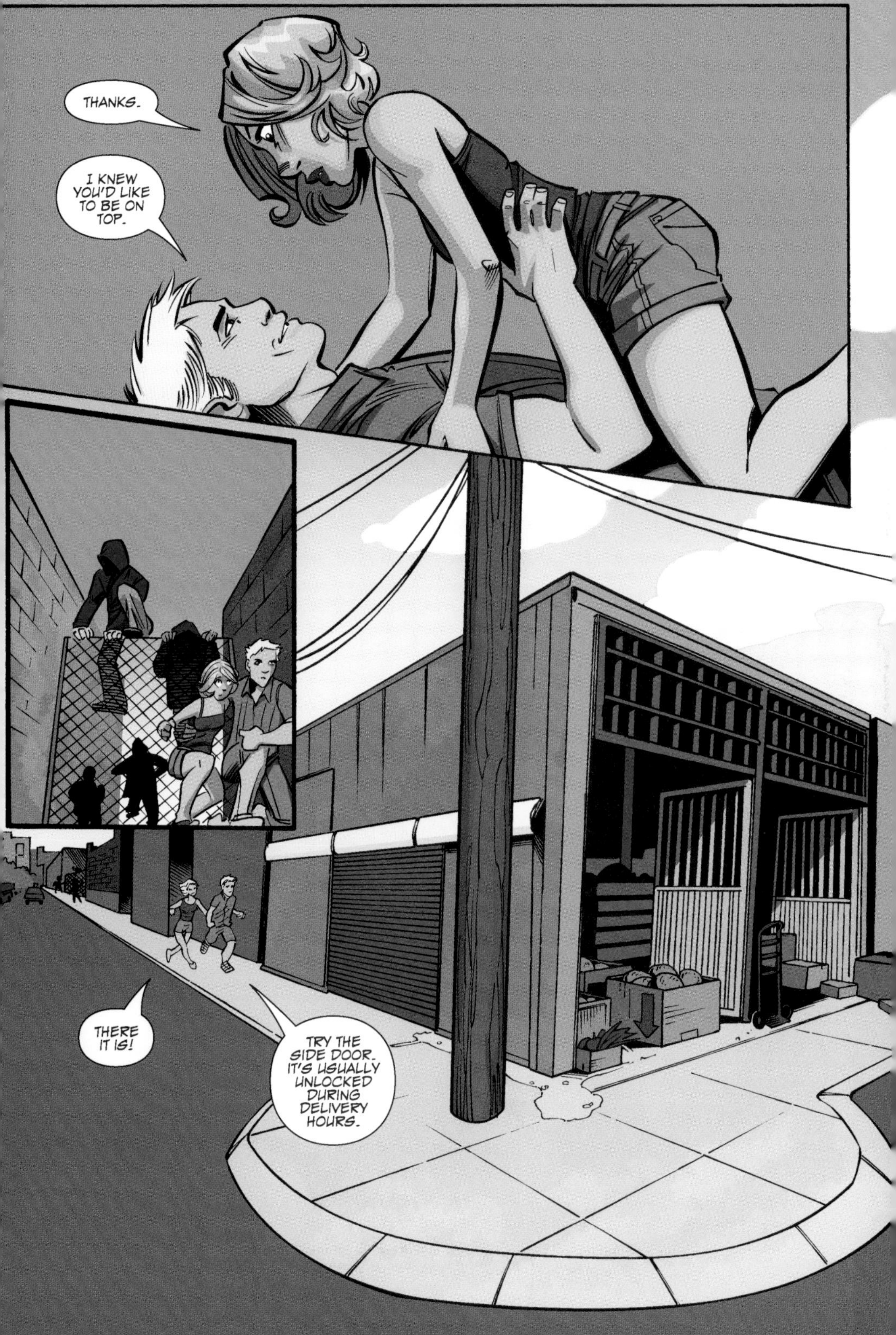
THANKS.
I KNEW YOU'D LIKE TO BE ON TOP.
THERE IT IS!
TRY THE SIDE DOOR. IT'S USUALLY UNLOCKED DURING DELIVERY HOURS.

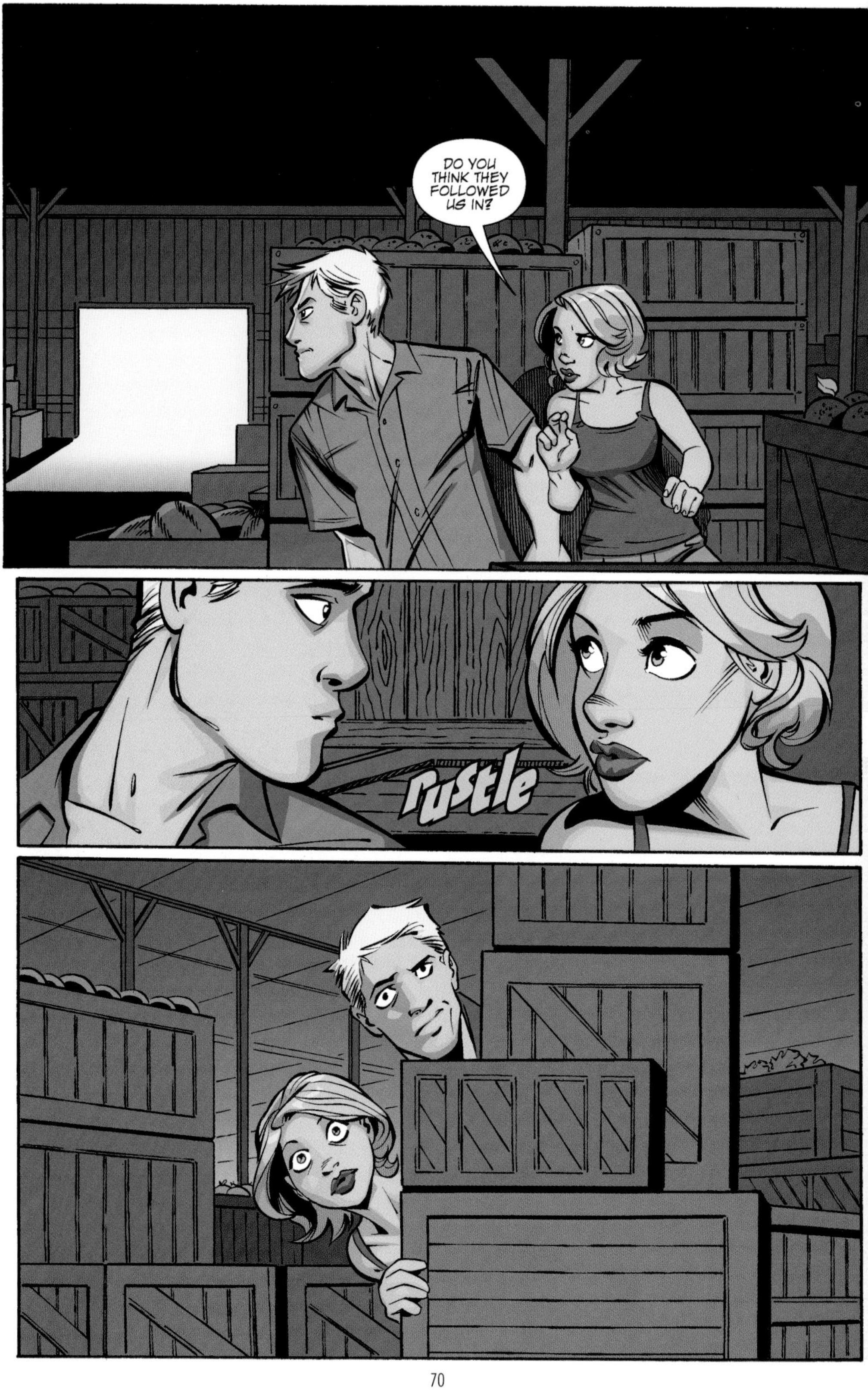
DO YOU THINK THEY FOLLOWED US IN?
RUSTLE

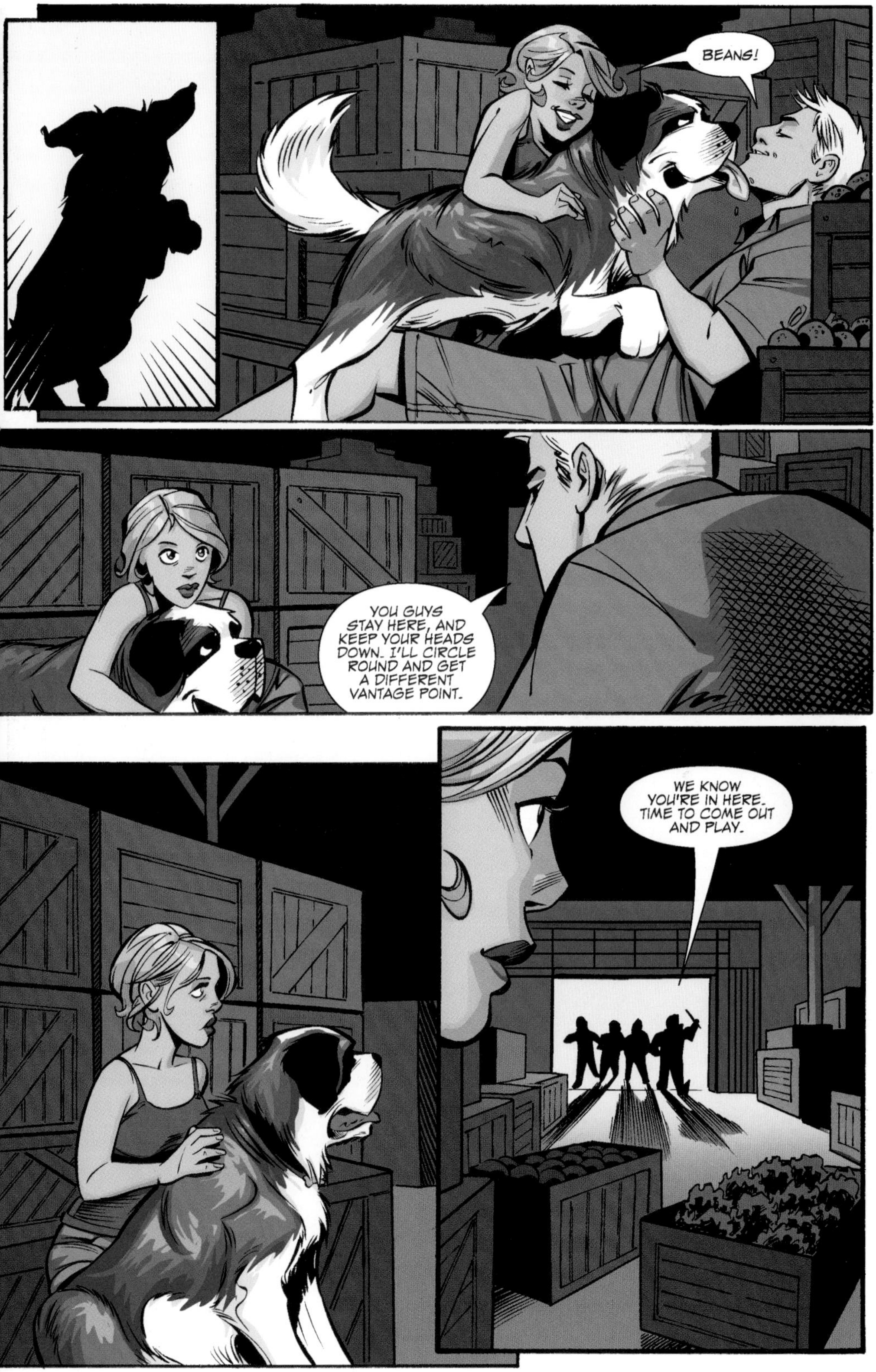
BEANS!
YOU GUYS STAY HERE, AND KEEP YOUR HEADS DOWN. I'LL CIRCLE ROUND AND GET A DIFFERENT VANTAGE POINT.
WE KNOW YOU'RE IN HERE. TIME TO COME OUT AND PLAY.

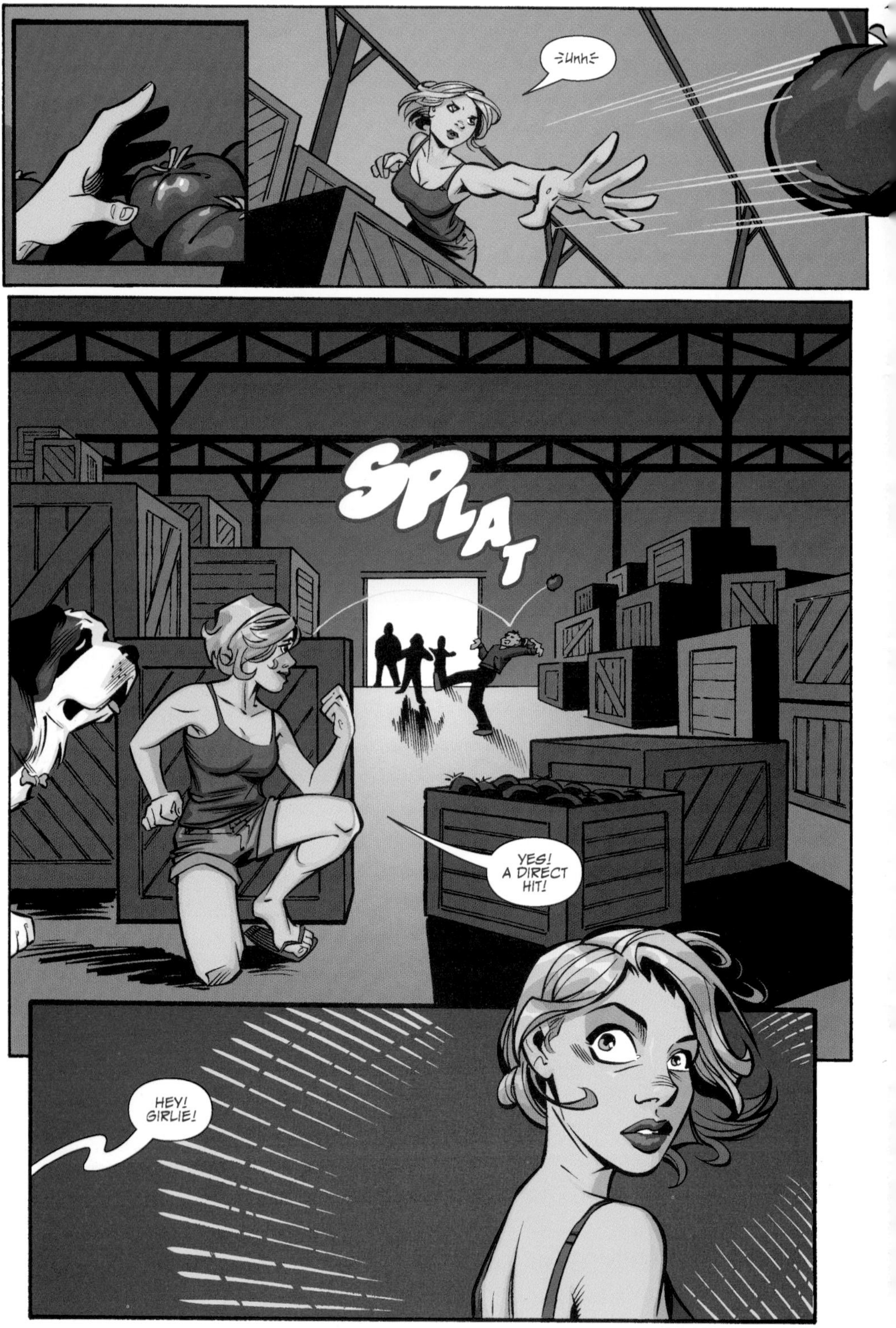
Unnh
SPLAT
YES! A DIRECT HIT!
HEY! GIRLIE!

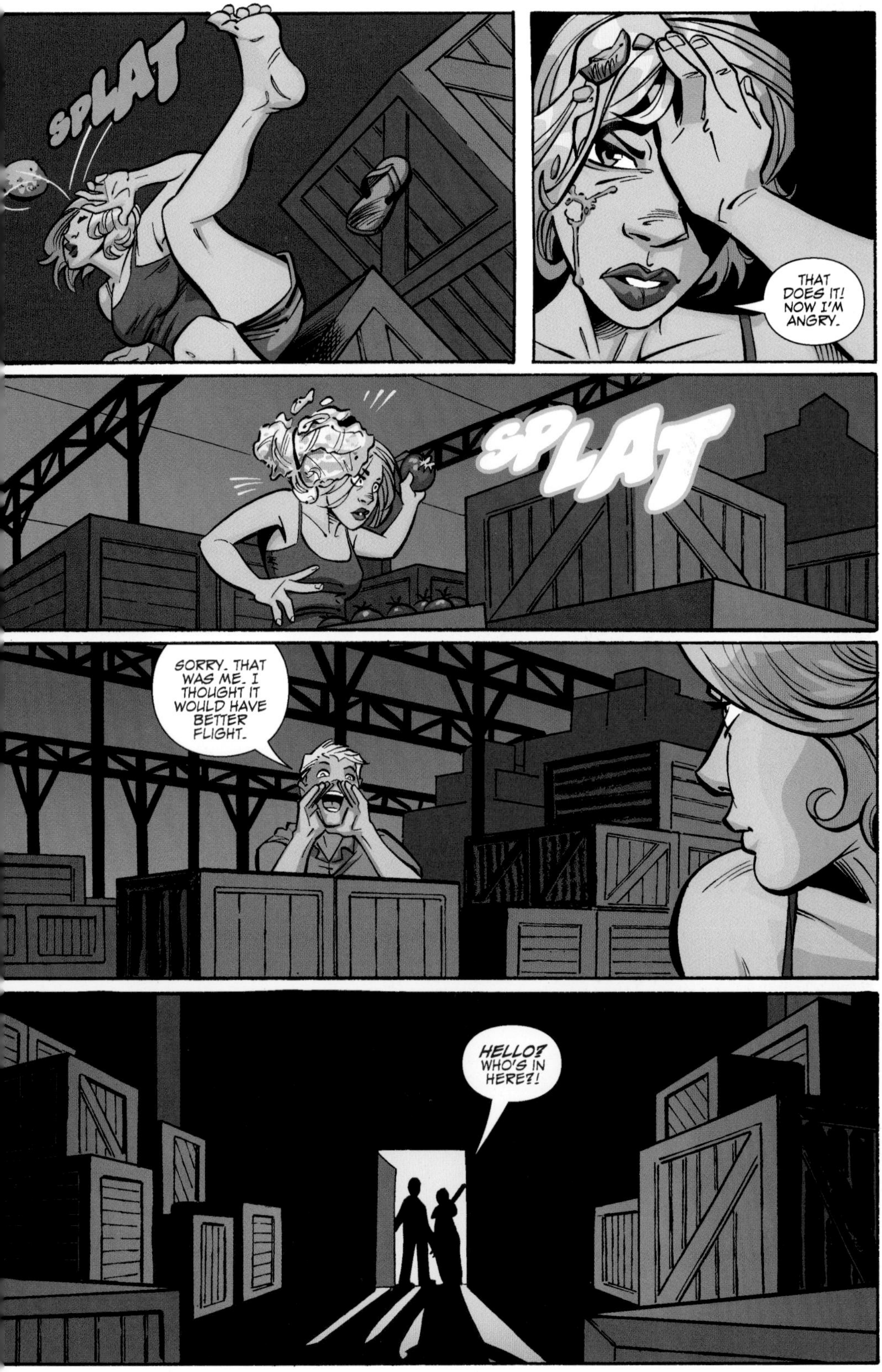
SPLAT
THAT DOES IT! NOW I'M ANGRY.
SPLAT
SORRY. THAT WAS ME. I THOUGHT IT WOULD HAVE BETTER FLIGHT.
HELLO? WHO'S IN HERE?!

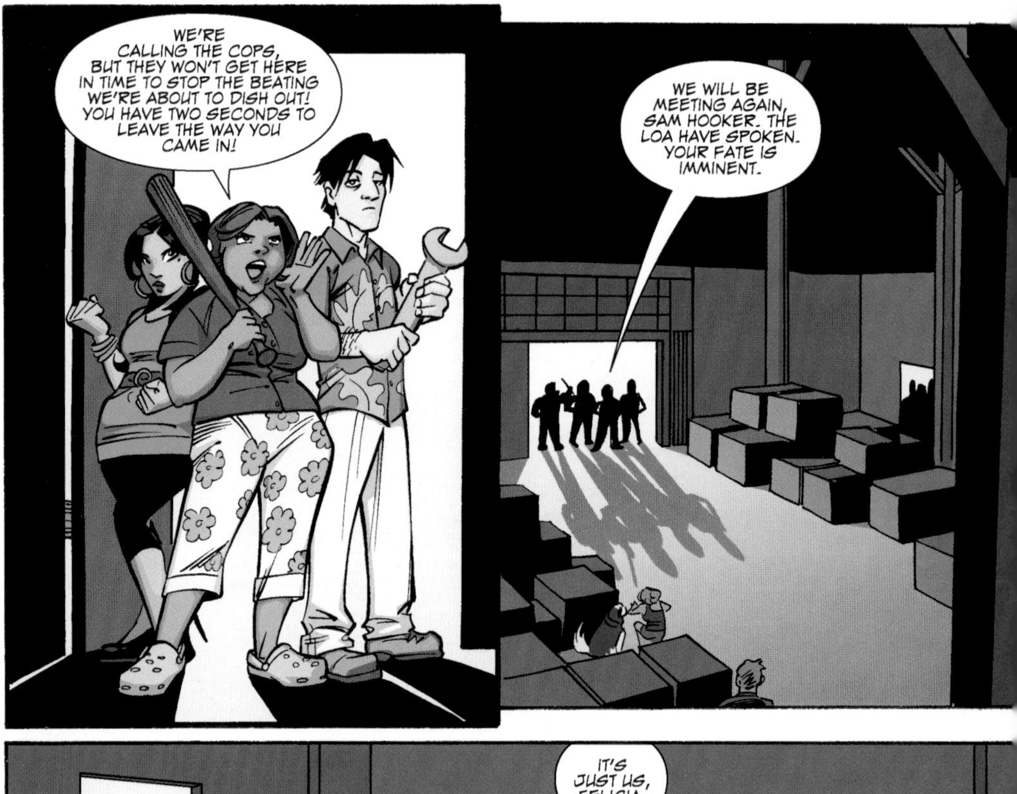
WE'RE CALLING THE COPS, BUT THEY WON'T GET HERE IN TIME TO STOP THE BEATING WE'RE ABOUT TO DISH OUT! YOU HAVE TWO SECONDS TO LEAVE THE WAY YOU CAME IN!
WE WILL BE MEETING AGAIN, SAM HOOKER. THE LOA HAVE SPOKEN. YOUR FATE IS IMMINENT.
IT'S JUST US, FELICIA.
WE HAD A LITTLE RUN-IN WITH SOME OF NITRO'S FOLLOWERS.

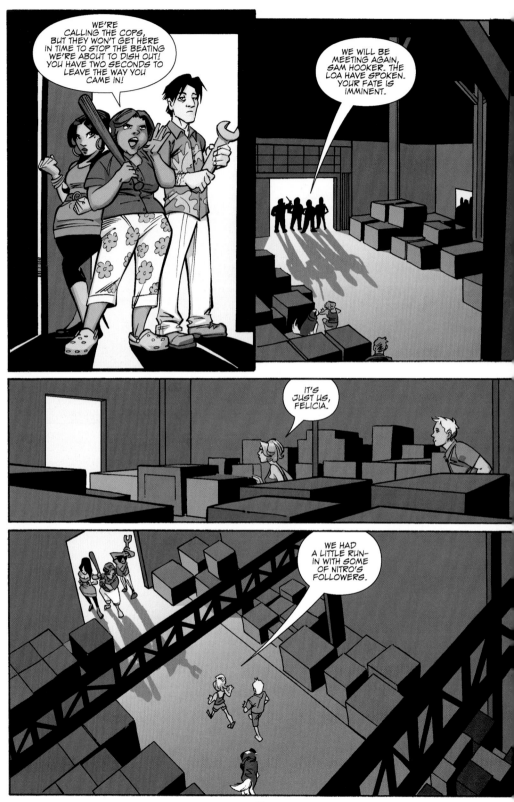

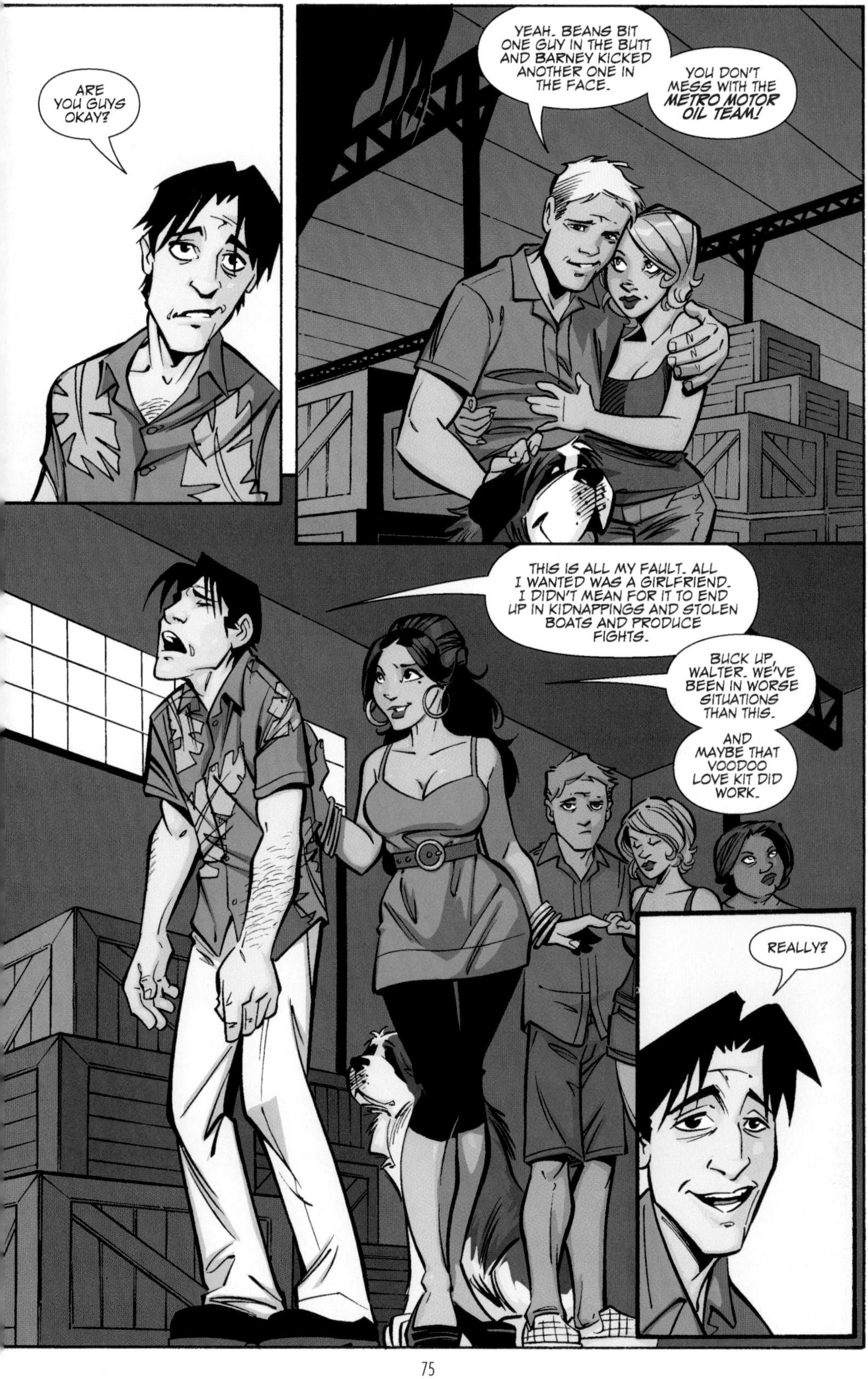
ARE YOU GUYS OKAY?
YEAH. BEANS BIT ONE GUY IN THE BUTT AND BARNEY KICKED ANOTHER ONE IN THE FACE.
YOU DON'T MESS WITH THE METRO MOTOR OIL TEAM!
THIS IS ALL MY FAULT. ALL I WANTED WAS A GIRLFRIEND. I DIDN'T MEAN FOR IT TO END UP IN KIDNAPPINGS AND STOLEN BOATS AND PRODUCE FIGHTS.
BUCK UP, WALTER. WE'VE BEEN IN WORSE SITUATIONS THAN THIS.
AND MAYBE THAT VOODOO LOVE KIT DID WORK.
REALLY?

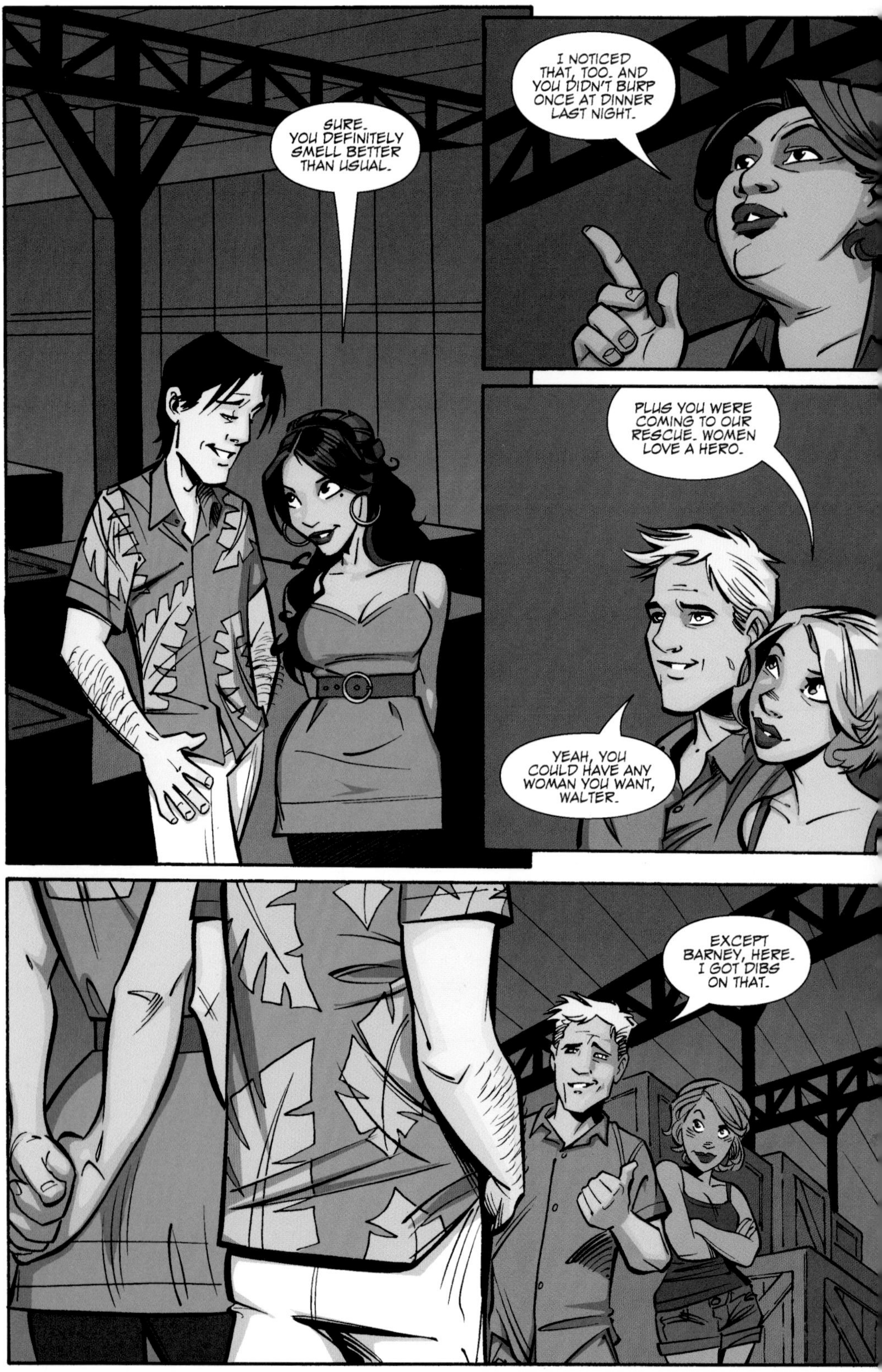
SURE. YOU DEFINITELY SMELL BETTER THAN USUAL.
I NOTICED THAT, TOO. AND YOU DIDN'T BURP ONCE AT DINNER LAST NIGHT.
PLUS YOU WERE COMING TO OUR RESCUE. WOMEN LOVE A HERO.
YEAH, YOU COULD HAVE ANY WOMAN YOU WANT, WALTER.
EXCEPT BARNEY, HERE. I GOT DIBS ON THAT.

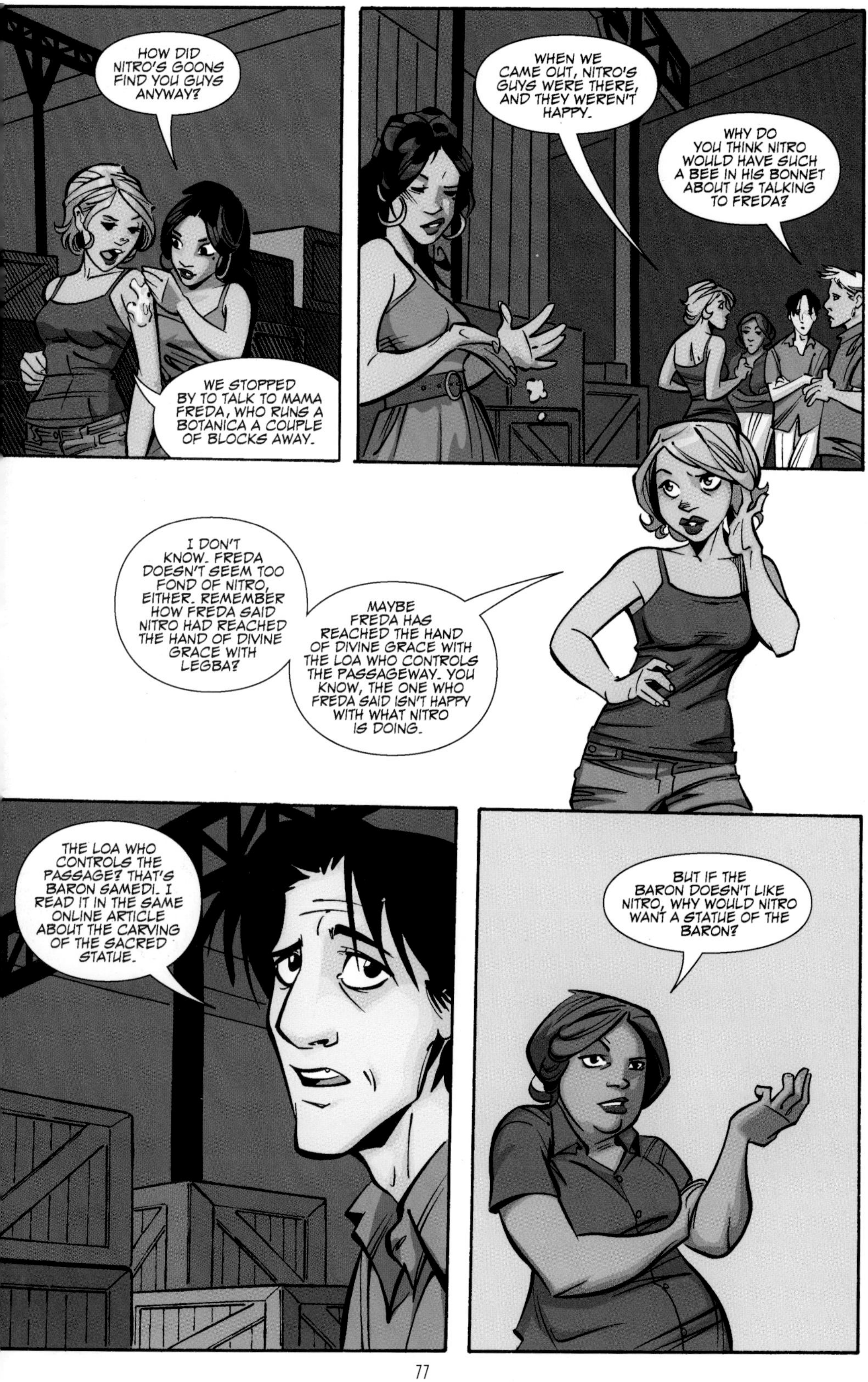
HOW DID NITRO'S GOONS FIND YOU GUYS ANYWAY?
WE STOPPED BY TO TALK TO MAMA FREDA, WHO RUNS A BOTANICA A COUPLE OF BLOCKS AWAY.
WHEN WE CAME OUT, NITRO'S GUYS WERE THERE, AND THEY WEREN'T HAPPY.
WHY DO YOU THINK NITRO WOULD HAVE SUCH A BEE IN HIS BONNET ABOUT US TALKING TO FREDA?
I DON'T KNOW. FREDA DOESN'T SEEM TOO FOND OF NITRO, EITHER. REMEMBER HOW FREDA SAID NITRO HAD REACHED THE HAND OF DIVINE GRACE WITH LEGBA?
MAYBE FREDA HAS REACHED THE HAND OF DIVINE GRACE WITH THE LOA WHO CONTROLS THE PASSAGEWAY. YOU KNOW, THE ONE WHO FREDA SAID ISN'T HAPPY WITH WHAT NITRO IS DOING.
THE LOA WHO CONTROLS THE PASSAGE? THAT'S BARON SAMEDI. I READ IT IN THE SAME ONLINE ARTICLE ABOUT THE CARVING OF THE SACRED STATUE.
BUT IF THE BARON DOESN'T LIKE NITRO, WHY WOULD NITRO WANT A STATUE OF THE BARON?

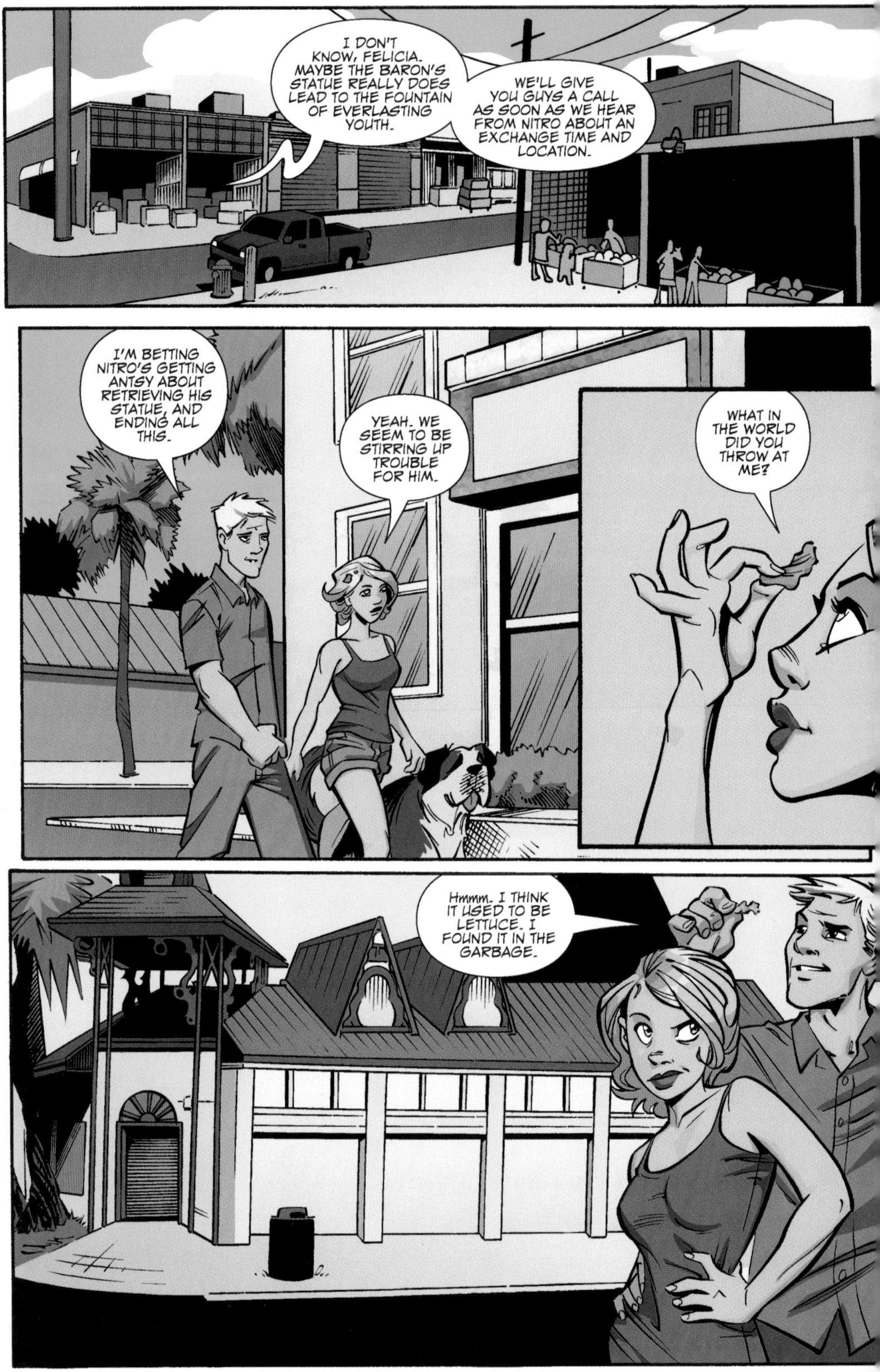
I DON'T KNOW, FELICIA. MAYBE THE BARON'S STATUE REALLY DOES LEAD TO THE FOUNTAIN OF EVERLASTING YOUTH.
WE'LL GIVE YOU GUYS A CALL AS SOON AS WE HEAR FROM NITRO ABOUT AN EXCHANGE TIME AND LOCATION.
I'M BETTING NITRO'S GETTING ANTSY ABOUT RETRIEVING HIS STATUE, AND ENDING ALL THIS.
YEAH. WE SEEM TO BE STIRRING UP TROUBLE FOR HIM.
WHAT IN THE WORLD DID YOU THROW AT ME?
Hmmm. I THINK IT USED TO BE LETTUCE. I FOUND IT IN THE GARBAGE.

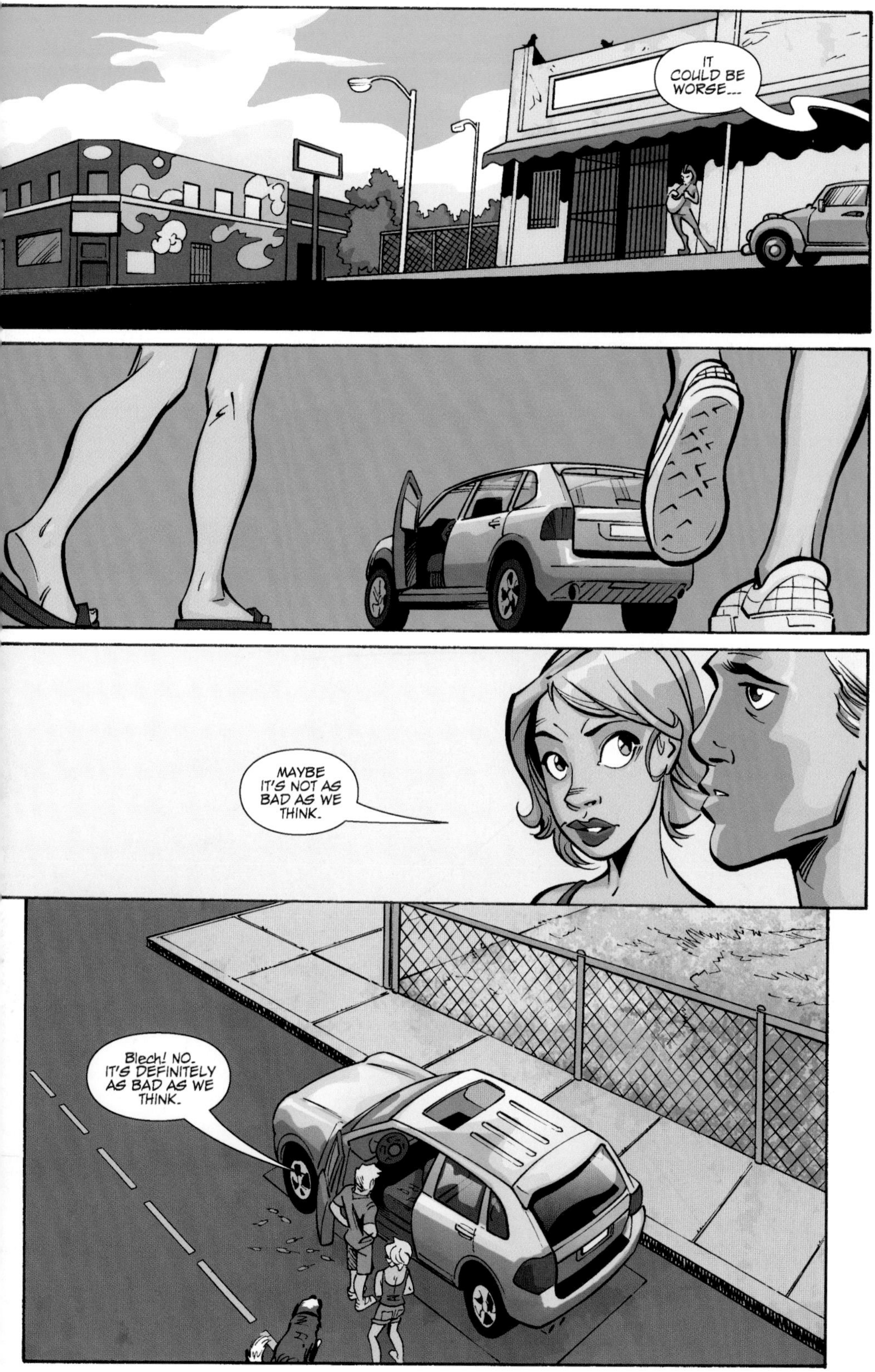
IT COULD BE WORSE...
MAYBE IT'S NOT AS BAD AS WE THINK.
Blech! NO. IT'S DEFINITELY AS BAD AS WE THINK.

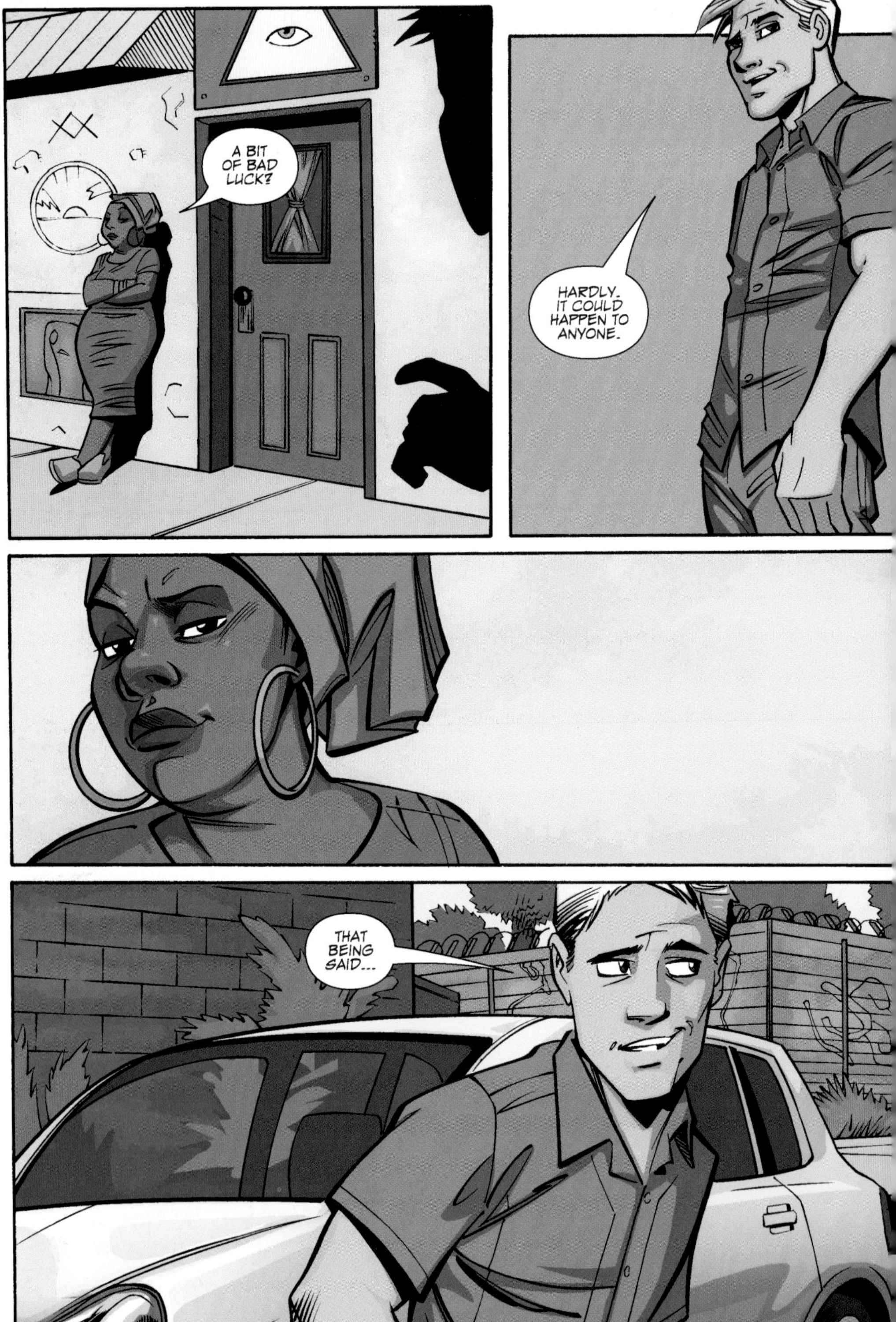
A BIT OF BAD LUCK?
HARDLY. IT COULD HAPPEN TO ANYONE.
THAT BEING SAID...

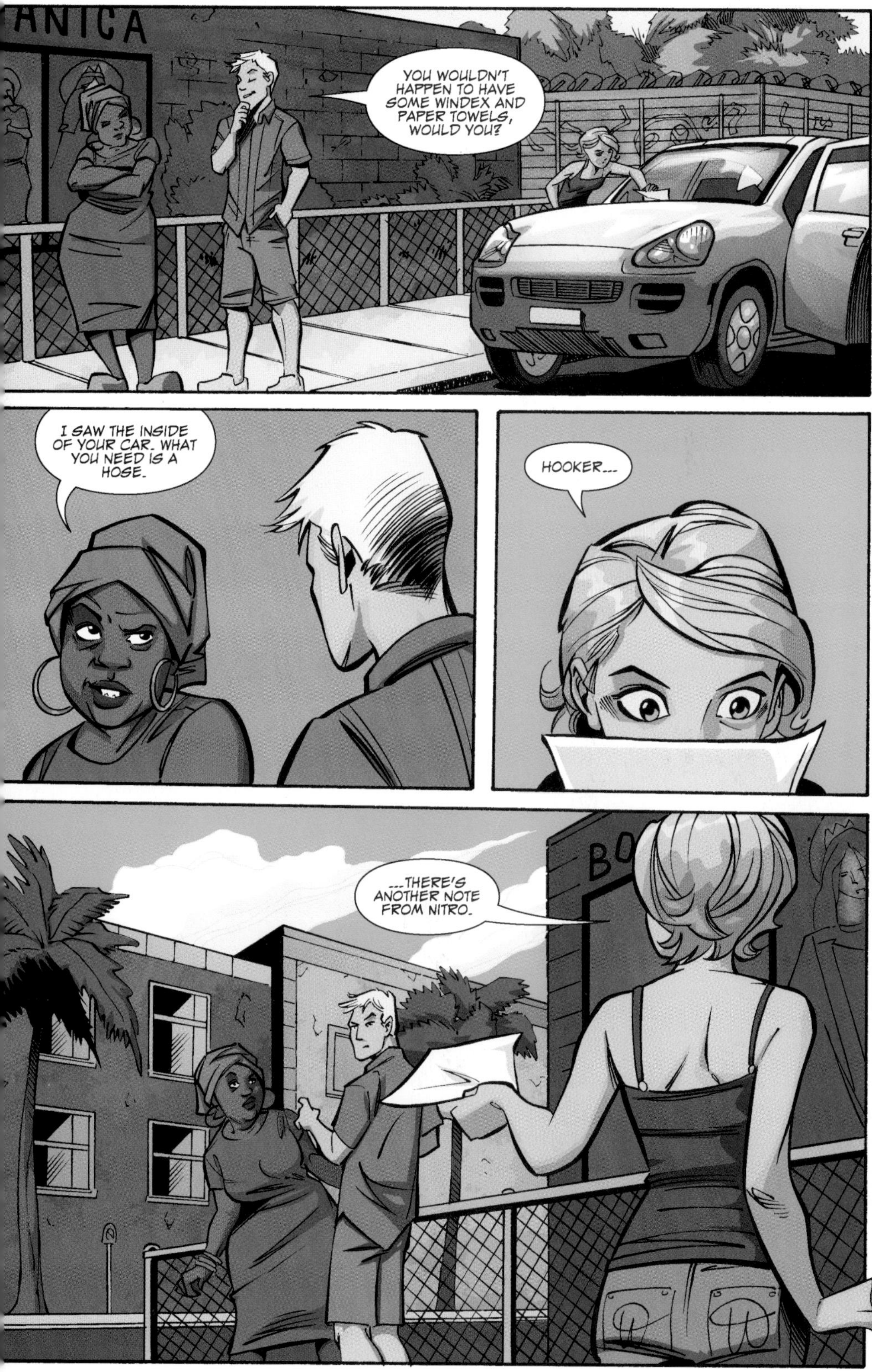
ANICA
YOU WOULDN'T HAPPEN TO HAVE SOME WINDEX AND PAPER TOWELS, WOULD YOU?
I SAW THE INSIDE OF YOUR CAR. WHAT YOU NEED IS A HOSE.
HOOKER...
...THERE'S ANOTHER NOTE FROM NITRO.

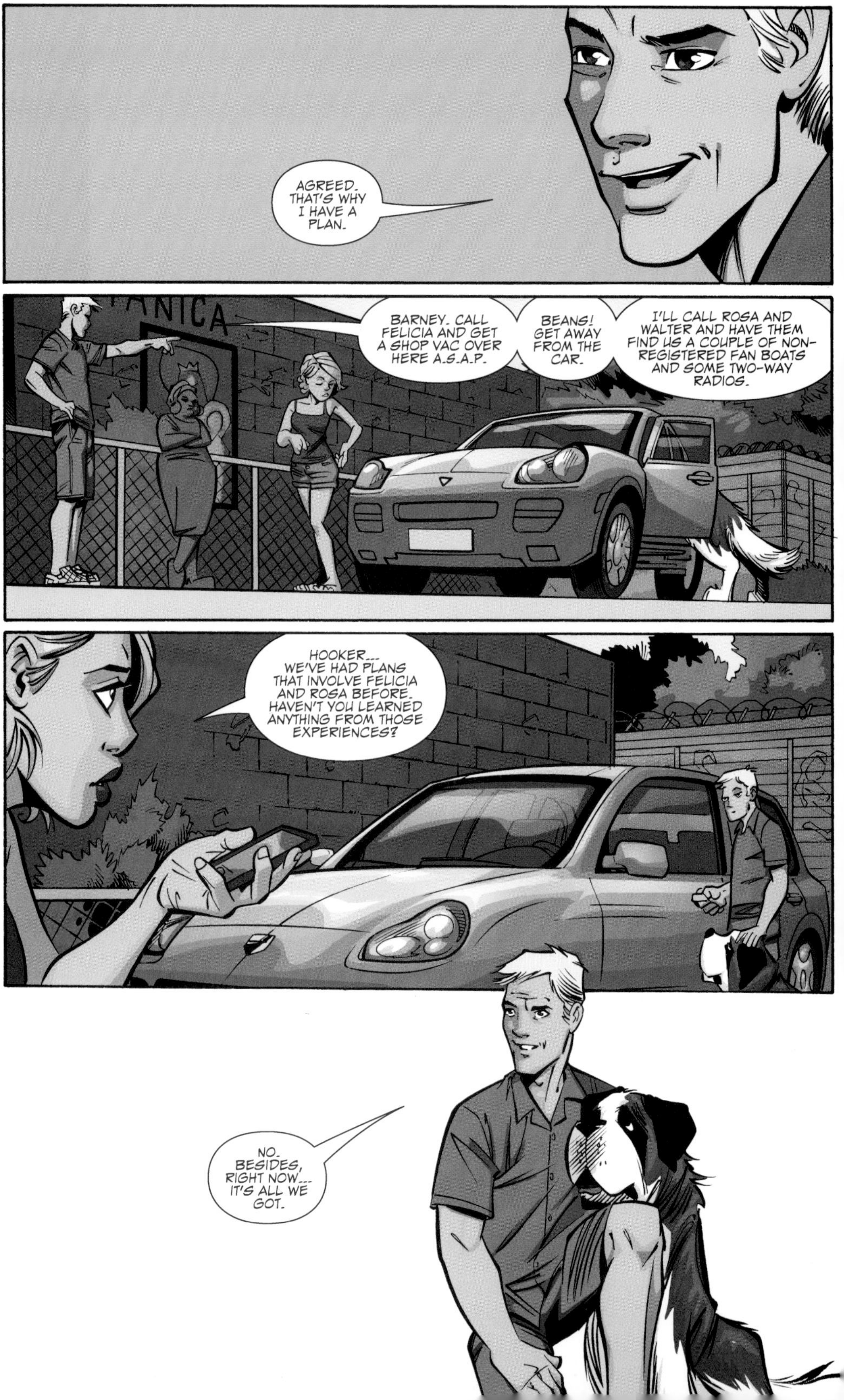
AGREED. THAT'S WHY I HAVE A PLAN.
ANICA
BARNEY. CALL FELICIA AND GET A SHOP VAC OVER HERE A.S.A.P.
BEANS! GET AWAY FROM THE CAR.
I'LL CALL ROSA AND WALTER AND HAVE THEM FIND US A COUPLE OF NON-REGISTERED FAN BOATS AND SOME TWO-WAY RADIOS.
HOOKER... WE'VE HAD PLANS THAT INVOLVE FELICIA AND ROSA BEFORE. HAVEN'T YOU LEARNED ANYTHING FROM THOSE EXPERIENCES?
NO. BESIDES, RIGHT NOW... IT'S ALL WE GOT.

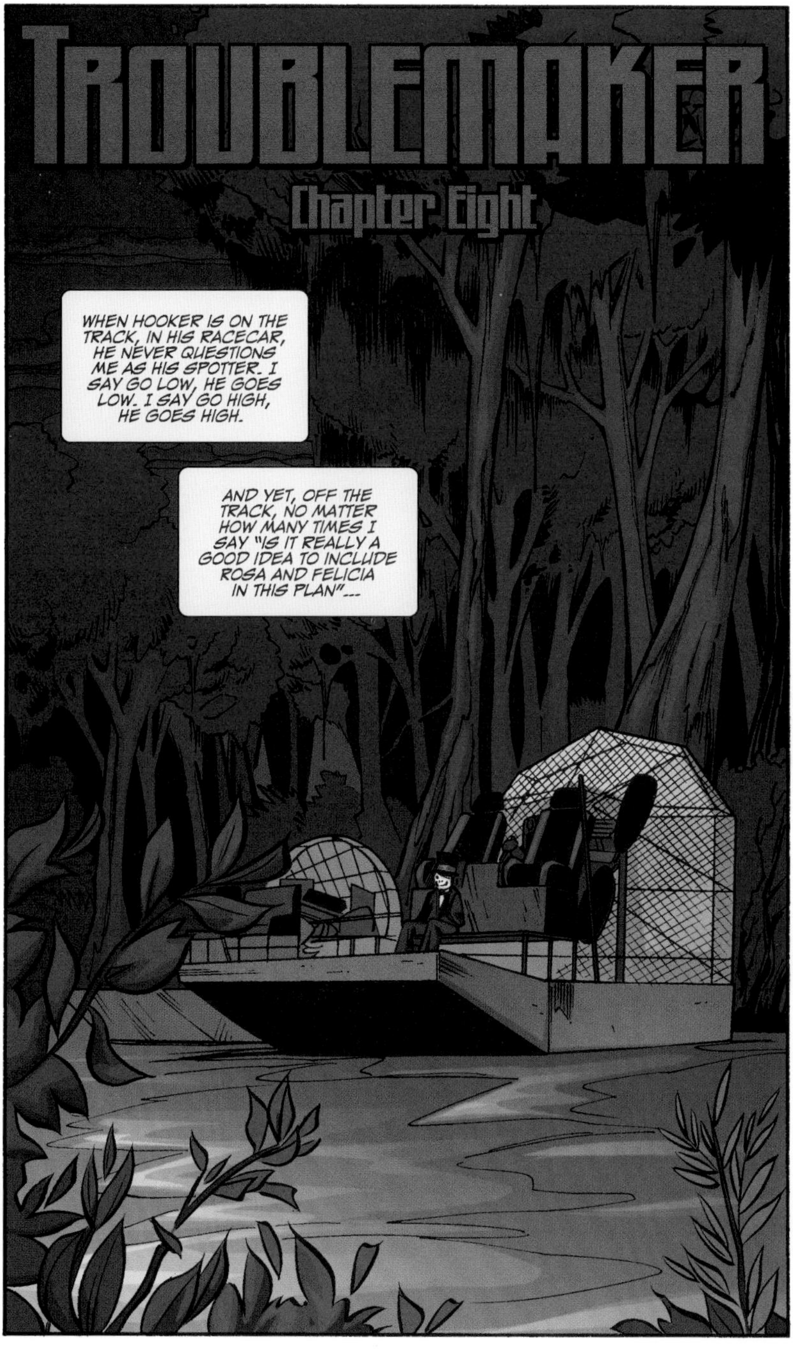
TROUBLEMAKER
Chapter Eight
WHEN HOOKER IS ON THE TRACK, IN HIS RACECAR, HE NEVER QUESTIONS ME AS HIS SPOTTER. I SAY GO LOW, HE GOES LOW. I SAY GO HIGH, HE GOES HIGH.
AND YET, OFF THE TRACK, NO MATTER HOW MANY TIMES I SAY "IS IT REALLY A GOOD IDEA TO INCLUDE ROSA AND FELICIA IN THIS PLAN"---

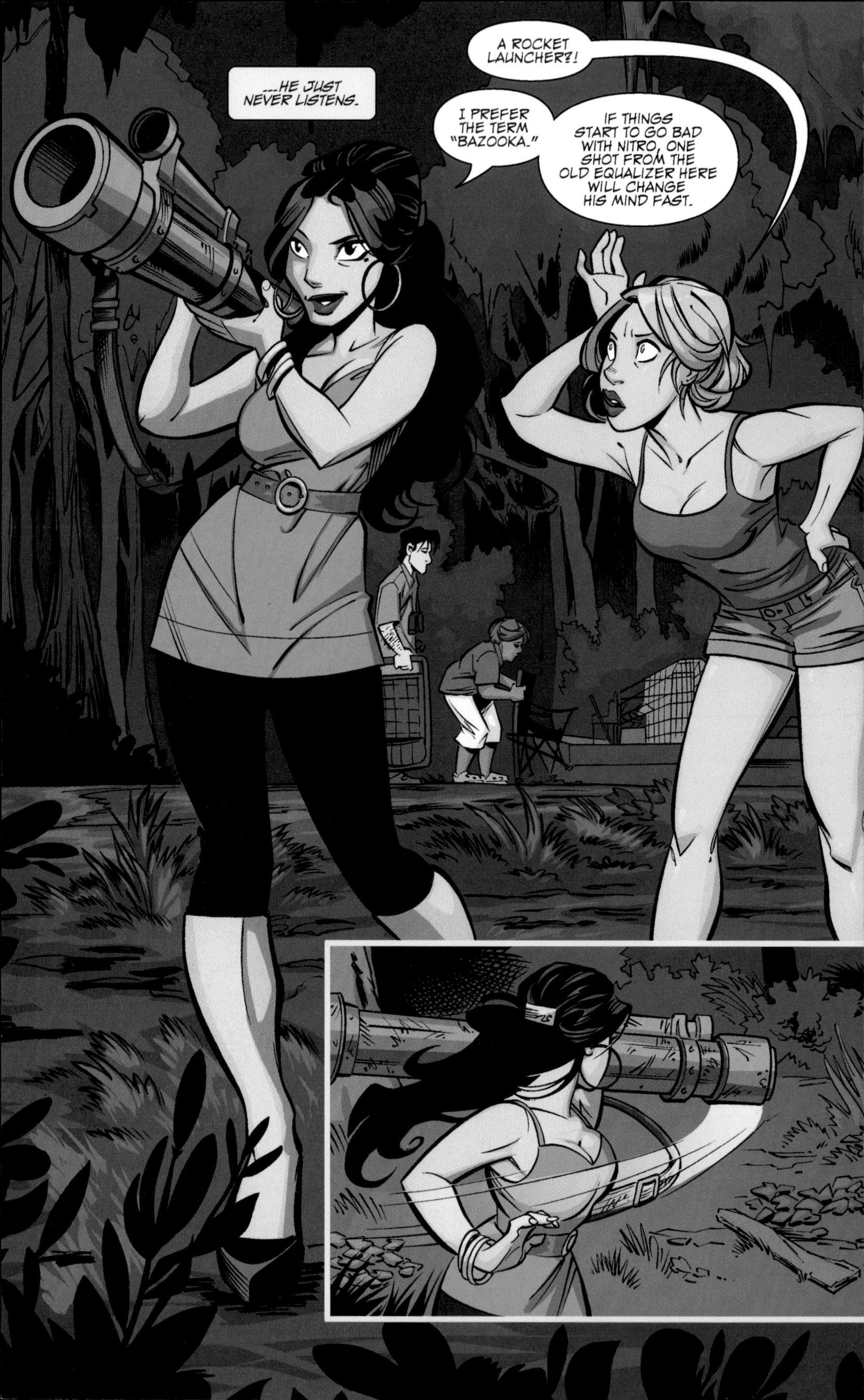
...HE JUST NEVER LISTENS.
A ROCKET LAUNCHER?!
I PREFER THE TERM "BAZOOKA."
IF THINGS START TO GO BAD WITH NITRO, ONE SHOT FROM THE OLD EQUALIZER HERE WILL CHANGE HIS MIND FAST.

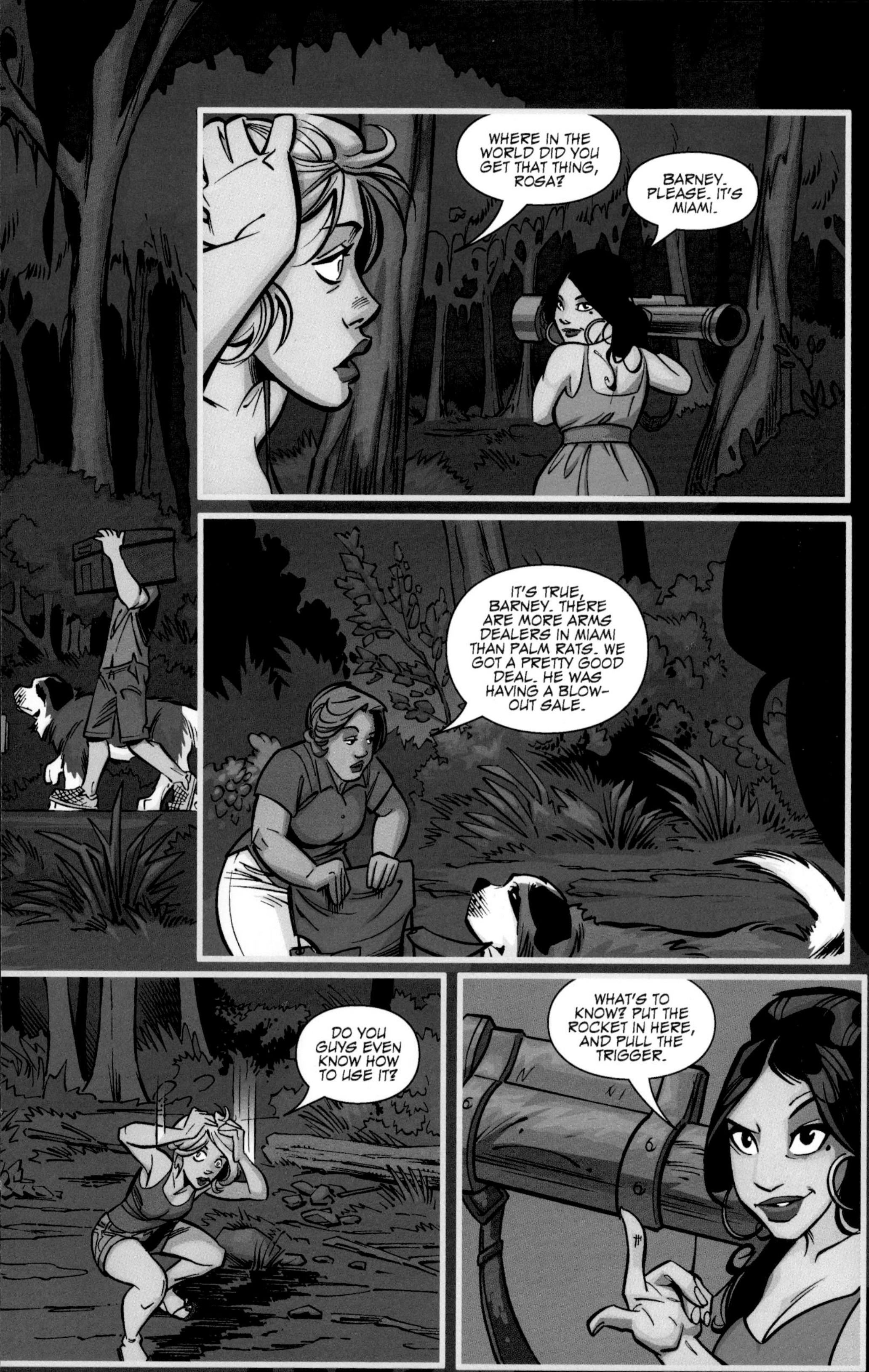
WHERE IN THE WORLD DID YOU GET THAT THING, ROSA?
BARNEY. PLEASE. IT'S MIAMI.
IT'S TRUE, BARNEY. THERE ARE MORE ARMS DEALERS IN MIAMI THAN PALM RATS. WE GOT A PRETTY GOOD DEAL. HE WAS HAVING A BLOW-OUT SALE.
DO YOU GUYS EVEN KNOW HOW TO USE IT?
WHAT'S TO KNOW? PUT THE ROCKET IN HERE, AND PULL THE TRIGGER.

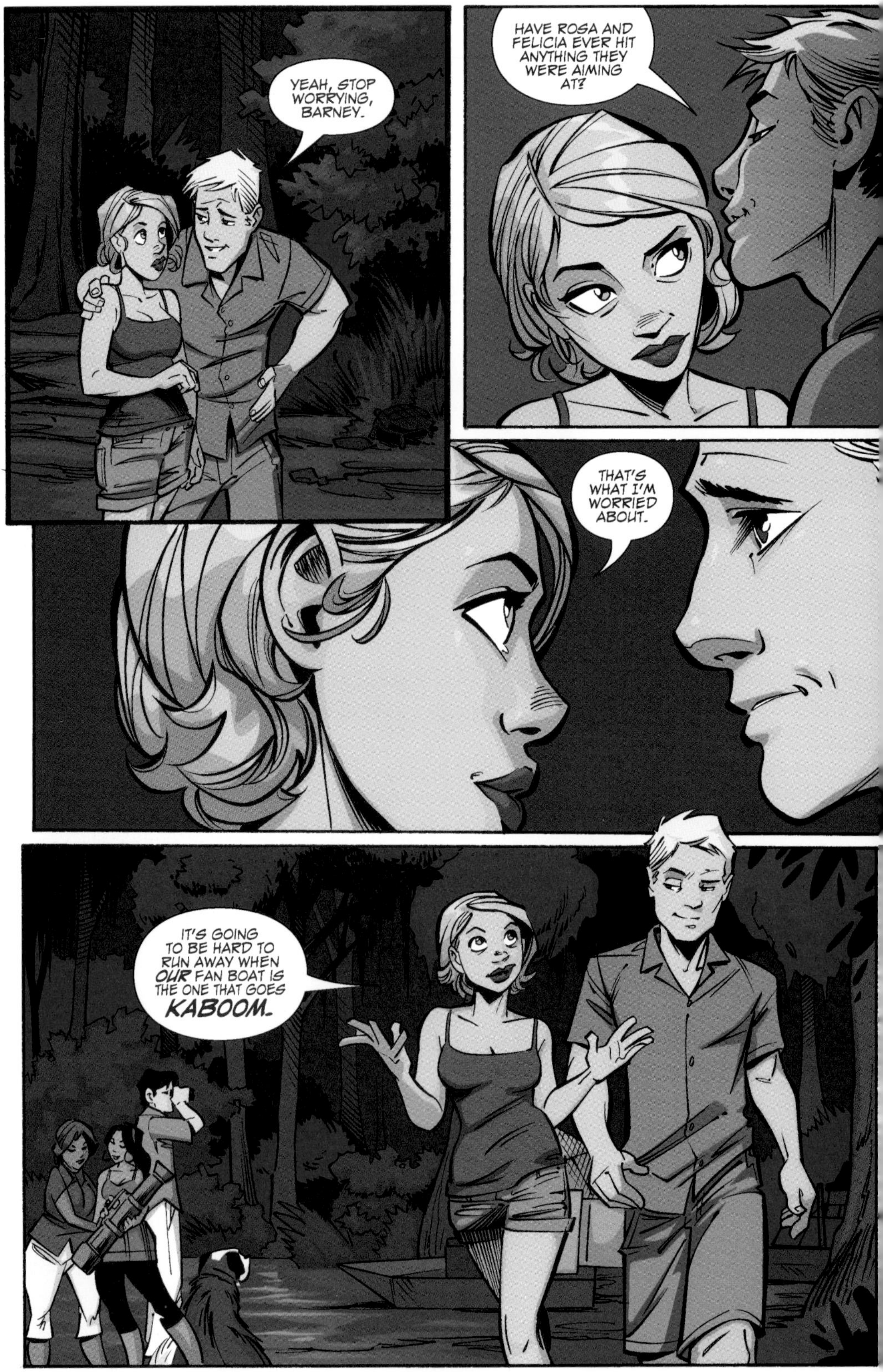
YEAH, STOP WORRYING, BARNEY.
HAVE ROSA AND FELICIA EVER HIT ANYTHING THEY WERE AIMING AT?
THAT'S WHAT I'M WORRIED ABOUT.
IT'S GOING TO BE HARD TO RUN AWAY WHEN OUR FAN BOAT IS THE ONE THAT GOES KABOOM.

EVERYONE KNOWS WHAT TO DO, RIGHT?

KEEP AN EYE ON YOU THROUGH THE BINOCULARS--

SORRY ABOUT NOT BEING ABLE TO GO AFTER THE TREASURE, WALTER.

THAT'S OKAY. I WOULDN'T KNOW WHERE TO START LOOKING ANYWAY. I JUST WANT TO DO THE RIGHT THING.

IF EVERYTHING GOES RIGHT, AS SOON AS YOU LEAVE NITRO'S CAMP, THE GIRLS PUT THE CHAIRS IN THE BOAT AND I SEND OUT AN EMERGENCY SIGNAL THROUGH THE TWO-WAY RADIO.

I LEAVE THE RADIO HERE WHILE WE HIGH-TAIL IT OUT OF THE SWAMP, AND HOPE THAT THE POLICE SHOW UP IN TIME TO GET NITRO AND THE BARON.

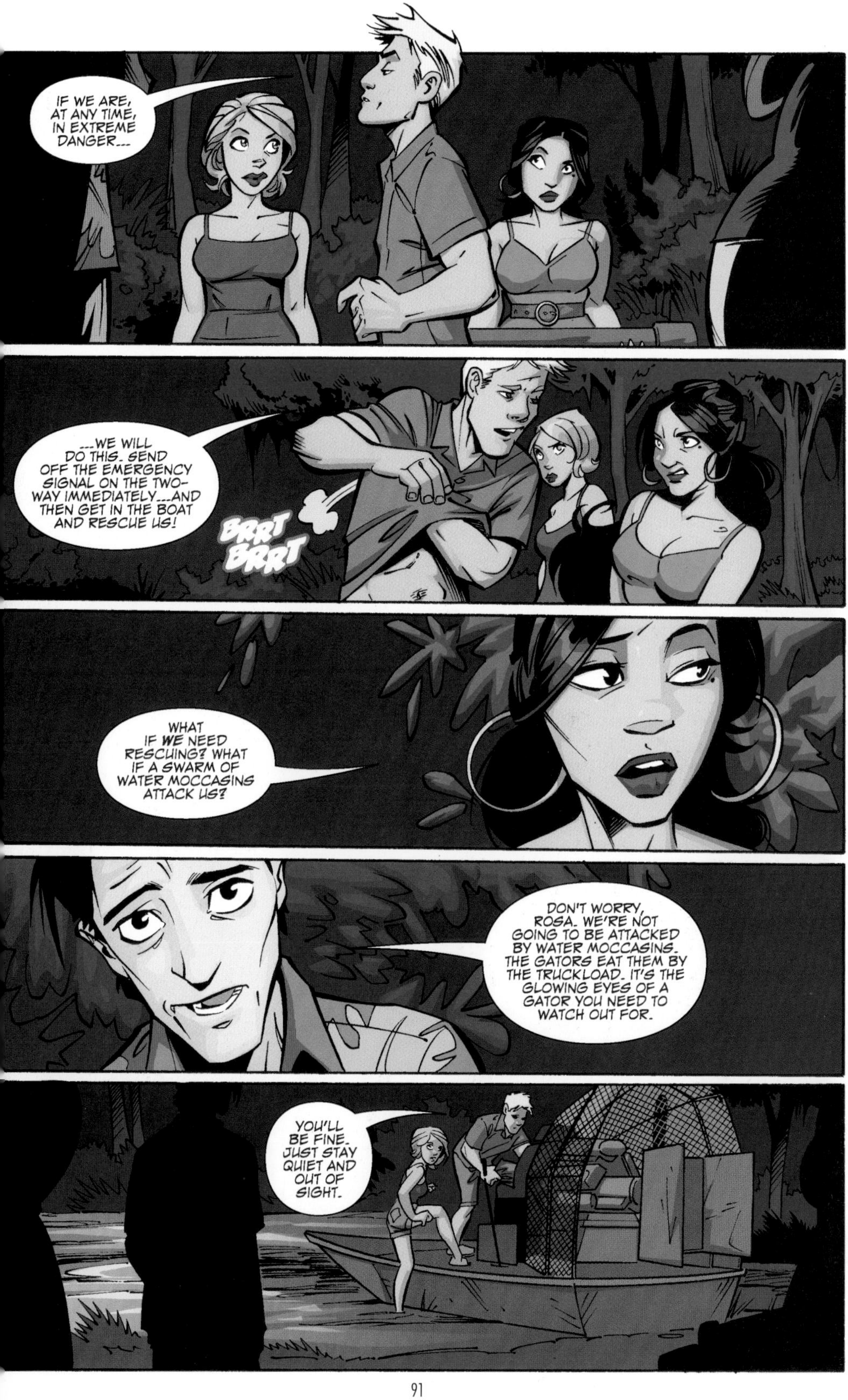
IF WE ARE, AT ANY TIME, IN EXTREME DANGER...
...WE WILL DO THIS. SEND OFF THE EMERGENCY SIGNAL ON THE TWO-WAY IMMEDIATELY...AND THEN GET IN THE BOAT AND RESCUE US!
BRRT BRRT
WHAT IF WE NEED RESCUING? WHAT IF A SWARM OF WATER MOCCASINS ATTACK US?
DON'T WORRY, ROSA. WE'RE NOT GOING TO BE ATTACKED BY WATER MOCCASINS. THE GATORS EAT THEM BY THE TRUCKLOAD. IT'S THE GLOWING EYES OF A GATOR YOU NEED TO WATCH OUT FOR.
YOU'LL BE FINE. JUST STAY QUIET AND OUT OF SIGHT.

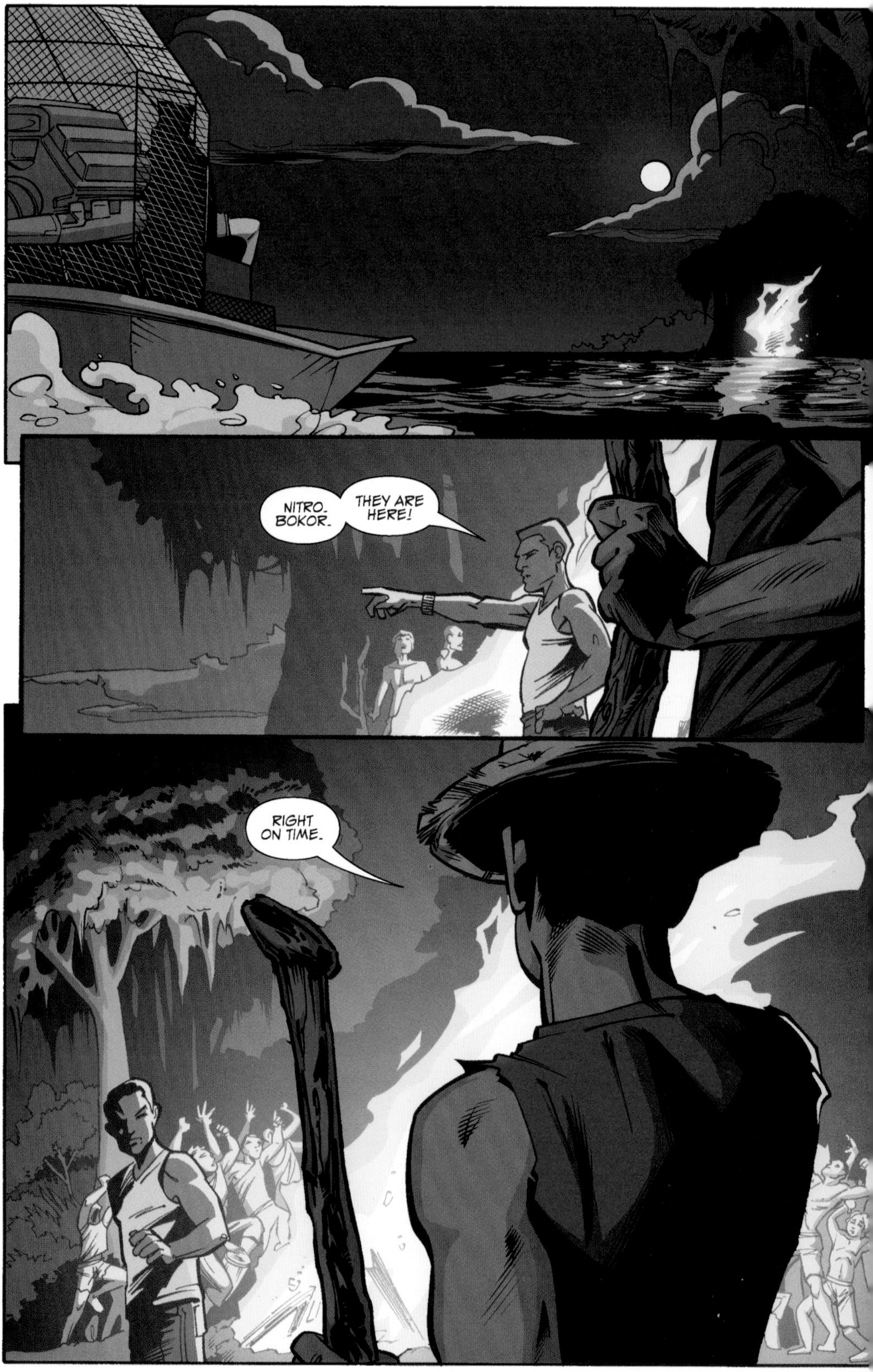
NITRO-BOKOR.
THEY ARE HERE!
RIGHT ON TIME.

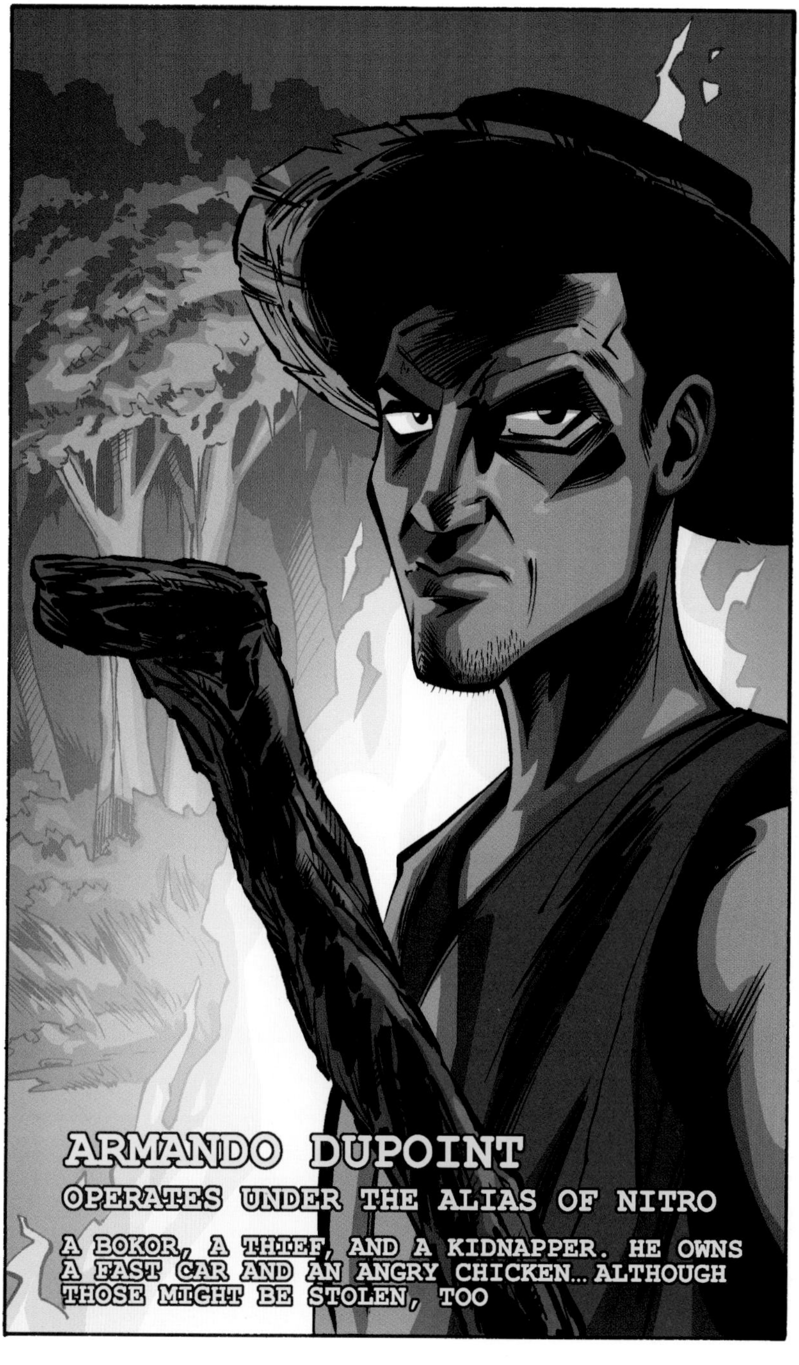
ARMANDO DUPOINT
OPERATES UNDER THE ALIAS OF NITRO
A BOKOR, A THIEF, AND A KIDNAPPER. HE OWNS A FAST CAR AND AN ANGRY CHICKEN... ALTHOUGH THOSE MIGHT BE STOLEN, TOO

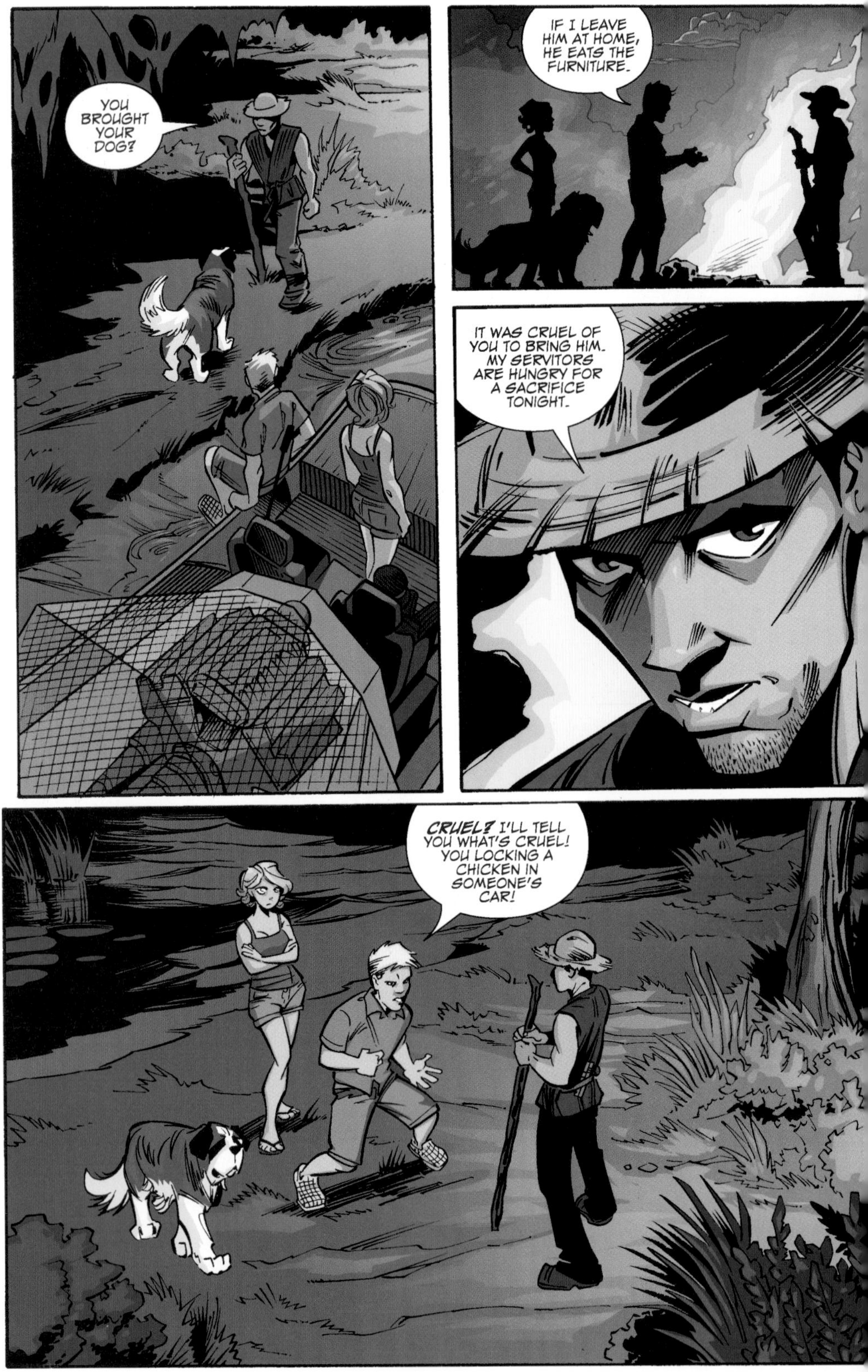
YOU BROUGHT YOUR DOG?
IF I LEAVE HIM AT HOME, HE EATS THE FURNITURE.
IT WAS CRUEL OF YOU TO BRING HIM. MY SERVITORS ARE HUNGRY FOR A SACRIFICE TONIGHT.
CRUEL? I'LL TELL YOU WHAT'S CRUEL! YOU LOCKING A CHICKEN IN SOMEONE'S CAR!

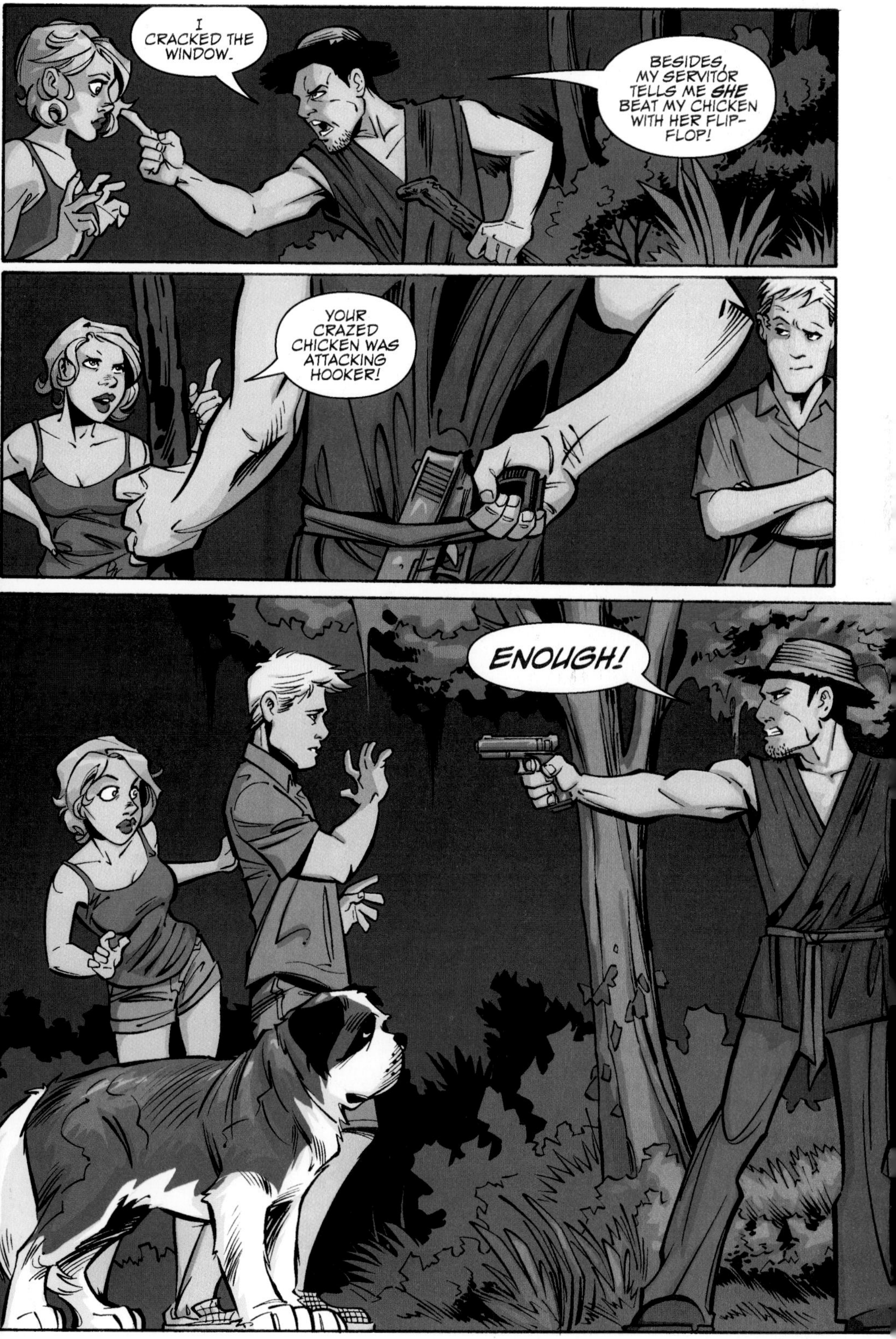

I CRACKED THE WINDOW.
BESIDES, MY SERVITOR TELLS ME SHE BEAT MY CHICKEN WITH HER FLIP-FLOP!
YOUR CRAZED CHICKEN WAS ATTACKING HOOKER!
ENOUGH!

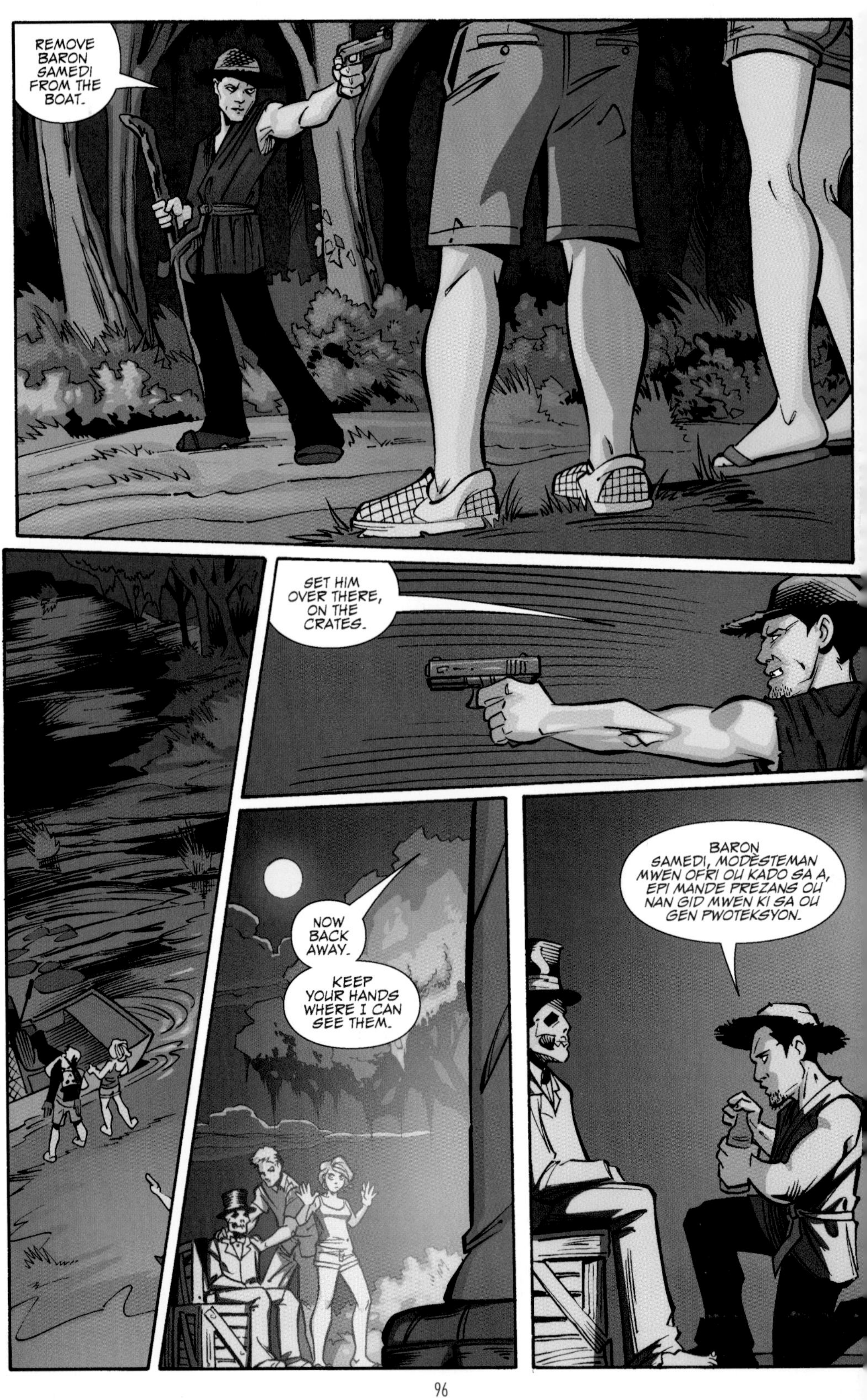
REMOVE BARON SAMEDI FROM THE BOAT.
SET HIM OVER THERE, ON THE CRATES.
NOW BACK AWAY.
KEEP YOUR HANDS WHERE I CAN SEE THEM.
BARON SAMEDI, MODÈSTEMAN MWEN OFRI OU KADO SA A, EPI MANDE PREZANS OU NAN GID MWEN KI SA OU GEN PWOTEKSYON.

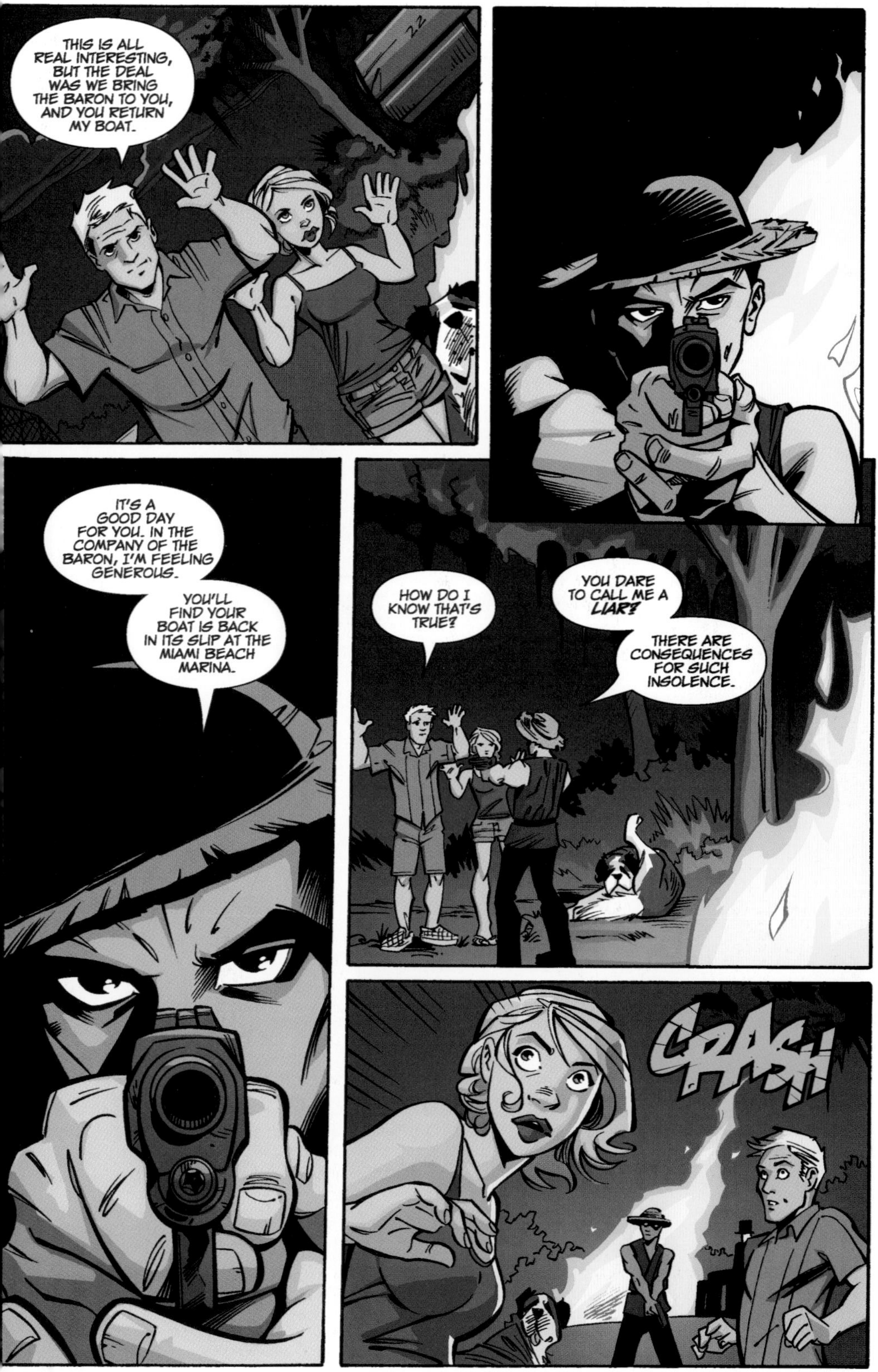
THIS IS ALL REAL INTERESTING, BUT THE DEAL WAS WE BRING THE BARON TO YOU, AND YOU RETURN MY BOAT.
IT'S A GOOD DAY FOR YOU. IN THE COMPANY OF THE BARON, I'M FEELING GENEROUS.
YOU'LL FIND YOUR BOAT IS BACK IN ITS SLIP AT THE MIAMI BEACH MARINA.
HOW DO I KNOW THAT'S TRUE?
YOU DARE TO CALL ME A *LIAR?*
THERE ARE CONSEQUENCES FOR SUCH INSOLENCE.
CRASH

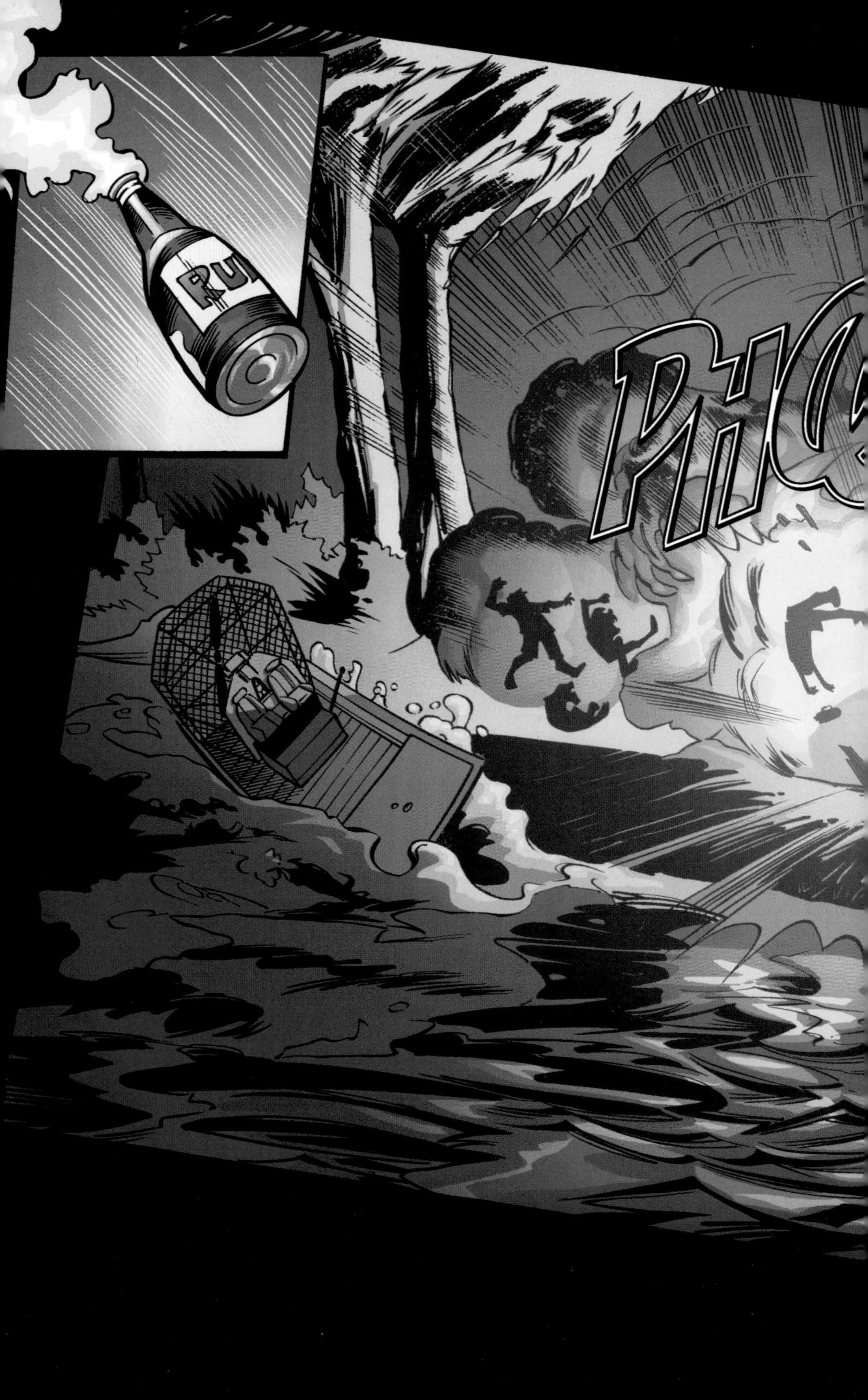

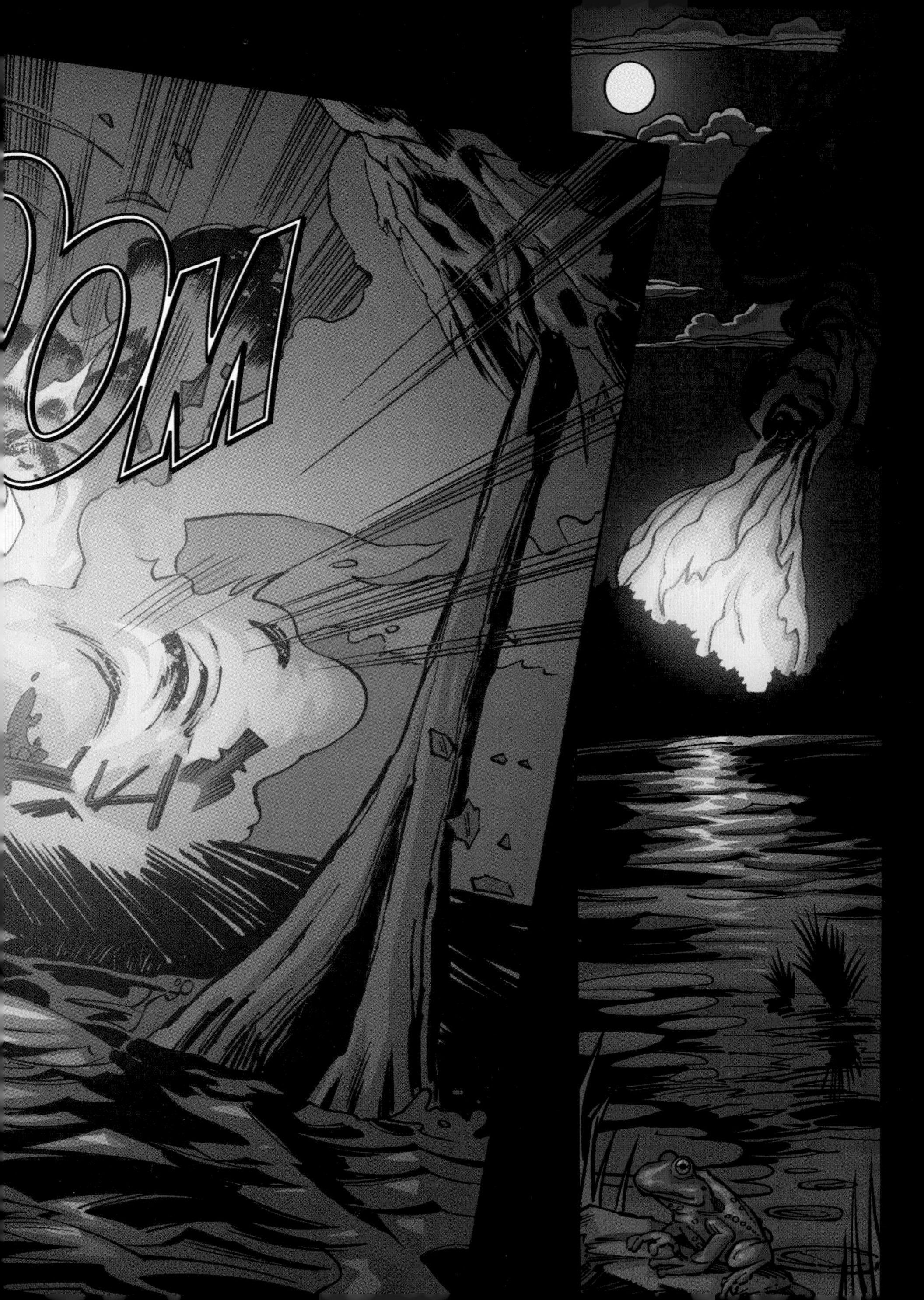

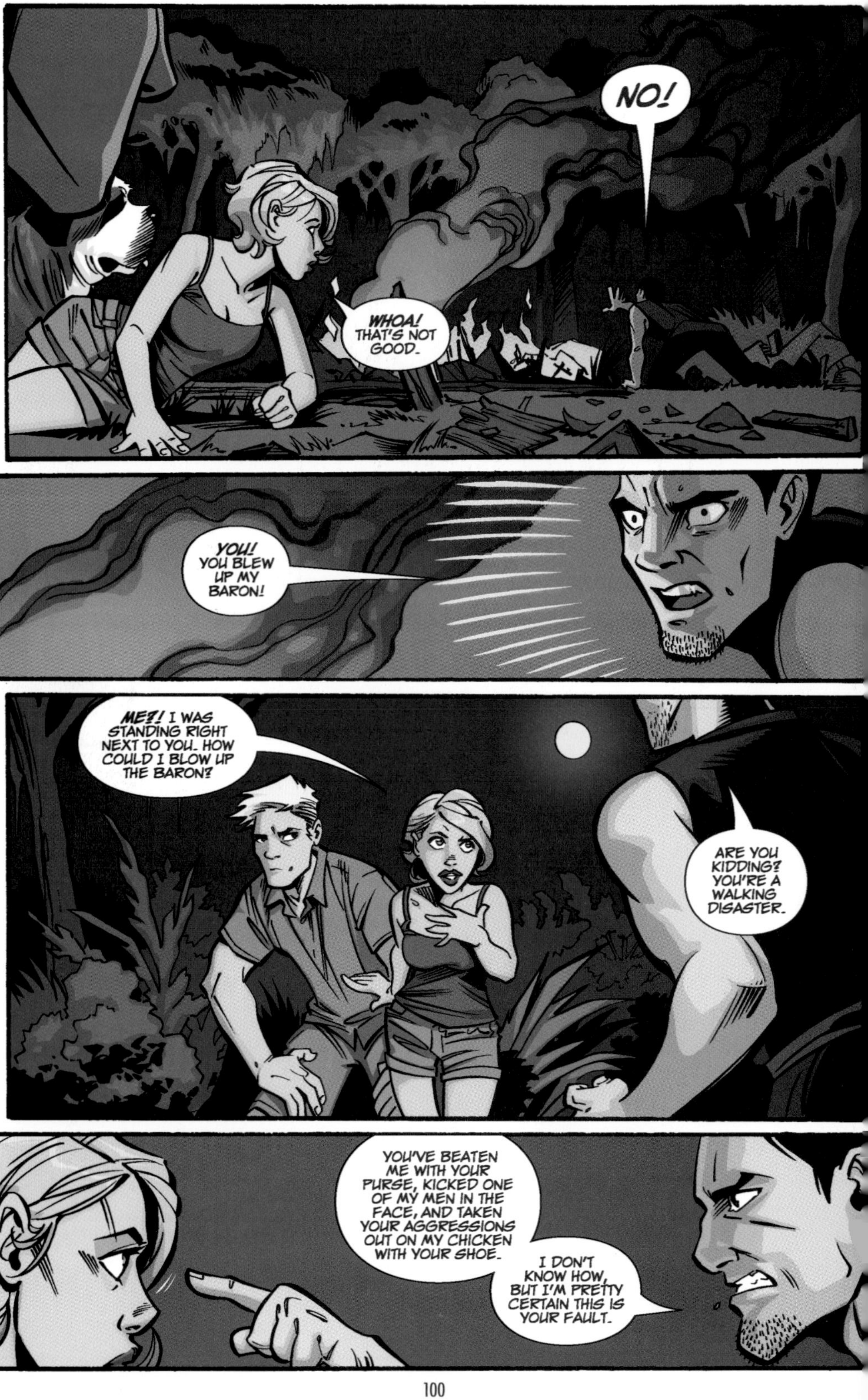
NO!
WHOA! THAT'S NOT GOOD.
YOU! YOU BLEW UP MY BARON!
ME?! I WAS STANDING RIGHT NEXT TO YOU. HOW COULD I BLOW UP THE BARON?
ARE YOU KIDDING? YOU'RE A WALKING DISASTER.
YOU'VE BEATEN ME WITH YOUR PURSE, KICKED ONE OF MY MEN IN THE FACE, AND TAKEN YOUR AGGRESSIONS OUT ON MY CHICKEN WITH YOUR SHOE.
I DON'T KNOW HOW, BUT I'M PRETTY CERTAIN THIS IS YOUR FAULT.

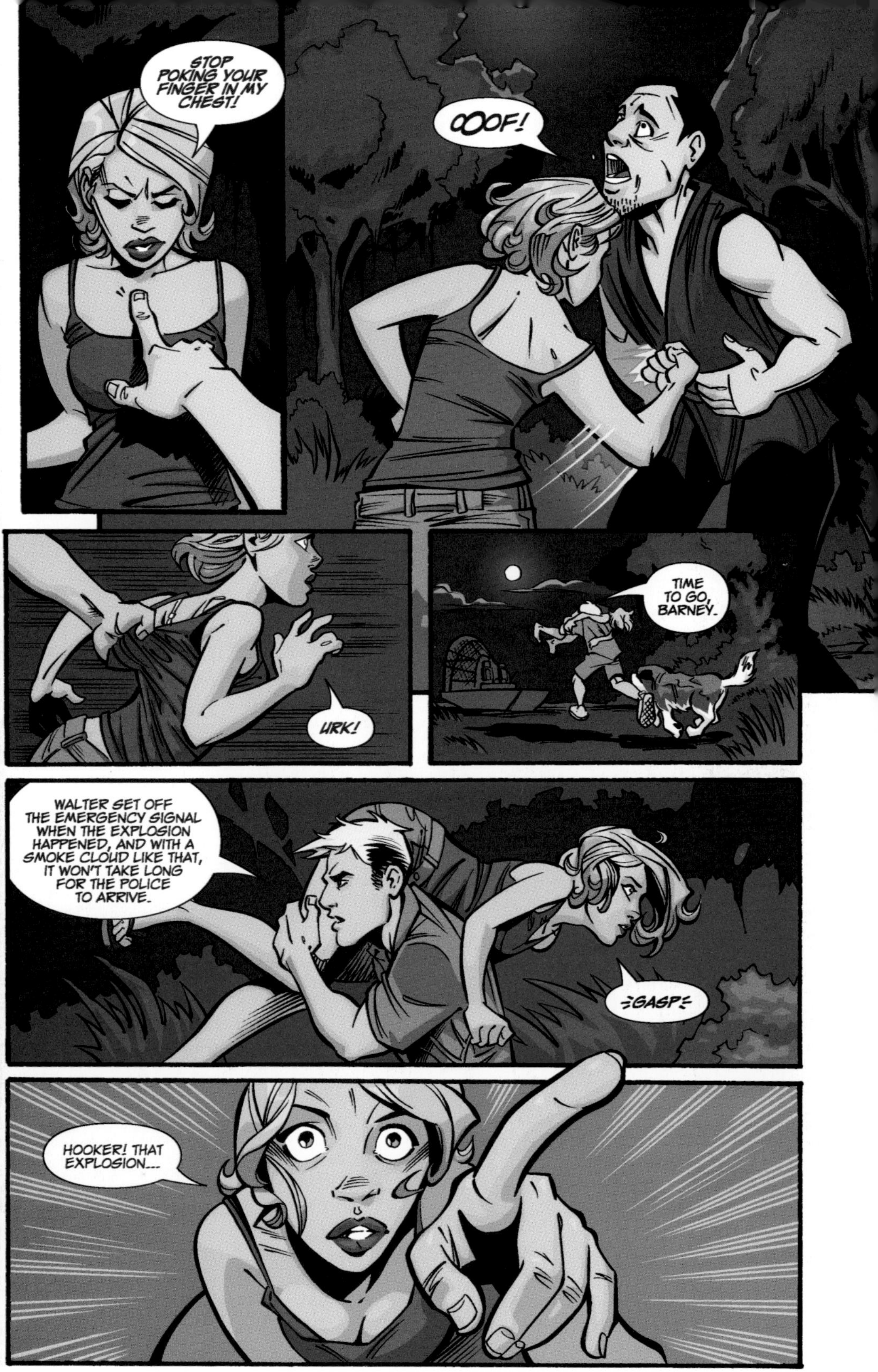
STOP POKING YOUR FINGER IN MY CHEST!
OOOF!
URK!
TIME TO GO, BARNEY.
WALTER SET OFF THE EMERGENCY SIGNAL WHEN THE EXPLOSION HAPPENED, AND WITH A SMOKE CLOUD LIKE THAT, IT WON'T TAKE LONG FOR THE POLICE TO ARRIVE.
GASP
HOOKER! THAT EXPLOSION...

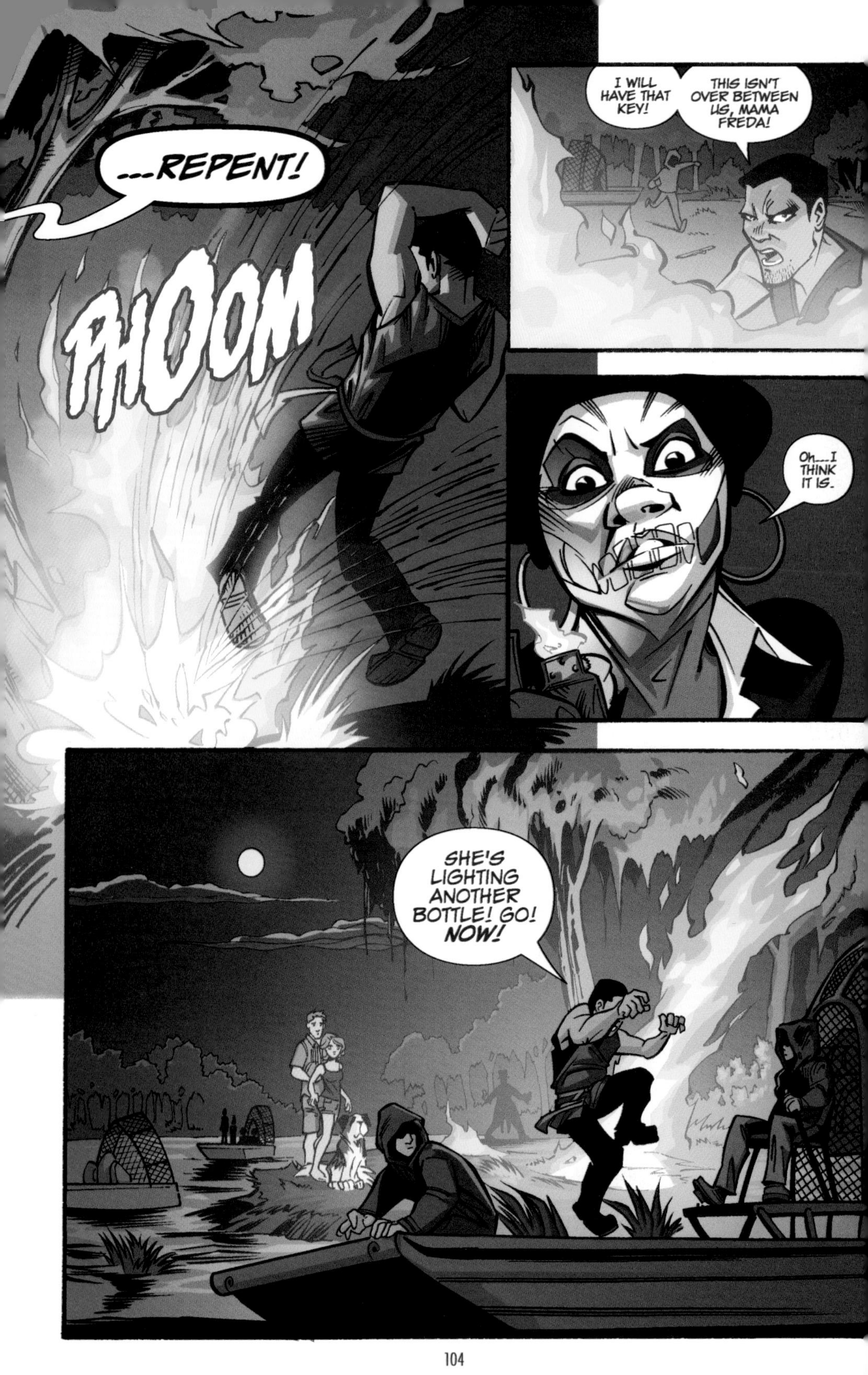
...REPENT!
PHOOM
I WILL HAVE THAT KEY!
THIS ISN'T OVER BETWEEN US, MAMA FREDA!
Oh... I THINK IT IS.
SHE'S LIGHTING ANOTHER BOTTLE! GO! NOW!

CREATOR BIOGRAPHIES

Janet and her granddog, Barnaby.

JANET EVANOVICH is the number-one *New York Times* best-selling author of the Stephanie Plum series, as well as the Alex Barnaby and Sam Hooker novels *Metro Girl* and *Motor Mouth*. Janet lives in Florida with her husband and her Havanese, Ollie. This is her first foray into writing comics.

ALEX EVANOVICH is the daughter of Janet Evanovich. She's been working with Janet for over fourteen years doing Internet work, newsletters, and editing, and is one of the coauthors of *How I Write*. She lives in Florida with her husband and her St. Bernard, Barnaby.

JOËLLE JONES debuted in comics in 2006, contributing a short story to the Dark Horse anthology *Sexy Chix*. She followed this a year later with the full graphic novel *12 Reasons Why I Love Her*, her first collaboration with author Jamie S. Rich. She went on to illustrate the crime graphic novel *You Have Killed Me* and most recently the teen-witch comedy *Spell Checkers*. Joëlle has also drawn the young-adult book *Token* with Alisa Kwitney, worked with Zack Whedon on a comic-book spinoff of the popular *Dr. Horrible's Sing-Along Blog* web series, and drawn two issues of the Eisner-nominated series *Madame Xanadu*, written by Matt Wagner. She is currently working on a long-form comic for DC/Vertigo called *The Starving Artist*. You can visit her online at www.joellejones.com.

BARNABY AND HOOKER HAD A BEGINNING. SOME WOULD CALL IT A PAST.

Janet Evanovich's
#1 *New York Times* Bestsellers
METRO GIRL and *MOTOR MOUTH*

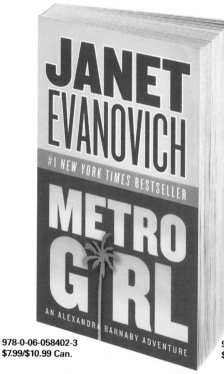

978-0-06-058402-3
$7.99/$10.99 Can.

978-0-06-058405-4
$7.99/$10.99 Can.

Read how Barnaby and Hooker blast through Florida to expose bad guys, right wrongs, and see that justice is done. And meet Rosa the cigar roller!

Now you are ready for **TROUBLEMAKER**, the first graphic novel in the series.

HARPER

AN IMPRINT OF HARPERCOLLINSPUBLISHERS

www.harpercollins.com

RECOMMENDED
DARK HORSE READING . . .

BUFFY THE VAMPIRE SLAYER SEASON EIGHT VOLUME 1: THE LONG WAY HOME

JOSS WHEDON, GEORGES JEANTY

Since the destruction of the Hellmouth, the Slayers—newly legion—have gotten organized and are kicking some serious undead butt. But not everything's fun and firearms, as an old enemy reappears and Dawn experiences some serious growing pains. Meanwhile, one of the "Buffy" decoy slayers is going through major pain of her own.

Buffy creator Joss Whedon brings Buffy back to Dark Horse in this direct follow-up to season seven of the smash-hit TV series.

$15.99
ISBN 978-1-59307-822-5

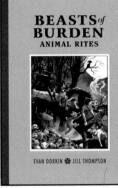

BEASTS OF BURDEN VOLUME 1: ANIMAL RITES

EVAN DORKIN, JILL THOMPSON

Welcome to Burden Hill—a picturesque little town adorned with white picket fences and green, green grass, home to a unique team of paranormal investigators. Beneath this shiny exterior, Burden Hill harbors dark and sinister secrets, and it's up to a heroic gang of dogs—and one cat—to protect the town from the evil forces at work. Can our heroes overcome these supernatural menaces? Can evil be bested by a paranormal team that doesn't have hands? And even more importantly, will Pugs ever shut the hell up?

$19.99
ISBN 978-1-59582-513-1

GIANT SIZE LITTLE LULU VOLUME 1

JOHN STANLEY, IRVING TRIPP

John Stanley and Irving Tripp's long run on *Little Lulu* is a milestone in American comics, as hilarious to grownups as it is to their children. With Stanley's popularity at an all-time high, Dark Horse is proud to take you back to the beginning of this legendary run. Collecting some of the earliest out-of-print volumes of Dark Horse's acclaimed reprint series, this massive 664-page omnibus contains the first fourteen issues where Little Lulu appeared.

$24.99
ISBN 978-1-59582-502-5

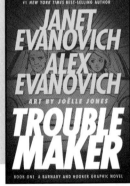

TROUBLEMAKER: BOOK ONE

JANET EVANOVICH, ALEX EVANOVICH, JOËLLE JONES

The first volume of *Troublemaker*, Janet Evanovich's first graphic novel, where all the trouble began for characters Alex Barnaby and Sam Hooker from the best-selling novels *Metro Girl* and *Motor Mouth*. A man has gone missing, and in order to find him Barnaby and Hooker will have to go deep into the underbelly of Miami and southern Florida, surviving Petro Voodoo, explosions, gift-wrapped body parts, a deadly swamp chase, and Hooker's mom.

$17.99
ISBN 978-1-59582-488-2